Bryn-mawr, Llanerfyl, Montgomeryshire : a *tyddyn* on the open moorland, a belt of trees sheltering its front from the prevailing winds. The roof is of rushes with a clod ridge

THE WELSH HOUSE

First published in 1940 (as Vol. LXVII of Y Cymmrodor)
Second (revised) edition, Liverpool, 1944.
New edition, Llanerch Press, 2004

Type Copyright © 2004, Llanerch Press.
Foreword Copyright © 2004, Dr. G. Stevenson.
Cover photograph, Copyright © Cadw

The publishers wish to thank the Honourable Society of Cymmrodorion for advice, Mrs. Eirlys Peate for permission to reprint this work, Cadw for use of the cover photograph, Dr. Greg Stevenson for the foreword and to all those who gave permission for use of their photographs in this new edition.

Published by

LLANERCH PRESS LTD

Little Court
48 Rectory Road
Burnham on Sea
Somerset
TA8 2BZ

www.llanerchpress.com

ISBN 978 1 86143 131 8

THE WELSH HOUSE

A Study in Folk Culture

BY

IORWERTH C. PEATE

M.A., D.Sc., F.S.A.

*Keeper of the Department of
Folk Culture and Industries in
the National Museum of Wales*

THIS VOLUME IS DEDICATED TO
THE MEMORY OF THE LATE
SIR DANIEL LLEUFER THOMAS, KT.,
M.A., LL.D., F.S.A.
1863-1940
HIS PIONEER WORK IN WELSH SOCIOLOGY
INSPIRED IT

'DYLED, PARCH, HOFFTER'

REPRINTED IN PAPERBACK
BY
LLANERCH PRESS LTD
2011

life for many. This was also the period that Sir Cyril Fox (Director of the National Museum for whom Peate worked) and Lord Raglan were undertaking their pioneering work recording the traditional houses of Monmouthsire (see Further Reading). After World War II most remaining thatch roofs were replaced with asbestos, corrugated iron or slate, electricity was making traditional fireplaces defunct, and ease of transport meant that building materials were losing their local distinctiveness. The rural homestead was gradually replaced by the modern bungalow designed on non-traditional lines using non-traditional materials.

Peate was witnessing a time in which the comparatively modern building traditions and materials of England were colonising even remote areas of rural Wales. Transport was greatly improved in the late nineteenth century, with railways in most areas, and bricks, Portland cement and concrete were replacing the local building materials of lime, stone, thatch and slate. This process was happening all over Britain, but it's easy to imagine why it would have been particularly alarming in Wales, for many areas had maintained their traditional buildings remarkably intact. The sense of loss must be similar to that felt by the Irish in the last decade of the twentieth century as their otherwise remarkably intact vernacular built heritage has been swamped by an economic boom and the geographically and stylistically anonymous bungalows that Wales first saw half a century ago.

Peate wasn't the first to write about Welsh vernacular architecture, but *The Welsh House* was the first pan-Wales survey of traditional buildings. It proposed that Welsh architecture was in fact the vernacular architecture of Wales, rather than the architect-designed polite architecture that was largely influenced from outside. Peate believed that the *gwerin* (folk) were inseparable from their homes and traditions, and so for him this text was an exercise in celebrating his nation. In a period when most would have looked to the 'English' castles of Edward I if you had asked them to name a Welsh historic building, Peate introduced the idea that the traditional cottages and farmsteads of Wales are the Welsh heritage. He was influenced by the celebration of folk architecture in Ireland, Sweden and Norway, but built on the work of people like Sir Cyril Fox and J. Romilly Allen who had undertaken detailed studies of regional architectures in Wales.

In preparing this book Peate collated all the current thinking on traditional Welsh architecture, and used his field study to develop his theories on the evolution of the Welsh house. For example, he describes in Chapter III how he retraced the steps of Sir Lleufer Thomas in describing the 'ink-bottle' houses of squatter districts in Meirionydd and

Montgomeryshire. Forty-five years separated Peate's visit from Sir Lleufer's, and Peate reports that he found none standing. Where Peate found that old housing types had been lost or altered he used material from the original reports, such as that prepared by the Royal Commission on Land in Wales which is the source of the older images of long-houses (Plates 11, 13, 17). J. Romilly Allen's article on the '*Old Farm-Houses with round chimneys near St Davids*' was largely reproduced by Peate for the section in Chapter VII on the farms of that area.

The Welsh House was years ahead of its time in that it contextualised houses in their natural and social landscapes, and yet in other ways it is very much a child of its time. Peate believed that Wales had a pristine culture, not one formed by centuries of inmigration, emigration and assimilation of foreign cultures. He writes of an upland '*refuge of ancient racial types, of bygone customs and forgotten things*'. It was this same naïve idea that Wales was home to rural life 'as it used to be' that fuelled our tourism industry at the time. The 1930s saw an unprecedented volume of writing about the rural idyll, and Peate's earnest research occasionally falls foul of romanticizing peasant life in days gone by. Wales was a country experiencing huge changes, industrialization and much Anglicisation in the inter-war years, and Peate's book was one small escape into the realm of a wholly Welsh, almost utopian past. People were travelling more and more by motor car and train, and a publishing industry had developed that provided a tour guide to the most romantic, historic villages. This was the period when most new houses were being built in pastiche cottage styles with half-timbered cladding, ceramic designers such as Clarice Cliff were producing tea-sets with cottage images on them, and women's magazines provided free cross-stitch patterns of rustic thatched cottages for housewives to decorate their antimacassars. Peate was undoubtedly part of this wider movement to preserve the idea of the 'good old days', but his motivations were greater than this. *The Welsh House*, was a chance to define a heritage that Peate felt was of national importance to the Welsh people, and he succeeded in this goal.

More than anyone, Peate was responsible for raising interest in Welsh folk traditions, from houses to furniture, agriculture to traditional songs. We could frown on Peate for his romantic view of the *gwerin*, and for harking back to '*yr hen ffordd Gymreig o fyw*', but we must remember the political and cultural circumstances of his time. This book was written in a time of increasing Welsh nationalism; it is titled *The Welsh House* rather than say *The Traditional Houses of Wales*. Plate 86, a section of partitioning from a house destroyed by the Air Ministry at Penyberth, was doubtless included as a vehicle for Peate to subtly criticise the unwelcome occupation of much of rural Wales by the English military, and their senseless destruction of ancient buildings. In the same way that Sir Cyril Fox and Lord Raglan were prompted into their research by the destruction of an ancient house (Wern Hir) to make way for the construction of an Ordnance factory, Peate uses Penyberth to remind people of the destruction of Welsh heritage. Like Saunders Lewis, Peate felt that he was part of a culture that needed fighting for, and it was an honourable battle to represent the *gwerin* (rather than the English who governed Wales) as the true inheritors of her cultural traditions. This is clear from the first pages where he tells us that the Welsh house is an *'expression of Welsh life – indeed, a facet of it, for the folk life is always indivisible'*.

The first edition was published in 1940 as volume XLVII of *Y Cymmrodor* for The Honourable Society of Cymmrodorion, and sold out in a couple of months. Such was the interest that a second edition was published in 1944, despite the fact that Britain was still at war, and a third followed in 1946. Perhaps the War itself reminded readers that the Welsh way of life was under threat. Since the 1940s the book has grown into a classic text for students of both Welsh architecture, and folk studies, and has an international significance as an example of how vernacular architecture can be studied from a sociological perspective.

The Welsh House isn't a comprehensive survey (and nor did Peate pretend it was), rather a call to others to take up the challenge of recording the remnants of the national folk heritage. Read the text and you will hear his voice, and feel his passion for the subject. Peate would no doubt have denied that he was an expert on Welsh vernacular architecture, but obviously he had an eye for vernacular detail, and enough knowledge to understand the value of what was being lost. This book doesn't try to take the reader on a parish-by-parish journey of local traditions, rather Peate emphasises the links between the *gwerin* and their homes. These, he suggests, are the real heritage of Wales, the houses that built a nation. And so in this text you won't find the names of architects and designers, for these are home-made homes that are built using locally available materials in local styles.

Peate's vision of Wales was a wholly rural place, and one that existed some time before the twentieth century began. Despite the fact that he was writing at a time when most people in Wales lived in the industrialised south-east, this is a book that looks from Cardiff (where he worked) to the rural hinterland of his family. With hindsight we can see that there was far more at stake in 1940 than the loss of our earliest and most ancient cottages and farms. *The Welsh House* is mostly concerned with traditional homes from before 1800, but we now include nineteenth century buildings which we consider worthy of protection. However, it is this group of Victorian rural cottages and farms that remains most at risk today. Largely unprotected by Statutory Listing, the simple mid-nineteenth century 'two up, two down' stone and slate rural cottage with sash windows is now a rare beast (photo 13). Individually they are rarely remarkable, but this is where their beauty lies, in being representative of a once common building type.

The sixty years that sit between this edition and the last do not devalue the original as a text for anyone interested in Welsh folk architecture. However, a few of the dates in the original can now be improved, for in general there seems to have been a trend to have dated the more rustic homes as earlier than they probably were. For example, although Peate states that cruck-construction ceased by the 17th century, we now know that scarfed-crucks were still being erected in Carmarthenshire and Ceredigion into the second quarter of the nineteenth century. In fact one of the unusual things about the built heritage of these counties is the paucity of buildings that date from before 1750. Dendrochronology (tree-ring dating) has now provided accurate dates for several of the earlier houses featured in the book, and we can now state with confidence that Abernodwydd (plate 9) was built from timber felled in AD 1678, Llannerch-y-Cawr (plate 34) in 1588, and Rhyd-y-Carw (plate 64) in 1515 (see Suggett 2003 in the 'Further Reading' for further Welsh dates).

The structure of the book is interesting in that it avoids the obvious route of following either geographical regions, or a chronological timeline. Most readers won't expect to see a discussion of iron-age round-houses in Chapter III, but this fitted with Peate's idea of a national building tradition. If the iron-age people were 'Celtic' (which they undoubtedly were, even if the term 'celtic' is a problematic one), then Peate included their homes to demonstrate the 'Welshness' of the building traditions of Wales. His sequencing evolution of round to rectangular houses is tenuous, and it is unlikely that houses with central chimneys actually represent a link between circular and rectangular forms. However, all the houses that you expect to be here are here, including wonderful detail on traditional farms and cottages.

Although *The Welsh House* is probably Peate's best known work, a glance at his full bibliography (see Jenkins 1969) reveals that he actually published very little on architecture. It is probably because of his involvement with the Welsh Folk Museum at St Fagans, that we associate him so much with buildings. Just as the Museum of Welsh Life is remembered for its buildings (when it is a storehouse for all Welsh cultural life), Peate's literary output and other publishing is over-shadowed by this work on just one of his many interests. Those who want to know more about Peate the man should turn to the recently published biography by R .Alun Ifans (published by Barddas 2003), and his literary achievements as summarised by Catrin Stevens (University of Wales Press, 1986).

Setting out to trace the footsteps of Peate some 60 years after his field survey, I saw a different Wales from the country that he knew. Peate recognised that Wales was losing its traditional architecture at an alarming rate, and recent decades have shown that this fear was indeed founded. I am grateful to the many owners who allowed me to visit their properties to undertake this research; to Jon Meirion Jones for permission to reproduce the englyn 'Y Murddun' describing the ruined clom cottages at Cwmtydu; and also to the readers of *The Western Mail* who answered my request for information. Robert Wall, Chief Architect of Cadw and Gerallt Nash, Curator of Historic Buildings at the Museum of Welsh Life, were particularly helpful, and Sandra Jones, Built Heritage Conservation Officer for Montgomeryshire went out of her way to assist with the buildings in her area.

Despite being celebrated in the book as being buildings of national importance, most of the houses from the original have collapsed, been demolished, or have been modernised beyond recognition. The lucky few have been moved to the Museum of Welsh Life, but these now exist out of context, and it is difficult to imagine the relationship with their original landscape. The buildings that were moved are the pigsty in plate 3, Abernodwydd in plate 9, Cilewent (referred to in the book as Ciloerwynt) in plate 31, and Llainfadyn in plates 46 & 74. Abernodwydd in particular underwent considerable reconstruction, with large sections of its timber frame being replaced.

Some of the houses had disappeared even before Peate published the book, and were included for their illustration of an old type. Llwyn-Rhys, Llanbadarn Odwyn (plates 15, 16 and 72) is one such example, although the platform for the house is still visible to this day. Lymore near Montgomery (plate 58) and Penrhos in east Montgomeryshire (plate 59) had also been demolished before Peate went to print. The cottage at Pontrhydfendigaid (plate 36) is an old postcard from 1910, and it is likely the house had collapsed by WWII. The outline of the building remains to this day, just south of the village.

Others had been abandoned shortly before Peate's visit, such as Tŷ'n-coed Uchaf, Blaencaron (plates 19 & 20) (now collapsed, photo 2) and Bryn Mawr, Llanerfyl (frontispiece & plate 48) which has mostly disappeared (photo 1). However, unlike the majority, both these houses are on land still farmed by the same family that was in residence when Peate visited. Peate's photograph of Bryn Mawr used as the frontispiece captures what must have been a common scene in Wales for the best part of a millennium, yet today no examples survive in this condition. We owe him a debt of thanks for capturing the last days of this ancient tradition.

The most shocking find is when buildings have gone, such as Pensarn-mynach, Cribyn (plate 37) which has been replaced by a modern bungalow (photo 6). Cribyn has seen several such thatched cottages demolished in order to make way for bungalow ribbon-development. Gwndwn (fig. 17 and plate 22) in Pencader, Carmarthenshire was empty (but untouched) when Peate visited, but has now been demolished to make way for silage storage on the farm. Ffynnon Goy Isaf (plate 39), Llain-wen isaf (plates 41 & 42) and Carn-deifog fach (plates 43 & 44) at Llanychaer were all flattened by the construction of the Royal Naval Arms Depot at Trecwn at the outbreak of WWII. The wonderful cruck barn at Lloran Ganol, Llansilin (plate 71) has gone, and the nearby cruck-framed Lloran Isa (not featured by Peate) has been de-Listed and also demolished. The Llansilin area was rich in early buildings (many now lost), but a recent resurvey of the area has introduced seven new Grade II* Listings.

Only the footings remain of some of the houses, such as Blaenwaun, Llansadwrn (plate 13), and Great Mains, Llaethdy (plate 38). Cae Crwn, Glanmorfa (plate 73) is assumed lost as it was in poor condition in 1940, and research has failed to identify remains. Others survive in part, such as the long-house Nant-y-ffin, Llandeilo (plate 17) which has had the byre demolished, but the house stands.

Many have been modernised, and have lost their original character in the process. Coedlannau, Pencader (plate 23) is one such example, where the original house is now cased in a hard cement render and with modern windows (photo 4). In some cases, such as Whithen, Pencader (plate 24), it is difficult to even recognise the original openings. Maes-y-bidiau, Abergorlech (plate 25) remained intact into the 1970s but now has huge picture windows and altered doorways (photo 5). Such alterations could always be reversed in the future if the owner was prepared to sacrifice a view for tradition.

Paradise Cottage, Leighton (plate 40) has also been altered, but drawings were made of the original before work was undertaken. Tŷ'n-rhosgadfan, Rhosgadfan (plate 45) was modernised as early as 1936 (meaning that Peate must have taken his photograph before then), and has been modernised again since. However, the house is still in local hands, and the present owner's father fondly remembered the visit from 'Dr Peate'. The traditional farmhouses around St Davids have been modernised, such as Gwrhyd Bach (plate 50), Llaethdy (plates 51 & 52) and Hendre Eiynon which lost its thatch c.1920, but still has its chimney (photo 7). Of the eight farms with round chimneys mentioned in this book, only Hendre Eiynon and Rhoson retain their's and two others not recorded by Peate have also been lost.

The largest of the houses in Peate's book have fared the best, such as Maes-Mawr near Caersws (plate 61) now a hotel with substantial extensions (photo 10), and Rhydonnen (plate 55) near Denbigh which has had replacement windows and a porch, but is otherwise intact (photo 9). Income from tourism has helped maintain these expensive structures. Both of these are Listed buildings, as is Hepste Fawr, Penderyn (plates 27 & 28), the circular pigsty at The Downs, Llantwit Major (plate 5) and Trewern, Buttington (plate 60) among others. Glan-'rafon, St. Harmon's (plate 33) has also fared well, although is sadly no longer farmed.

It is not just buildings that have gone, but their contents with them. Peate describes box-beds in Caernarfonshire cottages in Chapter V, but all have now gone aside from the few that have been rescued by museums. Very few beds that would have been seen in vernacular cottages from before 1830 have survived at all, suggesting perhaps that people slept on straw in the poorest of homes. Further examples of painted wall murals such as illustrated in plate 76 have recently come to light at Rhiwson at Cwrtnewydd and Treberfedd in Ystrad Aeron (both Ceredigion). Both houses have had major renovations in recent years, and at Rhiwson the paintings have been damaged in the process. The pitch floor illustrated in plate 78 at Pen-rhiw, Trefeglwys, has been removed and/or replaced by quarry tiles, but the same house does retain a square patterned pitch floor to the parlour of the original early house (not illustrated by Peate). Other details have been lost such as the roof at Tan-yr-ardd, Rhostryfan (plate 79) which went when the building was extended to two-storey height. The wattled chimney louvre illustrated in plate 81 has long gone, as have many hundreds of others in Ceredigion and Carmarthenshire. I have often knocked on doors to photograph original examples only to find that they had recently been removed because 'it was ugly' (Bryngolau, Dyffryn Aeron) or 'I kept banging my head on the thing' (Pen-y-Gaer, Bwlchllan). Original thatched chimneys (see plates 82 to 84) were all reduced or lost when roofs were capped in corrugated iron in the 1930s and 1940s, but reconstructed examples can now be seen at Troedrhiwfallen (photo 20) and Ffynnon Oer (photo's 17 - 24) and in Dyffryn Aeron.

There is also some good news, and several of the structures have fared well or been restored, such as Braichmelyn, Dinas Mawddwy (plate 1) and Llannerch-y-cawr, Cwm Elan (plate 34). Galch Hill, Denbigh (plate 56) appears untouched (photo 8), as does Penarth, near Newtown (plate 62), Talgarth, Trefeglwys (plate 63), and Rhyd-y-carw, Trefeglwys (plate 64) which has had a swimming pool and tennis courts added to the grounds.

Cefncloddiau, Llawr-y-glyn (plate 65) has recently been sold after having spent most of the last century owned by the same family but, fortunately, the new owners appear to be sympathetic to the building (photo 11). Others, such as Gwastod, Abermeurig (plate 21) which has been derelict for years and has partially collapsed (photo 3), now seems to have a brighter future with owners who intend to renovate and restore (including re-thatching) in 2004/5.

The depressing story of the fate of the houses chosen by Peate is a reflection of the fate of Welsh vernacular architecture in general since WWII. Unfortunately the last few decades have seen the wholesale destruction of traditional buildings. Hundreds if not thousands of simple cottages have been demolished to make way for modern houses and bungalows that reflect nothing of local traditions. Others lie empty and derelict (photo 12). Plastic windows replace the Georgian and Victorian originals that used to add character to our villages and towns. Limewashes have been sand-blasted off walls or cemented over. Despite attempts by Cadw to list the best examples, houses full of historic features are still being demolished and 'modernised' beyond recognition on a daily basis. Within the space of a single month in Ceredigion I have seen two thatched roofs stripped and replaced with concrete or plastic tiles (photo 14). With the thatch went the ancient crucks and wickerwork chimney hoods. What makes this destruction harder to bear is that it is often done for no good reason. I have witnessed the destruction of beautiful early eighteenth century wall-paintings because 'the wall leaned', the demolition of a cruck cottage to allow for an extra parking space on a bungalow plot, and a beautiful oak inglenook ripped out because the owner wanted 'light oak' coloured fittings to match her modern furniture. Features which have lasted for centuries are being destroyed in the name of improvement as people strive to make their mark on their homes. But good can come from even wanton vandalism, and a farmer who ripped out 17th century splat balusters and newel posts from his Knighton home, has inspired a builder in Castlemaine, Australia, to replicate the originals (photo 18).

The future for our remaining traditional buildings must be a better one. Some, but by no means all, counties now employ conservation officers who help protect traditional details through the planning process. Other counties have initiated heritage townscape initiatives, with particularly successful projects having been undertaken in Newport (Monmouthshire),

Cardigan and Denbigh. Listing now protects a good number of houses, but vernacular buildings tend not to be afforded the higher levels of protection (Grade II*, Grade I), and internal changes often go un-noticed. There are others that remain un-protected because they were by-passed in a Listing process that easily misses buildings that are invisible from public highways. The Historic Buildings Council for Wales offers hope through its grants for building conservation, via Cadw, and recent years have seen a swing towards funding more and more vernacular projects, such as the restoration of Yr Hen Siop, Treteio near St Davids (pictured on the dust-jacket). The Heritage Lottery Fund has also assisted some large projects in public ownership, but equally impressive results are seen when individual owners take care in maintaining their buildings and use traditional materials in their renovation (photos 15-25).

Organisations such as the National Trust have done good work in preserving traditional buildings in Wales, and they manage many cottages and farms of regional type. The Landmark Trust rescues historic buildings at risk and hires them for holidays, and has restored fifteen properties in Wales, including Dolbelydr near St Asaph (photos 22-23). This late sixteenth century gentry house is an inspiration to those who stay there, and an instructive example of high quality conservation repair. The newly established Faenol Building Conservation School near Bangor will hopefully train a generation of students in the practical skills of using lime and traditional materials in building renovation. For decades there has been a shortage of skilled builders and difficulties in gaining supplies, but now we have centres such as Tŷ Mawr near Brecon, ideally placed for supplying all of Wales.

Peate's warning against the loss of traditional buildings remains as relevant today as when it was first published over sixty years ago, as does his assertion that these traditional homes and their owners are inseparable from the traditional Welsh way of life. Despite the fact that Peate described this book as '*no more than a prolegomenon to a fuller study*', it wasn't until Peter Smith's *The Houses of the Welsh Countryside* was published in 1975 that Wales had a substantial national survey of its traditional buildings. Despite being reprinted and expanded in 1988, this great work is sadly now out of print, and there is thus no substantial book available on traditional Welsh architecture. Despite its age, *The Welsh House* remains a useful text for anyone curious to learn more about the rich architectural heritage of Wales. Peate speaks to his reader in a way that few architectural historians have, for this book is about far more than architecture. Peate's interest in Welsh houses was one informed by a comprehensive understanding of the crafts that went into their production, the furnishings that they housed, and the people that made them. It is this message that the meaning of houses cannot be separated from the people and circumstances that built them that gives this text its lasting value.

In my quest to trace the houses photographed by Peate I have been encouraged by the enthusiasm of people in helping me find these buildings. I never cease to be impressed by the sense of community ownership that people have for their local buildings. Like Peate in 1940, people today are aware that it is 'one minute to midnight' in the challenge to save our traditional buildings. If we can encourage communities to work together to identify, record and celebrate their best remaining examples, then hopefully we can secure their future. Then if another edition of *The Welsh House* is published in another half century, I hope that the picture won't be quite as bleak as it is today.

Greg Stevenson

Rhydlewis (Ceredigion), January 2004

Further Reading

(see also Peate's bibliography to the rear of this book)

Bevan-Evans M. 1964 *Farmhouses and Cottages* Flints Record Office

Britnell W.J. (ed.) 2001 'Tŷ-mawr, Castle Caereinion' *Montgomeryshire Collections* Vol. 89

Brooksby H. 1968-78 'The Houses of Radnorshire', in *Transactions of the Radnorshire Society*, pt I, 1968; pt II, 1969; pt III, 1970; pt IV, 1971; pt V, 1972; pt VI, 1973; pt VII, 1978.

Butler L.A.S. 1962 A Long-hut Group in the Aber Valley in *Transactions of the Caernarfonshire Historical Society* 1963 'Excavations of a Long-hut near Bwlch yr Hendre' in *Ceredigion*

Cadw 2003 *Small Rural Dwellings in Wales. Care and Conservation* Cadw

2004 *Stone in Wales.* Cadw

CPRW 1999 *The Cottage Tradition* Campaign for the Protection of Rural Wales

Davies M. 1991 *Traditional Qualities of the West Wales Cottage* (published privately)

Davis P. 1983 'Pen-y-banc, Aberarth' in *Ceredigion*

Fitzgerald M. 1993 *Pembrokeshire Architecture* Michael Rosedale Publications

Fox C. 1942 'Some South Pembrokeshire cottages', *Antiquity*(December 1942) pp 307-319

1951 'The round-chimneyed farm-houses of northern Pembrokeshire' pp124 -143 in W F Grimes, ed. *Aspects of Archaeology in Britain and Beyond – Essays Presented to O G S Crawford,* London

1951 'Three 'round-gable' houses in Carmarthenshire. Reprint from *Archaeologia Cambrensis*

Fox C. & Lord Raglan. 1994 *Monmouthshire Houses. Vols. I-III* (1951-4) (2nd edition) Merton Priory Press

The Gower Society. 2003 *Vernacular Gower* Swansea: The Gower Society

Hague D.B. 1958 'Giler, Cerrig-y-drudion, and Plas Chambers; an account of two 16th and 17th century Manor Houses' in *Transactions of the Denbighshire Historical Society*

Hayes P. 1968 'Some cottages in the Hawarden District: archaic types of cottages, some with cruck frames.' in *Flintshire Historical Society Publications*, 1967-8

Hogg A.H.A. 1954 'A 14th century house-site a Cefn-y-fan, Dolbenmaen' in *Transactions of the Caernarfonshire Historical Society*

Howells B. & J. Howells. 1980 'Peasant Houses in Stuart Pembrokeshire', *National Library of Wales Journal* Vol.21 (1979-80) pp. 357-365

Ifans R. Alun. 2003 *Bro a Bywyd : Iorwerth Cyfeiliog Peate 1901 - 1982* Barddas

Jenkins G. (ed.) 1969 *Studies in Folk Life. Essays in honour of Iorwerth C. Peate* Routledge

Jones S.R. 1969 'Ciloes-isaf, a late medieval Montgomeryshire Long-house' in *Montgomeryshire Collections*

Jones S.R. & J.T. Smith. 1971 'The Houses of Breconshire', in *Brycheiniog* ix-xiii (1963-69), xv

Lewis J.M. 1968 'The excavations of the 'New Buildings' at Montgomery Castle: an early 17th-century brick house in the Castle' in *Archaeologia Cambrensis*

Lloyd F., Vernon M.P., & M. Bevan-Evans. 1962 'The Long-house in Wales' in *Flintshire Historical Society Publications* 1967 'Penisardre: a Flintshire Farmhouse of the Great Rebuilding' in *Flintshire Historical Society Publications*

Lowe J. 1993 *Welsh Country Workers Housing* 1775-1875 National Museum of Wales Press 1994 *Welsh Industrial Workers Housing* 1775-1875 National Museum of Wales Press

McDermott K. 1978 'Two examples of Vernacular Architecture in Aberarth and Llansantffraid' in *Ceredigion*

Moore K.A. 1996-7 'A Vanishing Vernacular' (8 parts published in *Camarthenshire Life,* September 1996-April 1997)

Morris B. 1966 'Old Farmhouses and Cottages in Gower, Glamorganshire' in *Journal of the Gower Society*

1998 *Old Gower Farmhouses and their Families* The Gower Society

Nash G.D. 1989 'Up at Dawn: The Experimental Erection of a Squatter's Cabin' 57-70 in *Folk Life* Vol. 27

1995 *Timber-framed Buildings in Wales* National Museum of Wales Press

Owen T.M. 1969 'Historical aspects of Peat-cutting in Wales, in *Folk Life*
1970 'Social perspective in Welsh vernacular architecture',pp.108-115 in Moore, D. (ed), *The Irish Sea Province in Archaeology and History*

Parkinson A.J. 1975, 'A master carpenter in north Wales: a study of some carved screens and associated inscriptions of the late sixteenth century', pp.73-101 in *Archaeologia Cambrensis* Vol. 124

Pattison I. R. (ed.) *A Bibliography of Vernacular Architecture* Vol. III 1977-89 & Vol. IV 1990-94

Peate I. 1962 'Hendre'r wydd Uchaf' in the *Transactions of the Denbigh History Society*

1972 *Tradition & Folk Life. A Welsh View.* Faber

Phillips W.S. 1967 'Lower House and Cottage Farm: a study of two Timber-framed Houses in the parish of Evenjobb' in *Transactions of the Radnorshire Society*

RCAHMW. 1988 *Farmhouses and Cottages of Glamorgan* Royal Commission for Ancient and Historical Monuments, Wales

Smith P. 1963 'The Long-house and Laithe House' in *Culture and Environment*

1964 'Early Welsh Houses with reference to Dyfed' in *The Lands of Dyfed in Early Times*

1988 *Houses of the Welsh Countryside* HMSO (2nd edition)

Smith P. & E.M. Gardner. 1957 'Two Farmhouses in Llanbedr: 16th-17th century regional houses in Merioneth' in *Journal of the Merioneth Historical and Record Society*

Smith P. & D.B. Hague. 1958 'Tŷ Draw: a 14th century Cruck House from South Denbighshire' in *Archaeologia Cambrensis*

Smith P. & P. Hayes. 1964 'Brithdir Mawr, Cilcain: a Hall-house of 1589' in *Flintshire Historical Society Publications*

Smith P. & C.E.V. Owen. 1958 'Traditional and Renaissance elements in some late Stuart and early Half-timbered Houses in Arwystli' in *Montgomeryshire Collections*

1964 'Penarth: a Montgomeryshire Ailsed-hall?' in *Montgomeryshire Collections*

1965 'Architectural notes on Ystradfaelog, Bryn and Lower Gwestydd: three 17th-century central-chimney half-timbered houses in *Montgomeryshire Collections*

Smith J.T. 1963 'The Long-house in Monmouthshire' in *Culture and Environment*

Stevens C. 1986 *Iorwerth C. Peate* (Writers of Wales series) University of Wales Press

Stevenson G. 2002 'Discovering the Traditional Cottages of Wales' pp. 24-27 in *Walking Wales* Autumn edition

Suggett R. 1996 'The Chronology of Late-medieval Timber Houses in Wales' pp. 29-38 in *Vernacular Architecture*, vol.27

2003 Dendrochronology: progress and prospects' pp. 153-69 in C. Stephen Briggs (ed.) *Towards a Research Agenda for Welsh Archaeology* (BAR British Series 343. [This gives a consolidated list of all Welsh tree-ring dates].

Wiliam E. 1973 'Adeiladau Fferm Traddodiadol yng Nghymru', pp.2 – 14 in *Amgueddfa* Vol. 15

1973 'Farm Buildings in the Vale of Clwyd, 1550 – 1880', pp. 34 – 59 in *Folk Life* Vol. 11

1975 'To keep the devil at bay' pp. 34 – 6 in *Country Quest* May

1975 'Straw-Rope Underthatch in South-West Wales: a note' pp. 84-9 in *Folk Life,* Vol. 13

1975 'The vernacular architecture of a Caernarfonshire rural community, 1700 – 1900: the houses of Mynytho' pp. 173-94 in *Transactions of the Caernarfonshire Historical Society* Vol. 36

1975 'A Pair of Eighteenth-Century Labourers' Cottages at Banc Tai Newydd, Pontyberem', pp.125-32 in *Carmarthenshire Antiquary* Vol. 11

1976 'A Cruck Barn at Hendre Wen, Llanrwst, Denbighshire' pp. 23-31 in *Transactions of the Ancient Monuments Society* Vol. 21

1976 'A Guide to old farm buildings, a fast vanishing feature of our rural heritage', pp. 9 – 11 in *Country Quest* June

1977 'A Straw-Rope Partition at Trallwyn House, Pencaenewydd', pp.177-79 in *Transactions of the Caernarfonshire Historical Society* Vol. 38

1978 'Yr Aelwyd' the architectural development of the Hearth in Wales', pp. 85-100 in *Folk Life* Vol. 15

1979 'The protection of the House: Some Iconographic Evidence from Wales', pp.148 – 53 in *Folklore* Vol. 89

1979 'Tŷ'n y Braich, Dinas Mawddwy', pp. 303-9 in *Journal of the Merioneth Historical and Record Society* Vol. 18

1979 'North Devon Clay Ovens in Wales' pp. 30-48 in *Medieval and Later Pottery in Wales*

1979 'Where have all the pigsties gone?' pp. 18-20 in *Country Quest* September

1980 'Toi â brwyn yn ardel Bronnant, Ceredigion', pp. 175 – 8 in *Y Genhinen* 29/4 (1979 – 1980)

1981 'The Cottages of Rural Wales: A cultural challenge' pp. 5-9 in Period Home Vol. 2, No. 3

1982 *Traditional Farm Buildings in North-East Wales 1550-1900* National Museum of Wales Press

1982 'Peasant Architecture in Caernarfonshire' in the *Transactions of the Caernarfonshire Historical Society* Vol. 43

1986 *The Historical Farm Buildings of Wales* John Donald

1988 *Home-made Homes* National Museum of Wales Press

1989 'Cartrefi'r Cymry, 1200-1900' pp. 61-89.in Jenkins, G.H. (ed), *Cof Cenedl iv. Ysgrifau ar hanes Cymru*

1989 '"Let use be preferred to uniformity": domestic architecture' pp. 159-96.in Jones, J.G. (ed), Class, community and culture in Tudor Wales

1992 *Welsh Long-Houses* National Museum of Wales Press

1992 *Hen Adeiladau Fferm* Gwasg Carreg Gwalch

1994 *Welsh Cruck Barns* National Museum of Wales Press

1995 'Home-made homes': Dwellings of the Rural Poor in Cardiganshire' pp. 23-41 in *Ceredigion* Vol.XII No. 3

CONTENTS

PREFACE TO THE FIRST EDITION

THIS work is based on a field survey and the facts so collected have been supplemented by material from various written sources. Where it has been found possible, the evidence has been compared with that from other countries. The book is therefore for the greater part a systematic statement of facts actually observed in the field or collected in research. The accumulation of facts has led to several conclusions, but when theories have been put forward which cannot be proved conclusively, their tentative nature—as merely working hypotheses which may be disproved when our knowledge is fuller—is noted in each case.

It will be observed that no distribution-maps are included in the book. The omission is deliberate. It was felt that such maps would not only be useless for the purpose intended but might be very misleading unless every example in existence of the various types were marked on each map. Even then, such maps could only indicate the 20th century distribution of the types: that is, their only value would be as a record of modern conditions. For example, distribution-maps of existing timber-framed houses or long-houses or cruck-constructed houses would give little indication of the former incidence of these types in Wales. Some critics feel that the value of distribution-maps in archaeological work is grossly over-estimated: be that as it may, it is certain that some of the methods adopted in archaeological research cannot be applied to the study of a living culture.

No apology is needed for writing the book in English although an explanation may be of value. I should have preferred to have written it in Welsh; but there is an increasing and welcome tendency amongst research-workers who are members of small nations to write scientific works in one or other of the great international languages. (The only exceptions to such a rule are works dealing with language and literature which can be of use only to those who have mastered the language concerned). As an instance of this practice, *Folk-Liv*, the only journal of Folk Culture in existence, is published from Stockholm in English, German and French. In the present instance, quotations in Welsh in the work have been printed, for the sake of accuracy and as a true record, in that language and translated into English.

In the preparation of a study of this nature, any worker must depend to a high degree upon the co-operation of a large number of helpers in various directions. I acknowledge with gratitude the co-operation of many friends throughout Wales who in several ways facilitated my field-work. Sir Leonard Twiston Davies, K.B.E., F.S.A. (Pembrokeshire and Monmouthshire), Mr. W. Fergusson Irvine, M.A., F.S.A. (Merioneth-shire),

Mr. J. B. Willans, F.S.A. (Montgomeryshire), Mr. E. Emrys Jones (Montgomeryshire), Mr. W. Gilbert Williams, M.A. (Caernarvonshire) and Mr. Harold Davey (Denbighshire) gave me every facility to visit houses in certain parts of the counties mentioned. The names of persons who have helped me with individual houses and problems are mentioned in the text and footnotes, but special mention must be made of Mr. Llew. Morgan, Ystradgynlais, who photographed a number of houses for me and provided me with many details concerning them; Mr. Sam Ellis, Utica, New York, who has spared no trouble in giving me detailed descriptions of houses in north Montgomeryshire as he knew them in his boyhood days ; the Rev. E. Lewis Evans, M.A., Pontardulais ; Mr. J. J. Evans, M.A., St. David's ; Mr. Theodore Gibbins, Neath; the Rev. T. Jones, Trecastle; Mr. Hugh Owen, M.A., F.S.A., Llanfair-pwll; the Rev. Gomer M. Roberts, Pontrhyd-y-fen; Mr. R. D. Webb, Cardiff; Mr. E. I. Williams, Whitchurch; Mr. W. Rees Williams, B.Sc., Aberdare and Mrs. T. Williams, Trimsaran. My father's expert knowledge of rural building and of the Welsh countryside proved of the greatest value.

On individual points of a technical nature, I acknowledge with gratitude the advice and opinions, freely given, of Dr. Sigurd Erixon, Stockholm; Mr. W. F. Grimes, M.A., F.S.A., Southampton; Professor Henry Lewis, M.A., D.Litt., Swansea ; Sir John Edward Lloyd, M.A., D.Litt., F.B.A., F.S.A.; Professor Alf Sommerfelt, D.-es.-L., Oslo and of my colleague, Mr. W. E. Howarth, F.G.S. My colleague. Dr. F. J. North, F.G.S., Keeper of the Department of Geology in the National Museum of Wales, kindly read through the typescript of Chapter II, and made many suggestions and corrections. He is not however responsible for any errors which may still remain in it. Throughout the period of the survey, my friend. Professor Ifor Williams, M.A., D.Litt., F.B.A., F.S.A., gave his advice unstintingly on many linguistic problems and his ready help is recorded gratefully. In the same way. Sir Cyril Fox, Ph.D., V.P.S.A., Director of the National Museum of Wales, was always ready to discuss any problem which arose: I am grateful to him for advice on many matters. Most of the subjects treated in this volume were discussed from time to time with my colleague, Mr. Ffransis G. Payne, who has made many helpful suggestions. Miss E. H. Edwards, F.L.A., Librarian of the National Museum of Wales, was of the greatest service in securing for my use many of the books consulted, copies of several of which were difficult to obtain; my debt to her is great.

The greater part of the field-work was undertaken during vacations and week-ends : some of it was carried out during short periods of leave kindly granted me for that purpose by the Director and Council of the National Museum of Wales, who are also to be thanked for allowing me to reproduce a number of the plates. I acknowledge with gratitude the help of the Board of Celtic Studies of the University of Wales which made an annual grant over several years towards the cost of the survey. The following are thanked for allowing me to use certain illustrations and, in the cases mentioned, for lending blocks : the Editors of *Archaeologia Cambrensis* (for the blocks of figs. 2,32-52,56-7, and plates 50-3 and 71); Mr. Leonard Monroe, A.R.I.B.A. (fig. 56-7 and plate 71); Mr. C. W. Phillips, M.A., F.S.A. (fig. 2); Mr. Herbert Felton, F.R.P.S. (plate 54) and Messrs. B. T. Batsford, Ltd. (who generously supplied a duplicate of the block from *The English Cottage* by H. Batsford and C. Fry); Mr. M. F. H. Lloyd (fig. 6) and The Powysland Club; Mr. B. H. St. J. O'Neil, M.A., F.S.A. and H.M. Office of Works (fig. 3) and the Society of Antiquaries (who supplied the block from *The Antiquaries Journal*, July, 1936); Miss M. Wight; The Directors of the Gregynog Press (figs. 53-4); Mr. W. J. Hemp, M.A., F.S.A. (plates 68, 70); The Cambridge University Press (for lending the blocks of plates from *The Development of English Building Construction* by C. F. Innocent); H.M. Stationery Office (plates 11, 13, 17, 81-4); Mr. Ifan ab Owen Edwards, M.A. (plate 72 from *Cymru* edited by his father) and Mr. J. Watts (plates 57-64, photographs by his father). The Editors of *Antiquity* generously made available the sixteen blocks of the illustrations accompanying my paper on 'Some Welsh Houses' which appeared in the December 1936 issue of that journal.

Finally, my warmest thanks are due to Mr. Llewelyn Wyn Griffith for his constant encouragement and to Mr. T. C. Hart and the printing staff of Messrs. William Lewis (Printers) Limited for their personal interest and co-operation in the production of this volume.

IORWERTH C. PEATE

March, 1940

PREFACE TO THE SECOND EDITION

WHEN the Honourable Society of Cymmrodorion published this work in 1940 as Volume XL VII of *Y Cymmrodor* the greater part of the edition consisted of subscribers' copies and a few hundred copies only were for sale to the general public. The complete edition was sold in a few months. But the demand for the volume continued and it is felt that a second edition can no longer be delayed. The Society however has its annual commitments in the matter of publications but through its Council, it generously allowed me to prepare a new edition for publication elsewhere and, by lending all the necessary blocks, made it possible for the present publishers to offer this edition for sale at a price considerably lower than that of the first edition. I am deeply grateful to the Society for both its permission and its generosity.

As I have stressed in its pages, this volume is no more than a prolego-menon to a fuller study. No drastic revision was therefore necessary at this stage, but minor revisions and additions have been made. Travelling restrictions and other difficulties have stringently curtailed my field-work since 1940 and there is therefore no considerable body of new material to be incorporated. When detailed work has been carried out on an adequate scale, a volume of a different character will be necessary.

The sub-title of this work is 'A Study in Folk Culture.' Much of it is concerned with the 'unlearned artistry' of the 'common people,' but it must be stressed (in view of misconceptions in unexpected places) that the study of Folk Culture is not merely a study of the *vulgus in populo* but of 'alle maner of men.' For that reason, and because they form an integral part of the argument of this book, the homestead-group hut-circles of prehistoric chieftains, the palaces of the Welsh Kings and the half-timbered houses of a few 'gentry' are dealt with. In each case the building-tradition discussed is a vital part of the subject-matter of this book. The fact that the occupants of the houses were, or are, 'aristocrats,' is of no importance. Indeed to the folk-culturist the distinction between 'aristocrat' and 'peasant' is unscientific and inadmissible. The houses of the king and the bondman were built on the same principle; so were the half-timbered manor-house and cottage: the difference was in degree not in kind. To suggest that Folk Culture is concerned only with the bondman's dwelling and the labourer's cottage, is to misunderstand completely the meaning and scope of the subject and to introduce into scholarship an odious distinction of social snobbery. The only types excluded from the present study are those (see p. 132) which bear no relation to the traditional Welsh house: when the national survey is complete, they too can be dealt with as a part of Folk Culture.

For the early history of the rectangular house in Wales, the only body of evidence is that adduced in Chapter VI. It has been suggested-on the strength of one questionable example from Anglesey-that the Roman house made 'a deep impression on the native consciousness' and that I should have traced the early history of the rectangular form. In my judgement, the impression was very slight: indeed a pre-Roman type persisted (pp. 115-6) until early medieval times. In the absence from Wales of all but fragmentary data, I am not prepared to theorize on the early history of the rectangular form.

All the plans in this work (except where otherwise stated) are my own work. A full scale was prepared for each plan. Most of the blocks however (e.g. of long-house plans) were made for other publications and, in the interest of economy, re-used here. For reasons beyond my control, the blocks were made, in the first instance, without incorporating the scales prepared. To rectify this omission, the total length has been indicated in each caption: this will be found adequate except, possibly, for the fastidious critic to whom a *drawn* scale is still a fetish.

My use of Figures 32-36 has been criticised and, because these do not show the crucks referred to in the contemporary description, the illustrator has been held to be 'inventing.' Two comments only are necessary: (*a*) the illustrations are used (see p. 118) to show the 'hurdles, wattling, poles, rods' etc. of the Laws, and not to illustrate cruck-construction: (*b*) I believe the drawings to be faithful reproductions of a ruinous house, when its cruck feet had rotted and the house held up by a 'crazy array of supports.'

The first paragraph of Chapter VIII explains why only outstanding features of construction are discussed. Much detailed work will have to be carried out before the necessary data is available to make possible a full treatment of construction. When I am advised to lay the principal stress on construction as 'the grammar' of my 'language,' I can only reply that, with the best teachers, grammar comes last if indeed it is ever taught as such. It must perforce come last, whatever our views on the teaching of linguistics, until a school of students of native Welsh building will lavish on their subject the attention to detail long given to potsherds and earthworms. In the meantime, I resolutely refuse to theorize on insufficient data. Finally, I must emphasize that this is a study in Folk Culture, not in architecture *per se.*

IORWERTH C. PEATE

May, 1944

LIST OF ILLUSTRATIONS

Plates (at end)

63. Talgarth, Trefeglwys, Montgomeryshire.
    Photo : James Watts.
64. Rhyd-y-carw, Trefeglwys, Montgomeryshire.
    Photo : James Watts.
65. Cefncloddiau, Llawr-y-glyn—Staylittle district, Montgomeryshire.
    Photo : I. C. Peate. Copyright : National Museum of Wales.
66. Timbering of a barn in south Yorkshire.
    Copyright : Cambridge University Press (from C. F. Innocent: The Development of English Building Construction).
67. Glan-y-wern, Llandyrnog, Denbighshire.
    Photo : I. C. Peate. Copyright : National Museum of Wales.
68. Cruck constructed building, Yale district, Denbighshire.
    Photo .- W. J. Hemp, M.A., F.S.A.
69. Cruck-constructed cottage, Hawarden, Flintshire.
    Copyright: Cambridge University Press (from C. F. Innocent: The Development of English Building Construction).
70. Y Gilfach, Llanfihangel-y-Pennant, Merionethshire.
    Photo : W. J. Hemp, M.A., F.S.A.
71. Cruck construction, Lloran Ganol, Llansilin, Montgomeryshire-Denbighshire border. From *Arch. Camb.*, 1933.
72. Llwyn-rhys, Llanbadarn Odwyn, Cardiganshire : interior view of cruck.
    From *Cymru*, 1901, by courtesy of Ifan ab Owen Edwards, M.A.
73. Cae Crwn, Glanmorfa, Portmadoc, Caernarvonshire.
    Copyright : Cambridge University Press (from C. F. Innocent: The Development of English Building Construction).
74. Llainfadyn, Rhos-isaf, Caernarvonshire: showing use of large boulders in the walling.
    Photo : I. C. Peate. Copyright : National Museum of Wales.
75. Porch of a cottage near Waterfall Station on the Snowdon Mountain Railway, Caernarvonshire : note the dry-walling.
    Photo : I. C. Peate. Copyright : National Museum of Wales.
76. Painted mural decoration, of early 17th-century type at Brogynin, Penrhyn-coch, Cardiganshire, now in the National Museum of Wales.
    Photo : I. C. Peate. Copyright : National Museum of Wales.
77. Pitched floor, Plasau Duon, Llanwnnog, Montgomeryshire.
    Photo : I. C. Peate. Copyright : National Museum of Wales.
78. Pitched floor, Pen-rhiw, Trefeglwys, Montgomeryshire.
    Photo : I. C. Peate. Copyright : National Museum of Wales.
79. Tan-yr-ardd, Rhostryfan, Caernarvonshire : detail of roof showing rods tied together, surmounted by clods.
    Photo : I. C. Peate. Copyright: National Museum of Wales.
80. Pair of interlocking ridge-tiles from Caerphilly, Glamorganshire, now in the National Museum of Wales.
    Copyright : National Museum of Wales.
81. Wattling of a chimney louvre, Carmarthenshire.
82. Thatched chimney-'pot', Carmarthenshire.

Colour

Photographs

Photo: Elen Davies

Photo 1: Bryn-Mawr, Llanerfyl, Montgomeryshire: front view in 2003. The house was vacated in May 1939, and has since collapsed. Compare with plate 48 (same view) and the Frontispiece (rear view).

Photo: Greg Stevenson

Photo 2: Ty'n-coed Uchaf, Blaencaron, Ceredigion: rear view, 2003. The house was vacated shortly before Peate's visit, and has since collapsed. Compare with plate 20 (same view).

Photo: Greg Stevenson

Photo 3: Gwastad Gwrda, Abermeurig, Ceredigion: view of rear c1999.
This photograph was taken a couple of months before the gable collapsed.
The house is currently in poor repair, but the owners have plans to renovate
and re-thatch in 2004/5. Compare with plate 21 (front view).

Photo: Penelope Clarke

Photo 4: Coedlannau, Pencader, Carmarthenshire, 2003.
Although heavily modernised, this long-house has fared better than most of
the others illustrated in the first edition. Compare with plate 23 (same view).

Photo: David Roe

Photo 5: Maes-y-bidiau, Abergorlech, Carmarthenshire, 2001.
Original openings have been altered and extended, changing the character of the original. Compare with plate 25.

Photo: Greg Stevenson

Photo 6: Pensarn-mynach, Cribyn, Ceredigion, 2003.
A modern bungalow replaces the original cottages. Compare with plate 37.

Photo: Mrs R.A.Jamieson

Photo 7: Hendre Eiynon, St Davids, Pembrokeshire, 2002.
Although modernised, this is one of only two surviving round chimneys once typical of the peninsula. Compare with plate 53.

Photo: Roy Thomas

Photo 8: Galch Hill, Denbigh, 2003.
One of the least changed houses, the front elevation is virtually identical to how it looked in 1940. Compare with plate 56.

Photo: Buddug Jones

Photo 9: Rhydonnen, Gellifor, Denbighshire, 2003. A porch has been added that matches the existing architecture, and there are replacement windows, but this important early house survives remarkably intact. Compare with plate 55.

Photo 10: Maes-mawr, near Caersws, Montgomeryshire, 2003
Although massively extended, the original house remains largely intact. Compare with plate 61.

Photo 11: Cefncloddiau, Llawr-y-glyn, Staylittle, Montgomeryshire, 2003. Despite the cement render and modern porch, the house is largely intact. Having recently sold, the new owners appear sympathetic to the building. Compare with plate 65.

Photo 12: Cottage at Gwyddgrug, Carmarthenshire.
Typical of the eighteenth century cottages that have survived into the 21st century, this humble building retains thatch under a corrugated iron roof, and even has original window frames (for shutters). It is currently used as a shelter for farm stock.

Photo 13: Cottage at Penrhiwpal, Ceredigion.
Planning law in Ceredigion encourages new-build houses (usually bungalows), rather than renovation of existing housing stock, such as this pleasantly proportioned 19th century cottage.

Photo 14: Fron Dolau, Bwlchllan, Ceredigion.
Derelict and having suffered partial collapse, this clom cottage retained oak crucks and thatch under the corrugated iron. Currently being 'renovated' by a property developer, and to have a slate roof.

Photo: Greg Stevenson

Photo 15: Treleddid Fawr, St Davids.
Unlike so many vernacular cottages on the peninsula, this example has remained in the same hands since the 1930s, and has been traditionally maintained with limewash to the roof and walls.

Photo: Andrew Vaughan-Harries

Photo 16: Cottage at Abereiddy.
Another fine example of the Pembrokeshire vernacular, this one now stands in a hamlet where every house is a second or holiday home. Note the grouted roof with wire forming the ridges.

Photo: Jason Spragg

Photo 17: Eighteenth century underthatch of smoke-blackened oak and gorse at Ffynnon Oer in Dyffryn Aeron

Photo: Rob Hadden

Photo 18: New balusters in a house near Castlemaine, Australia, faithfully copied from originals from a farmhouse near Knighton (Powys). The 17th century originals were being ripped out and destroyed, the visiting Australian was so taken with them that he copied the splat template and produced his own in local hardwoods.

Photo 19: Troedrhiwfallen, Cribyn, photographed in 2002.
The last thatched house in Cribyn, this humble vernacular cottage had five applications to demolish it before it was rescued by its present owner.

Photo 20: Troedrhiwfallen, Cribyn, during conservation in 2003.
Support from the Historic Buildings Council of Wales made renovation possible, including a new layer of longstraw thatch on top of the existing layers. The finished cottage is now let for holidays, with profits going to fund other rescue projects.

Photo 21: Interior of the hall at Plas Uchaf, Corwen, Powys.
The unusually grand hall was built around 1400, with the fireplace being added in the sixteenth century.

Photo 22: Dolbelydr, a late sixteenth century manor house near St Asaph in Denbighshire, photographed here before repairs and restoration were undertaken by the Landmark Trust.

Photo 23: Dolbelydr in 2003

Substantial repair and some reconstruction has guaranteed a future for this important historic house where Henry Salesbury wrote his *Grammatica Britannica*, giving the house a claim to be the birthplace of the modern Welsh language.

Photo: www.underthethatch.co.uk

Photo 24: The author of the foreword finishing the surface on a newly built clom (earth) wall at Ffynnon Oer in the Vale of Aeron. Thousands of clom cottages were built across West Wales in the 18th and 19th centuries, but few have survived unaltered.

Photo: Andy Warren

Photo 25: Belam, Glynbrochan, Powys.
Recently renovated using conservation building techniques and traditional lime products, this is a good example of the revival of traditional skills in rural areas.

THE
WELSH HOUSE

CHAPTER I

Introduction

FOLK CULTURE as a subject for serious scientific research has only recently come into its own in this island and that, to a high degree, only in Wales. It follows that most of the problems relating to the cultural development of the British peoples have been looked upon as topics either subordinate to aspects of political or economic history or as 'bygones' elucidating the study of prehistoric archaeology. The miscellaneous collections of 'bygones' in so many national and provincial museums, displayed as appendages to archaeological research and the complete neglect of Folk Culture in all our universities are proof of this neglect of the subject as an independent science.

The 'dependent existence' to quote Professor Sigurd Erixon[1] of Folk Culture 'as an ambulating guest of certain branches of science' down to our own time has resulted in difficulties which have now become almost insuperable but which did not exist even fifty years ago. The unparalleled development of what has been aptly called the Machine Age, and the application to social needs of scientific invention in all its branches have resulted in a metamorphosis of country life to a degree beyond comparison with the growth of civilization in any other age. The development of transport has put the most inaccessible moorland village within the reach of populous areas: the mechanisation of industry, agriculture in particular, has caused the overflow of many traditional methods: the centralization of authority both in marketing and in local government has resulted in a phenomenal change in the social economy of the countryside. Side by side with these factors in the transfiguration of our rural life must be considered the growth of education and a quickening social consciousness which have resulted in the improvement of the countryman's living conditions and in the large-scale abandonment both of methods of labour and of houses and outbuildings which could only be described as primitive. While all these developments have been in varying degrees beneficial, their cumulative effect for the student of Folk Culture was to destroy a mass of evidence of the greatest importance in unravelling the story of our traditional culture.

---

[1] *Folkliv*, I, 1937, p. 5.

This is in no way better exemplified than by the changes affecting houses in Wales. Down to the last decade of the 19th century. Government Blue Books and other authoritative sources contain descriptions of houses of a most primitive character in the Welsh countryside. But in the present century most of these houses have disappeared completely. In another chapter, it will be seen how it has been impossible to discover in the past few years a type of house described in detail as existing in 1893.[1] Country landlords of large estates, conscious of their social duties to their tenants, have carried out extensive schemes of rebuilding farm-houses or of restoring them to such a degree that their traditional features have been completely eliminated. The progress made in sanitary and similar laws- although much remains to be accomplished[2] - has made necessary the reconstruction of hundreds of houses. A less pleasant feature of this transformation in country housing was the introduction, principally after the European War 1914-18, of 'council houses.' In many instances these replaced old cottages which were native to their environment however much their internal accommodation could be criticized. The new houses however seem too often to conform to a standardized pattern adopted indiscriminately by local authorities without thought for the particular requirements of their own areas. There are notable exceptions, but it is unfortunately true that in many areas, the new housing schemes have no regard for 'decency' in architecture nor is any serious attention paid to the relationship of houses to their environment.

This deplorable attitude, so well illustrated in modern housing schemes, is not an entirely new factor in the history of Welsh housing. During the 19th century, evictions for political reasons and emigration to America and to industrial areas of south Wales, together with the effects of the enclosure movement, resulted in many districts in large numbers of farm-houses and cottages becoming untenanted. A contemporary observer[3] in the parish of Llanbrynmair, Montgomeryshire, lists as many as 106 such houses which became unoccupied in that parish within his own memory. That this should happen at a time-the mid 19th-century- when a general vitiation of good taste in architecture was apparent was nothing short of a tragedy. The result, later in the century, was the building of a large number of houses distinguished only by their lack of decency in design and of good taste in materials. Judging by the widespread distribution in Wales of

---

[1] See p. 39.

[2] See the *Report of the Committee of Inquiry into the Anti-Tuberculosis Service in Wales and Monmouthshire* (1939).

[3] Peate, David: *Hen Ffyrdd a Hen Dai adfeiliedig Llanbrynmair* (in MSS), 1887.

houses of the second half of the 19th century, this development in building must have been almost universal.

Coinciding as it did with the development of rail transport and the production in great quantities of Welsh slates and of red and yellow pressed bricks[1] it changed the whole character of the Welsh countryside and created for Welsh villages, in particular, a reputation of unattractive ugliness which many of them deserve. The unintelligent use of such materials as corrugated-iron, in the present century, completed the tragedy.

The student of the Welsh house has therefore to work under serious disadvantages. Much of the material has been destroyed and much so tampered with as to be valueless. The original material with which he is concerned-the traditional types-outcrops only here and there from beneath a deep stratum of a later overlying culture. So extensive is this layer that some students have maintained from time to time that Wales has no architecture. Since this view is fundamental to the subject of this book-the Welsh House-it must be examined here.

Wales is a country of high undulating moorland and of deep valleys, with a consistently high rainfall. Until recent times it has had no large cities or towns. Its community has always been essentially peasant in character. For the last three hundred years it has had no separate political existence and its social and economic life therefore has been linked with that of England, which is not separated from it by any natural boundary.

These, in brief, are the important factors in assessing Welsh architectural attainment. A wet moorland does not lend itself to the development of architectural forms based on the rich cultures of the sunny Mediterranean. A cityless peasant community does not foster the erection of noble public buildings. A nation bereft of its sovereignty cannot promote the growth of the fine arts except by indirect and generally innocuous means. In such a country, incorporated moreover since 1536 in a neighbouring virile state, the only national architecture is the non-professional architecture. In the 18th and 19th centuries when the professional architect had emerged as a necessary member of most European communities, his influence in Wales was felt only on the houses of the rich and on the public buildings of the prosperous towns and cities. But the rich in Wales were almost universally anglicized and the prosperous towns were those of the industrial areas which were then breaking away from the traditional Welsh peasant culture to become anglicized but *deraciné* areas. There was no incentive or need for a school of professional architects in the Welsh rural community. Consequently the mansions of the country squires and the buildings of the

---

[1] See Chapter II.

anglicized towns are almost without exception English in inspiration, but mildly conditioned at times by the particular needs of their environment. And when the time came for the erection of national structures on a grand scale, most of them found a home in the new city of Cardiff, others in Aberystwyth and Bangor and Swansea, but all conforming to a well-established classical tradition and divorced in conception, design and materials from the unpretentious architecture of the traditional Welsh community. In this respect, it is true to say that there is no Welsh architecture. Such buildings indeed are the work of Welsh- or English-born architects working in a supra-national tradition which has not found a peculiar Welsh expression.

Is there then such an expression in any Welsh building? The answer is to be found in the dwelling-houses of the Welsh people. 'In peasant architecture the fundamental issues in building are made more clearly apparent. Social, climatic and geographical conditions all combine to produce an architecture in which fashion or style play little or no part. The primitive need for shelter from the sun and rain induces the peasant folk to build shelter for themselves and their cattle. There are no architects. The peasant knows his wants and builds. With his meagre resources he builds as simply as possible in the local material available. He is able to conceive and create his work because of the simplicity of his life and needs. It is a clear expression of his life, simple and direct... The abstract and purely aesthetic beauty of a column, the decorative effect of a frieze are outside his comprehension. A plain white wall, a dark window-opening, a red-tiled roof, these he understands not for their aesthetic but for their practical value. Utility comes first. Beauty follows, resulting naturally from the constructive elements and the colour and texture of the materials.'[1]

The Welsh house-be it farmhouse or cottage-is therefore an expression of Welsh life-indeed, a facet of it, for the folk life is always indivisible. It follows therefore that the folk dwelling varies according to the climatic and geographical conditions of the locality in which it is found *and also according to the social condition of its occupant or builder and his economic status.* In the same way, 'true peasant architecture knows no time: it represents the past, present and future.'[2] The creation of new social and economic conditions such as have been indicated on the preceding pages has resulted in a desire for the amelioration of country life and for the creation of styles artificially governed. As in every aspect of folk life, this departure from the natural or the traditional to the artificial has resulted in a

---

[1] Ling, A. G.: 'Peasant Architecture in the Northern Provinces of Spain' in *Journal of the Royal Institute of British Architects,* 1936, p. 845.

[2] *Ibid.,* p. 846.

betrayal of the normal decencies of the countryside. But the betrayal is an unconscious one and education in the value of the old tradition and in the methods of developing it to suit present social needs will provide the only solution for the present 'desecration of the countryside' which many deplore but which some only criticize un-intelligently.

This book is the story of a long pilgrimage extending over a period of twelve years. It has been of a dual nature: on the one hand wanderings through the thirteen counties of Wales in search of the houses to be described on the following pages. Many of the journeys were fruitless and all too frequently it was found that the houses searched for had disappeared or had been replaced by new buildings. An example may be quoted. Llwyn-rhys,[1] near Llangeitho, Cardiganshire, was photographed before the 1914-18 war by the late W. R. Hall of Aberystwyth. The photograph shows a long-house of great interest. Through great good fortune the house was examined shortly afterwards by Mr. W. J. Hemp, M.A., F.S.A., who pronounced it to be of 15th-century date, with a 17th-century addition built to serve as the first Nonconformist Meeting House in Cardiganshire. The house had a thatched roof. It was again photographed by Mr. D. J. Davies, of Lampeter, when it had a corrugated-iron roof. I visited the district in 1930 to make a detailed survey and plan of this important structure, but to my consternation discovered that it had completely disappeared. This is what had happened: during the last years of the war, corrugated-iron sheeting became scarce. The owner of the now-uninhabited Llwyn-rhys after valiant attempts (unfortunately directed to the wrong quarter) to have the house scheduled as an ancient monument, stripped the sheeting, which he required for other purposes, from the roof. The rain penetrated through the leaky thatch and completely ruined the mud walls which fell in. The timbering which endangered the farm stock was then pulled down and in this way one of the most important historical monuments in Cardiganshire disappeared for all time.

This is not an isolated example. In a large number of instances, I have followed in the wake of destruction of this nature, much of it thoughtless, and unnecessary. In some other instances, my visits were providential. Bryn-mawr, Llanerfyl (see p. 99, 100), visited in the summer of 1938, appeared to be secure for many years. It was occupied by a young farmer and his family and had the appearance of a snug and comfortable-although isolated-dwelling. A month or two after my visit, its occupants had left and the house was abandoned : it is likely that its fate will be that of several other homesteads in the locality. It will never again be occupied.

---

[1] See pp. 65-67.

This desertion of the open moorland-indeed in many cases, of the countryside-was one of the outstanding facts made obvious during the course of the survey. 'Of eighteen cottages visited and measured at Llanychaer [Pembrokeshire] . . . only three were still inhabited : it is still more significant that of the fifteen unoccupied cottages, seven had been deserted within the last few years. That this refusal of a traditional mode of life is primarily due to primitive conditions in the cottages is improbable: rather, it is the croft system that has broken down in the area. We must suppose that the life is too hard, the rewards too slight,. the inconveniences of isolation too manifest. The croft cannot today yield a "living".[1] This movement from the countryside is however, as has been stressed, continuous from the 19th century (see pp. 82-3). In 1899, a writer notes concerning a neighbouring district of north Pembrokeshire : 'Peth dynnai fy sylw oedd nifer mawr o fythynod a mân dyddynod wedi syrthio . . . Cyfrifais tros ddeugain'. [What drew my attention was the large number of ruined cottages. ... I counted over forty] .[2] Unfortunately in such areas as Llanychaer, in the Vale of Glamorgan, in Llyn, in Monmouthshire, in Merionethshire and in Cardiganshire, the destructive 'march of Time' has been hastened by the action of the British Defence Ministries which have occupied so many areas of rural Wales. The wanton and unintelligent destruction by the Air Ministry of Penyberth in Llyn, a house with 15th-century features, and with strong historical associations, is well-known. The timbering was hacked down and sold for firewood. Providentially, a neighbouring farmer acquired examples of the earlier features and through his generosity a wooden window-head and a length of oak panelling, both of late 15th-century date, are now in the National Museum of Wales. The Ministries have since come to an arrangement with the Museum whereby the Museum authorities examine the sites before they are 'developed', with a view to the preservation of antiquities. This is however little solace to a nation whose rural amenities and traditional culture are ruthlessly assailed by such 'developments'.

There is much to be said -if we wish to assess the extent of the survival in modern times of old types- for a careful survey of the distribution of every type of house in Wales, and the preparation of detailed distribution- maps of all such types, with measured plans and descriptions of each variation. It became obvious to me that such a survey was beyond the ability of a Museum official working on his own with but a few short weeks each summer in which to do the work. Indeed, most of the work on which this volume is based was carried out during short annual summer

---

[1] Fox, Sir Cyril: 'Peasant Crofts in North Pembrokeshire', in *Antiquity*, 1937, p. 439.

[2] *Cymru*, 1899, II, p. 112.

vacations sacrificed for this purpose. Such detailed surveying, parish by parish, is essential and will be carried out, if circumstances permit, over many years. But it was felt that this study should not be delayed until such work had been completed. By traversing every county enough information has been obtained to justify the present publication of a study of Welsh houses. The subsequent careful plotting of types will no doubt correct certain details but the main principles have thus been determined. It is hoped therefore that this work will induce other workers to assist in detailed surveys of their own areas to secure the plotting of minutiae beyond the scope of this volume.

The second aspect of the 'pilgrimage' involved an exhaustive study of references to Welsh houses in literature and in manuscript sources. The starting-point for such a study had to be the monumental *Report of the Royal Commission on Land in Wales*. Its exhaustive section on farm-dwellings and its Bibliography, both the work of the late Sir Daniel Lleufer Thomas, M.A., LL.D., F.S.A., have been invaluable in the preparation of this work. It was the present author's good fortune to come into close contact with Sir Lleufer in 1926 and it was on his advice and with his encouragement that this work was begun.[1] Sir Lleufer's breadth of vision and scholarship, discernible in every field of Welsh historical research, was nowhere more evident than in his careful record of farm-houses and cottages and his descriptions, always marked by scientific accuracy, of their structure and economy. No less important in every respect is Sir Lleufer's less-known work included in the *Report on the Agricultural Labourer in Wales,* one of the publications of the Royal Commission on Labour.[2]

Contemporary descriptions of houses in Wales are unfortunately not numerous. Many of the English travellers of the late 18th - early 19th centuries have contented themselves with dismissing the subject with phrases such as 'miserable hovels'. Occasionally, however, detailed descriptions are given. While it is well-known that most of the travellers who 'discovered' Wales at that period were deplorably ignorant of Welsh life and history which they therefore delineated in a prejudiced and garbled fashion, it is obvious too that where their descriptions depended on personal observation they are generally accurate. Consequently, it was found necessary to read through the voluminous literature of that period about

---

[1] The work took definite shape after a discussion in 1934 between Dr. Ake Campbell and Professor C. von Sydow of Sweden, Mr. Seamas Ó Duilearga of Eire, and the writer. Dr. Campbell's own work on the Irish house has been a valuable example in preparing this volume.

[2] It is a source of gratification to the writer that Sir Lleufer was able to read the present work when it first appeared (1940) and to express his delight that a work on Welsh houses had at last been published

Wales in English as well as all available references in Welsh. For the English works the exhaustive lists in the appendices to Mr. W. J. Hughes's *Wales and the Welsh in English Literature* formed a basis for my reading. The task was arduous and long. For the early 19th century too, the *Report of the Commission on the State of Education in Wales* (1847) and several other Blue Books gave many details. A complete bibliography of the relevant literary sources consulted is printed at the end of this work.

CHAPTER II

Building Materials

THE use and character of building materials in folk architecture can never be determined completely by one factor, although from time to time some writers have tended to emphasize certain factors at the expense of others. It has already been stressed[1] that the countryman builds as simply as possible in the local material available, but the nature of that material varies in most districts. The variation depends upon many circumstances amongst which may be mentioned geographical position, climate, height above sea level, soil and topography, geological conditions and the tractability of the materials available. It is intended here to discuss the materials used in Wales in relation to such factors as these.

Wales forms a part of the Highland Zone of western Britain.[2] It may be looked upon as an upland fortress on the edge of a lowland extending from the English Plain to the Ural Mountains. Over this 'sea of lowland' the tides of centuries have swept to break upon the fortress of the west. Wales has often been compared with Palestine: there are directions in which the comparison can be made. Much of the life of the Holy Land has been conditioned by that of the Syrian Desert beyond. Wales can be understood only by reference to the lowlands beyond its eastern fringe.

We are concerned therefore with an upland country of moor and mountain beyond a vast lowland area, an upland, too, that has become the 'refuge' of ancient racial types, of bygone customs and forgotten things. This moorland plateau has been dissected by rivers flowing north, east, south and west in deep-cut ravines and broad valleys which radiate from the upland like the spokes of a mighty wheel. One of the principal effects of this dissection, indeed of the geological formation of the country to which we shall refer later, has been to emphasize its highland character and to weaken its geographical unity. It has resulted in the creation of isolated communities dotted over the Welsh massif and around its fringes-to a high degree separated from each other by natural boundaries, deep valleys, high mountains and broad tracts of boggy moorland but united by an ancient culture and language. 'Continuity and persistence are remarkable features of the life of Wales.'[3]

---

[1] p. 4.

[2] For a survey of the significance of the Highland Zone in prehistoric and early historic times see Fox, Sir Cyril: *The Personality of Britain* (Fourth Edit., 1943).

[3] Fleure, H. J., in *Arch. Camb.,* 1923, p. 241.

To continue the simile, Wales opens most of its doors in a westerly direction. Its rivers, from the north around the western rim of the massif to the south, flow away from the eastern lowland; but several important rivers run north-eastwards, eastwards and south-eastwards. The entrances into Wales from the east, some of which are formed by the valleys of these rivers, must therefore not be overlooked. The upland plateau shaped almost like an hourglass is fringed, north and south, with tongues of lowland. In the north the present railway route from Chester to Holyhead indicates the extent of the lowland strip. In the south is the coastal plain of southern Monmouthshire and the Vale of Glamorgan with the estuaries of the Tawe and Tywi beyond, the lowland ending in 'Little England beyond Wales', again the route of east to west rail communication from London. In central Wales the broad valley of the upper Severn opens up the midland area of the Welsh massif to provide another cross-country railway route while the Dee 'cleft' at Llangollen and the projections of lowland occupied by the upper Wye and the Usk make inroads into the uplands.

These topographical features are of the greatest importance in any consideration of human culture in Wales. They help to clarify the reasons for the 'continuity of cultural character' on the one hand and 'the power of absorption, the tendency to fusion' in Wales, on the other. Both these characteristics are exemplified in the history of the Welsh house.

The climate of Wales is maritime, with mild winters and cool summers. 'This character is most pronounced in the coastal districts, particularly in the west, where severe frosts and snow are comparatively rare. More rigorous conditions prevail in the upland regions, and the higher mountains are frequently capped with snow during the winter and early spring months. The rainfall is closely related to the surface-relief... The highest mean annual rainfall is about 200 in. near the peak of Snowdon. A considerable area in north Wales receives a rainfall of over 100 in. per annum. . . . Typically, the Welsh climate is distinguished by an equable temperature, abundant and well-distributed rainfall, and a generally humid atmosphere. In the lowlands, frost occurs only occasionally . . . The climate of the uplands is more rigorous, but the proximity of the sea and the prevalence of mild south-westerly winds mitigate its severity. Although the rainfall is considerably higher in the uplands than in the lowlands, the shallow character of the soils intensifies the effect of drought, which actually becomes a limiting factor in the growth of grass and determines a heathy type of vegetation.'[1] For 1894 as much as 131.05 in. of rainfall were recorded at certain stations in Montgomeryshire, 100.8 in. in Caer-

---

[1] Robinson, G. W. : 'The Soils of Wales' in *Guide Book for the Excursion round Britain of the Third International Congress of Soil Science* (1935), pp. 260-2.

narvonshire, 107.51 in. in Merionethshire and 100.61 in. in Glamorgan-shire, as compared with 24.55 in. in Flintshire and 25.65 in. in Denbigh-shire.[1] These late 19th-century figures are quoted as indicative of the end of the period with which we are principally concerned but the variation in rainfall from period to period in recent times is slight, the average rainfall over the British Isles during the years 1901-30 being 103% of that of the period 1870-99.[2]

Excessive rainfall, such as falls over the greater part of the Welsh upland, has an important bearing both on agriculture and on the general life and habits of the people. Together with the surface conditions in the highland area it limits arable farming and encourages pastoral farming : it affects the distribution of population and is an important factor in the history of building. Nor must other related factors be overlooked : the great amount of cloud, the absence of sunshine and the constancy of winds which are all climatic factors, have their effect upon housing.

But in any consideration of factors affecting housing and, in particular, building materials, the geology of any area is of outstanding importance. Geology provides the clue to most local materials available for use in construction. 'The style of a national architecture' to quote Ruskin,[3] 'may evidently depend in a great measure upon the rocks of the country.' A treatment of the physique of Wales is therefore not adequate in itself, important though it is to illustrate conditions which modify the use of certain materials. It should be clearly understood too that geological 'districts' bear no relation to county boundaries and that these must therefore be ignored in considering house-types.

The superficial observer in these days of swift transport by road and rail may wonder why any great stress is laid upon local geology. The fact is of course that, as we have already indicated, the countryman 'builds as simply as possible in the local material available'. The last fifty years have witnessed a revolutionary change in this direction. The development of transport (in association with other causes such as the increase of mass-production and the social amelioration referred to in Chapter I) has made the local builder independent of local materials. Bricks are often found to be cheaper than stone quarried locally, even when transport costs are included. Corrugated-iron has ousted timber, and asbestos the native slate or tile.

---

[1] *Royal Commission on Land in Wales : Report*, p. 28.

[2] *British Rainfall*, 1937, p. 277.

[3] John Ruskin in Stones of Venice, quoted in J. Alien Howe : *The Geology of Building Stones* (1910), p. 2.

Consequently for the first time in the long history of building in Wales, no builder is now dependent upon the local material available. This change, as I have indicated, is revolutionary. It has dealt tradition a death-blow from which it may never recover. Traditional lay-outs and plans often conditioned by the nature of the materials used, have been discarded and traditional techniques and methods forgotten. Furthermore the end of this dependence upon local materials is the basic cause of the widespread bad taste in modern building-to be seen in the use of materials unsuitable for the areas concerned (e.g. pressed brick of a violent colour in grey-stone countrysides remarkable for their half-tones) and in the absence of the craftsman's skill in building and the craftsman's restraint in design, which so often happens when craftsmen abandon tradition[1] and have to handle new materials demanding a new technique. This transition converging upon the social developments referred to in Chapter I was undoubtedly the primary reason for the widespread transformation of the Welsh countryside in the late 19th-century.

The following treatment of the geological factors is mainly stratigraphical and it may be argued with much validity that a lithological treatment would be more pertinent. The writer is aware of this need. But such a study can only be undertaken by a competent geologist. Furthermore it would need a systematic collection of building stones actually used in every parish, studied by a geologist in relation to the lithology of Wales. It is surprising that such work has not long since been undertaken since it would form a valuable contribution to the economic geology of Wales. It is to be hoped that when such projects as the Soil Map of Wales have been completed, such tasks as a lithological survey from the point of view of building materials will be undertaken also. The students of anthropology and history cannot be expected to fill this gap in our knowledge.

In view of this difference between stratigraphy and lithology, the description in this chapter of the geology of Wales should be considered in the light of the following note, kindly supplied by Dr. F. J. North;, F.G.S.: 'The adaptability of a stone for building purposes depends upon its lithological characters, e.g., its hardness and durability, and the development of planes of weakness such as bedding, jointing and cleavage, that may facilitate the quarrying and dressing of the stone, or may, on the other hand, render it useless for constructional work. For some purposes, where a freestone is needed, softer stone with well-spaced planes of weakness is suitable.

---

[1] For craft deterioration of a similar nature in another field see the author's *Y Crefftwryng Nghymru* (1933), p. 32.

These lithological and structural characteristics are independent of the age of the rock and similar types may occur in stratigraphical series of widely different ages, and taking the Welsh rocks as a whole, the various rock-types enumerated are distributed as follows :-

(*a*) Hard massive rocks without pronounced structures are characteristic of the Pre-Cambrian Series, and of certain types of igneous rock of Ordovician Age.

(*b*) Hard rocks with more or less pronounced joints and bedding planes,. are present in all the formations represented in Wales, although they are absent over considerable areas : examples are the quartzites of the Pre-Cambrian and the Millstone Grit; the sandstones of Silurian, Old Red Sandstone, and Carboniferous Age, the grits of the Cambrian and Silurian Systems ; limestones of the Llandeilo and Llandovery Series, the Carboniferous Limestone and the Lias.

(*c*) Fissile sandstone, for tiles and paving in the uppermost Silurian beds, the Old Red Sandstone, and the Pennant Series.

(*d*) Slate locally in the Cambrian, Ordovician and Silurian.

(*e*) Softer sandstone and limestone for freestone in the Carboniferous Sandstones of North Wales, the Trias, the Rhaetic Series and the Lias.

(*f*) Relatively soft sandstones and conglomerates in the Trias.

(*g*) Marls, shales and clay for brick-making in the Old Red Sandstone Marls, the Upper Carboniferous Shales, the Trias and in certain alluvial clays.

(*h*) Limestones for mortar are locally developed in most of the formations in Wales, e.g., even in the Old Red Marls there are impersistent beds of impure limestone.

In many parts of Wales the "solid" rocks are masked by a covering of superficial deposits of alluvial or glacial origin. The alluvial deposits yield no building material except clay, but the glacial deposits often contain large or small boulders of rocks of types not native to the locality where they now occur. In such cases the available building material would have no relation whatever to the rocks that would be indicated on the "solid" geological map.'

The 'solid' geological map of Wales (fig. 1) reveals the following principal features:-

1. Three areas of Pre-Cambrian rocks. These are :

(*a*) Anglesey. Here is an extensive tract of Pre-Cambrian rocks -the Mona Complex- consisting of gneisses overlaid with a bedded series through both of which plutonic intrusives were thrust at a later period. This area also has Ordovician rocks laid down directly on the Mona Complex, small areas of sandstone, and Carboniferous Limestone cropping out over a quarter of the island area.

(*b*) The Llŷn Peninsula. Rocks closely similar to the Pre-Cambrian rocks of Anglesey appear in the south-west of the Llŷn Peninsula between Nefyn and Bardsey Island, constituting a 'complex' consisting of the three main groups of rocks recognized in the Mona Complex, whose outcrops are separated by Ordovician deposits. These are, however, so well covered with drift that in general their contribution to the local geological 'control' of building material is therefore reduced. There are also important outcrops of igneous and volcanic rocks in the Arfon-Snowdonia district and also in the Cader Idris area.

(*c*) A comparatively small area of north-west Pembrokeshire, particularly in the neighbourhood of St. David's. Here there are volcanic and plutonic rocks, the former consisting of variously-coloured tuffs with interbedded flows of lava and the plutonic intrusions consisting of such igneous rocks as granite, quartz-porphyry, etc., and also Ordovician rocks of volcanic origin.

2. Three areas of Cambrian rocks. These are :

(*a*) The Harlech Dome. This is 'the grandest mass of Cambrian rocks to be seen in Britain : they form a barren and desolate tract almost without habitation, with high, rugged, block-like mountains where thick banks of grit and conglomerate come to the surface. Sweeping round the Lower Cambrian rocks that form the centre of the Dome, the Middle and Upper Cambrian rocks from Criccieth to Cader Idris crop out in successive arcs.'[1]

(*b*) That part of Caernarvonshire which is separated from the Harlech Dome by the Ordovician rocks of Snowdon -the Bethesda- Llanberis-Nantlle-Pen-y-groes area.

---

[1] Smith, B. and George, T. N.: *British Regional Geology : North Wales* (1935), p. 20.

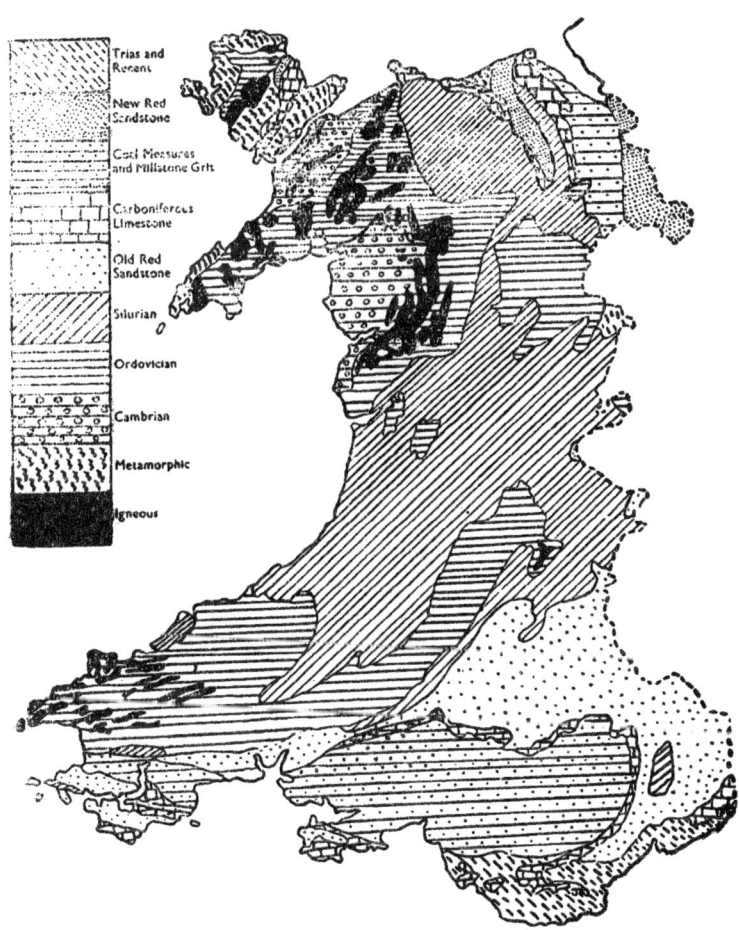

Fig 1. A simplified geological map of Wales.

(*c*) Pembrokeshire, where the Cambrian rocks occupy a larger area than do the Pre-Cambrian.

3. The moorland plateau of Wales extending from the Denbighshire moors to Carmarthenshire and north Pembrokeshire. This is a vast tract of Ordovician and Silurian rocks. In the Geological Map of Wales the Ordovician is bounded on the east by a prolonged band of Silurian rocks. These are found over the greater part of the Denbighshire moors and continue in a narrow belt in the Corwen-Llanuwchllyn district, separating the Ordovician dome of the Berwyn Hills from the western Ordovician tract. (It should be noted too that there is an important slate region between Corwen and Llan-gollen). The Silurian belt widens southwards into the highland of central Montgomeryshire and continues on the east over eastern Radnorshire narrowing again across Brecknockshire into the Tywi Valley, appearing again in small areas of Pembrokeshire. This line represents in certain areas a lithological boundary of importance, as will be seen later. In the present century however it has been shown[1] that Silurian rocks are widely distributed in the region, covering the larger part of Cardiganshire and north Carmarthenshire. The Ordovician and Silurian tracts consist mainly of shales, slate, mudstones, limestones, sandstones and conglomerates.

4. Two areas of 'sandstone': they are :

(*a*) The Devonian system known as the Old Red Sandstone which extends from the English borderland through Monmouthshire and Brecknockshire (where it assumes a monumental aspect) into a thin sliver projecting into the Carmarthen Bay and extending into south Pembrokeshire. It is a projection into Wales of great human importance of a rock which has profoundly influenced architecture in Britain. It should be noted that the term 'sandstone' however is here misleading to the uninitiated since Marls make up an important and, in some areas, the principal part of the Old Red Sand-stone formation (see p. 24).

(*b*) The Vale of Clwyd. 'The whole of the basin which forms the Vale of Clwyd is composed of new red sandstone [Trias] but around its edges there runs a thin band of... carboniferous limestone which crops up most prominently in the Eyarth Rocks in Llanelidan parish. It is also the chief geological feature of the Yale district. . . .

---

[1] See for instance British Regional Geology : North Wales and British Regional Geology : South Wales.

We have here "a piece of England let down . . . like a wedge amidst the more massive and ancient rocks, a remarkable fragment of genuine English scenery, a rich plain of new red sandstone beautifully wooded and watered and diversified by park-like slopes".[1] Geologically, the Vale of Clwyd is a piece of Cheshire-like scenery let down into the Silurian system in Wales.

5. The coalfields of south and north Wales :

(*a*) South Wales. The Coal Measures extend from the Bryn-mawr-Pontypool district 'across Glamorganshire to the Llanelly-Kidwelly area of Carmarthenshire and thence in a narrow band across Pembrokeshire. 'Over the greater part . . . the Pennant sandstone occupies the surface, and that rock is responsible for the smooth rounded hills so characteristic of the coalfield scenery.'[2] Encircling the Coal Measures are the outcrops of Millstone Grit and Carboniferous Limestone while the Vale of Glamorgan on the south of the coalfield shows large expanses of Keuper Marl and Lias.

(*b*) North Wales. The coalfields of Flintshire and Denbighshire present essentially the same features as those of the southern coalfield -Coal Measures, 'Millstone Grit' and Carboniferous Limestone flanked on the east by the Trias and on the west by the Silurian of the Clwydian Hills.

The general morphology of Wales therefore indicates this fivefold classification which must now be considered in more detail in relation to building materials.

1 (*a*). Anglesey is a flat, rolling county with soils derived chiefly from the metamorphic rocks but with limestone and sandstone soils also. 'The climate is insular, mild and humid and the whole island is characteristically windswept. Woodlands are therefore not common. In comparison with the South Wales counties, hedges and other forms of shelter belt are commonly replaced by earth banks and stone walls, the latter being a characteristic feature in north Anglesey.'[3] Most of the more durable members of the Mona Complex have been widely used for local building

---

[1] Thomas, [Sir] D. Lleufer: *The Agricultural Labourer in Wales* (1893), p. 113.

[2] North, F. J.: *Coal, and the Coalfields in Wales* (1931), p. 163.

[3] Stapledon, R. G. [edit.] : *A Survey of the Agricultural and Waste Lands of Wales* (1936), p. 56

purposes but the selection and treatment of the stone have to be carried out with care. 'The irregular surfaces and splintery edges of the corrugated schists render them quite undressable and their interspaces have to be liberally filled in with cement. Walls of this kind are usually faced with "rough-cast" [which] . . . adds greatly to the monotonous and dismal aspect of the houses.'[1] Indeed, the finer Ordovician sandstones, particu-larly those of the Llannerch-y-medd area are far more suitable for building and instances are known where the rural builders have used these rocks, for sites on the Mona Complex, rather than use the intractable schists on the site itself.[2]

But the best building material in Anglesey is to be found in the Car-boniferous rocks. There has been an extensive use of the Carboniferous Limestone in the island, especially its massive grey varieties, and of rocks in the Carboniferous Limestone Series which includes sandstones. It should be noted here that the castles of Beaumaris and Caernarvon were built in great part of one of the stones in this series-the Penmon rock. The use of local limestone in Anglesey as material for human habitations has continued from the Dark Ages at least. In the hut-group at Pant-y-saer, in Llanfair Mathafarn eithaf parish, excavated by Mr. C. W. Phillips in 1932-3, large slabs of the local limestone were almost invariably used[3] as they were for many of the prehistoric monuments.

Anglesey is therefore partly a stone county. But several of the small cottages were of 'mud' as well as stone. For such small peasant structures, supplies of quarried stones were not looked for when clay or mud could be used in conjunction with stone. We are told that 'all these mud houses in Anglesey have now disappeared' but that 'mud and stones, in proportions varying with the geology of the district' were used formerly.[4] The roofs, as one would expect in a wheat-growing county, were often of straw.

1 (b). The Llyn Peninsula. Here again, as we have seen, are to be found Pre-Cambrian rocks, but of restricted importance for building purposes. As in Anglesey, there is a thick mantle of glacial drift, consisting of boulder-clays, sands, silts and gravels, much of the country inland being almost entirely drift-covered to a height of some 200 ft.[5] The peninsula is low lying, most of the area being below 500 ft. and there are considerable

---

[1] *Memoirs of the Geological Survey (Anglesey II)*, pp. 851-3.

[2] *Ibid.*

[3] *Arch. Camb.*, 1934, p. 4.

[4] *An Inventory of the Ancient Monuments in Anglesey (1937)*, p. cl.

[5] Matley, C. A.: 'The Pre-Cambrian Complex of South-Western Lleyn' in *Quart. Journ. Geol. Soc.* (1928), p. 441.

marshy tracts. We find therefore the use of igneous rocks where they appear and stone from the glacial drift, for building. The solid farmhouses of Bardsey Island and many of the small mansions of the mainland are examples of this use of granite and such rocks and also of boulder-clay stone. Castellmarch near Abersoch is an example where the granite was obviously obtained from a nearby intrusion.

But in Llŷn too, clay or mud was formerly widely used for the small cottages so characteristic of the area. '[The peasants'] Habitations . . . particularly in Llŷn consist of walls built of what in Devonshire is termed *cobb* ; that is an argillaceous earth having straw or rushes mixed with it while in a state of paste, and then laid layer upon layer, between boards, till the whole are ready for the formed roof composed of thatch either of straw or heath.'[1] A cottage at Llithfaen, mentioned before the Land Commission[2] is typical of the district, 'the rent was £1 a year, the house was made of mud . . . there were only two rooms.'

1 (*c*) and 2 (*c*). North-west Pembrokeshire. The complex geology of this area has been dealt with by a number of workers[3] and for our present purpose, all that need be stated is that there are many resemblances between it and Llŷn. The substantially built farmhouses of the St. David's area, which may be compared, for instance, in some respects with those of Bardsey, provide evidence of the use of local granite stone. On the other hand, the purplish pennant-like sandstones in the old work of St. David's Cathedral came from the Coal Measures of Nolton Haven,[4] while Cambrian sandstones (Caerbwdy and Caerfai) have been used in more recent work. But in this district again, particularly in the uplands, mud-walled building used to be evident, and we shall see later that it was widespread through the county. The whitewashed cottage, either stone or mud, 'stands out clearly in the mountain landscape on the side of the Precelly (*sic*) range, such as at Maenclochog'[5] and the prevalent type was described in 1814 as 'a mud walling about five feet high, a hipped end, low roofing of straw, with a wattle-and-daub chimney, kept together with hay-rope bandages ... the disgrace of the country.'[6]

---

[1] Evans, J.: *The Beauties of England and Wales*, XVII (1812), p. 322.

[2] *Royal Commission on Land in Wales: Minutes of Evidence*, I, p. 528.

[3] See for instance Cox, A. H. and others: 'The Geology of the St. David's District, Pembrokeshire', in *Proc. Geol. Assoc.* (1930), pp. 241ff.

[4] Fenton, R.: *Historical Tour through Pembrokeshire* (1903 edit.), p. 155.

[5] Thomas, [Sir] D. Lleufer: *The Agricultural Labourer in Wales* (1893), p. 63.

[6] Davies, Walter : *General View of the Agricultural and Domestic Economy of South Wales* (1814), p. 144.

Culley,[1] writing in 1867, describes, the cottages of Pembrokeshire (and indeed a far wider area of south-west Wales) as of 'mud (clay and straw mixed)'.

It can be stated therefore without fear of contradiction, that the building materials of north-west Pembrokeshire, Llŷn and (to a high degree) Anglesey, have much in common. But it must not be overlooked that there are other areas of Wales which have much in common with these western regions from the point of view of the suitability of stone for building. For instance some of the cottages in the Trecŵn area are built of large blocks of dolerite or diabase and resemble in materials houses in the Dolgelley (Merionethshire) area where similar rocks occur. We shall see in Chapter VIII the importance of Pembrokeshire roofing-slates. Slate was also used in Pembrokeshire both for walling and for covering walls. George Owen writes[2]: 'This kinde of stonne serveth alsoe for wallinge stones.'

2 (*a*) and (*b*). The 'Harlech Dome' and its surrounding country and east Caernarvonshire. For our present purpose this area can be studied as a whole although there are some features which will have to be discussed separately. Nevertheless, there is an essential unity in the materials of the whole area as they appear to the tourist's eye. The whole area is stone country, almost always associated with slate or stone-tile roofing, while in a considerable part of the area, the older buildings show a frequent use of timber in association with stone. The cruck-construction of several medieval houses in the Snowdonian area (see pp. 158-64) has been described in detail by Hughes and North.[3] Such timbering which represented oaks of considerable size must have been obtained locally : we are told[4] that the medieval builders at Caernarvon, for instance, 'sent [carpenters] into the woods at Rhos, Llanrwst and Nant Conwy to fell trees and prepare big joists and large pieces of timber.'

The Harlech district itself is notable for its characteristic local stone. Even the field and mountain fences are of stone: this, of course, is a feature found elsewhere too, but not, I think, to such a degree as in this part of Wales. 'The local stone in its colour and weight and the massiveness of the square blocks re-echo the menacing severity of the bald hills and the grey

---

[1] *Third Report of the Commission on the Employment of Children, Young Persons and Women in Agriculture* (1867), p. 48.

[2] Owen, George : *The Description of Penbrokshire* (1892 edition), I, p. 82.

[3] Hughes, H. Harold and North, H. L.: *The Old Cottages of Snowdonia* (1908), pp. 5ff.

[4] Knoop, D. and Jones, G. P.: *The Medieval Mason* (1933), p. 48.

sea.[1] A modern example of its use is to be seen in Coleg Harlech, the work of George Walton.

In the greater part of Cantref Meirionnydd, Arfon and Arllechwedd (to use the old tribal names which are here apposite for the tract of country spreading-with Harlech as its focus-from the north coast of Caernarvonshire to the boundaries of Montgomeryshire), the material used falls into two classes, blocks of hard rocks and slate. The rocks of the Harlech district itself are mostly sedimentary, while around the edge of the dome, igneous rocks-mostly Ordovician-and slate occur. The igneous rocks are, for the builder, very intractable. Consequently big boulders, with little trace of trimming, were used. A small farmhouse in the Bwlch Oerddrws district of Merionethshire (plate 1) where such rocks occur, shows a considerable part built of less than three dozen such boulders (the faces of some of which, in this instance, have been roughly trimmed). Some of the peculiarities of this type of walling, which are due to the character of the stone used, will be discussed in a later chapter. Houses showing these peculiarities are found throughout the area where such rocks appear : the Dinas Mawddwy-Dolgelley .area may be looked upon as their southern limit and the Llanaelhaearn-Ormes Head coastline the northern.

The Cambrian rocks of central Caernarvonshire yield slate of excellent quality. The area includes Bethesda, Llanberis, Nantlle and Pen-y-groes, the Penrhyn and Felinheli slates from that district being well-known. The Ffestiniog area provides slate from the Ordovician rocks, as do the Abergynolwyn, Corris and Aberllefenni districts which can be conveniently included here. Slate is also found in the Silurian rocks to the south of Corris. Houses of slate blocks are found throughout the area and in towns and villages on its fringes, from the Conwy, Machno, Lledr and Llugwy valleys to Dolgelley and Machynlleth.

3. The moorland plateau of Wales. This extensive area of rolling upland with deep and often broad and fertile valleys presents a diversity in topography and at the same time a characteristic unity. Of the total agricultural area of Denbighshire, 16% is heather moor. Of molinia and nardus (including mountain flush bog) which generally dominate upland above the tree-level, Merioneth has 26½%, Montgomery 28%, Cardigan 27%, Radnor 22%, Brecknock 44% and Carmarthen 13%.[2] These figures indicate the extent and nature of moorland vegetation in this area, although the fact should not be lost sight of that lowland-pasture types also show a

---

[1] *Journal of the Royal Institute of British Architects*, 1939, p. 547.

[2] Stapledon, R. G.: *op. cit.*, p. 58.

uniformly high percentage in these counties (that of the whole of Wales being nearly half the land surface). In short, we are here dealing with a large agricultural unit of grass- and heather-growing upland and fertile lowland,[1] with a low percentage of woodland (apart from Monmouthshire with woodland as 12.8% of the total land area, Montgomeryshire is highest with 6.6%)[2] about 80% of the land being over 500 ft. above sea level.

Mud and clay (often equivalent when the terms are used by early writers) are materials general throughout the area, supplemented by stone, generally unquarried except where a good quarried stone is easily accessible, and by timber almost throughout the plateau but more markedly on the eastern borders. Cruck construction (see pp. 158-64) is found throughout the area in Denbighshire, Merionethshire, Montgomeryshire, Radnorshire, Cardiganshire and Carmarthenshire[3] while half-timbering (see Chapter VII) is characteristic of the eastern fringe of the uplands and a projection of the technique extends westwards in Montgomeryshire to within sight of Cardigan Bay.

We have already referred to the mud houses of Pembrokeshire. In Carmarthenshire in the 18th century, 'building a mud cabin costs 10*l*.'[4] Cardiganshire cottages in 1815 were 'mostly constructed of mud'.[5] The 1847 Commissioners have frequent references to 'clod houses' in Radnorshire[6] while throughout the area from Denbighshire to Pembrokeshire there are constant references by all the writers to the general use of wattle and brushwood (see pp. 166-7). A writer in 1887, describing the construction of houses in the west Montgomeryshire uplands[7] refers to the use of stone in clay for the gable ends, wattle and daub in timber-framing for the sides, and

---

[1] In Denbighshire, out of a total agricultural area of (approximately) 385,000 acres, 135,000 are rough and hill grazings ; Merioneth 230,000 out of 356,000; Montgomery 193,000 out of 451,000 ; Cardigan 173,000 out of 413,000 ; Radnor 129,000 out of 283,000 ; Brecknock 294,000 out of 465,000 , and Carmarthen 103,000 out of 504,000. See Stapledon : op. cit., p. 65.

[2] Forestry Commission : *Report on Census of Woodlands* (1924').

[3] C. F. Innocent's statement [in *The Development of English Building Construction* (1916), p. 35] that 'he has been unable to find it in south-west Wales' is surprising if he includes in that term Cardiganshire and Carmarthenshire.

[4] Young, A.: 'A Tour in Wales* [1776] in Annals of Agriculture, VIII.

[5] Rees, T.: The Beauties of England and Wales (1815), XVIII, pp. 407-8.

[6] Report of the Commissioners of Inquiry into the State of Education in Wales, 1847, p. 56.

[7] Peate, D.: *op. cit.* (in MSS.).

rushes over brushwood for the roof. Heather roofing is still to be found, e.g. at Bwlch Du, Mynydd Hiraethog, and was formerly widespread as an under-layer as was fern in areas where there were plentiful supplies.[1] In the towns, stone was more frequently used. Corwen, in 1797, however, had houses of 'stone ... cemented with clay and loam',[2] probably the technique described by Peate above. Llanidloes, impinging upon the half-timbered house region, had most of its houses in 1798 'built with laths and mud',[3] while Newtown in 1822 was a 'town composed chiefly of lath and plaster houses'.[4] But Aberystwyth in 1821 had 'houses of grey stone with whitened roofs'.[5]

In the more inaccessible upland regions where stone was available, it was often used in a primitive fashion. At Tal-y-llyn, Merionethshire (1847), on the edge of the slate country, the houses 'are formed of a few loose fragments of rock and shale, piled together without mortar or white-wash'[6] while at Llan-ym-Mawddwy in the same county (1798)'the 'cottages are built of fragments of [stone], piled one upon another in an irregular manner, with the interstices filled up with lumps of turf or peat. The roof is covered with broad coarse slates.'[7] In the same area of central Wales in 1775, Sir Thomas Gery Cullum refers to stone cottages with slated roofs and to 'timbered and plaistered' houses[8] which he contrasts with houses made 'entirely of Earth, and that not of Straw wrought up with it, but with sometimes a Layer of Straw' in Carmarthenshire.

Reference has already been made to the delineation (subsequently modified by recent work) on geological maps of the Silurian rocks. This line in Radnorshire and in part of Montgomeryshire seems to indicate, approximately, the western limit of half-timbered houses in that area though there may be no relation between the two facts. It is noted here as a matter of interest. But it should be observed that the timber-framing technique 'peters out' in the highland into houses with walls boarded in horizontal, overlapping lengths.

---

[1] *Royal Commission on Land in Wales: Report* (1896), p. 693.

[2] Wigstead, H.: *Remarks on a Tour to North and South Wales in 1798*, p. 21.

[3] Bingley, W. : *Tour round North Wales in 1798*,1, p. 484.

[4] Pinnock's County Histories : *North Wales* (1822), p. 83.

[5] Newell, R. H. : Letters on the Scenery of Wales (1821), p. 105.

[6] *Report of the Commissioners of Inquiry into the State of Education tn Wales,* 1847, p. 63.

[7] Evans, J.: *A Tour through North Wales in . . . 1798*, p. 66.

[8] Vaughan, H. M. : 'A Synopsis of Two Tours made in Wales in 1775 and in 1811' in *Y Cymmrodor,* 1927, pp. 49, 57.

4 (*a*). The Old Red Sandstone area of south Wales. This includes the land between the upper Wye and the fringe of the Carboniferous area of south Wales and therefore covers both the Black Mountains of Brecknockshire and part of the Brecknock Beacons. It covers a considerable part of Monmouthshire skirting the Carboniferous area north-east of Cardiff. Its westward extension from Brecknockshire into Carmarthenshire narrows into a band on the slopes of the Carmarthenshire Black Mountain into Pembrokeshire. In Herefordshire this rock is the home of half-timbered work at its best (Weobley, Eardisland, Pembridge, etc.) but except for its natural intrusion in the lowland valleys-into the Abergavenny district, for instance-the technique is generally absent from the Old Red Sandstone in Wales.

One reason for this concerns the problem of lithology as contrasted with stratigraphy to which we have referred. 'Old Red Sandstone' is a stratigraphical-not a lithological-term and the Old Red Sandstone in Herefordshire is lithologically different from the Old Red Sandstone of Brecknockshire and Carmarthenshire. In the Beacons and the Vans, for instance, there is a great local development of sandstones and conglomerates in the upper part of the Old Red Sandstone. The difference in building materials between the Herefordshire Plain and this part of Wales is due therefore to the stratigraphical succession in the Old Red Sandstone present in the respective areas and to the structure of the area, by reason of which the sandstones and conglomerates in the Welsh Old Red Sandstone make a great escarpment.

The Herefordshire Plain therefore ends abruptly at the Welsh border and in Wales one enters a countryside of a different character. Most of the Old Red Sandstone land is at a high altitude-only 6.2% of Brecknockshire is below 500 ft.-except for valleys such as that of the Usk where half-timbering has intruded as far as Brecon itself. But the Beacon country and the north Brecknockshire uplands are part of the moorland plateau and for the reasons stated it is to the moorland tradition that the houses there belong. Further west the Old Red Sandstone descends into the fertile Tywi valley, which is however so far removed from the John Abel country and lithologically so different that the technique of the 'black and white' house is not evident there. In fact, in the Carmarthen district, building stone for local purposes has been obtained from sand-stones in the Old Red Sandstone, some of them flaggy green sandstones-note, for instance, some of the cottages in the Myddfai-Gwynfe district.[1] In recent work it may be noted that the new church opened at Gwynfe in 1899 was built of a hard red

---

[1] *Memoirs of the Geological Survey (Carmarthen),* p. 157.

sandstone obtained from the Brown-stones of the Old Red Sandstone quarried on the Llangadock-Brynaman road. Llandyfan Church was rebuilt with a similar stone.[1]

In Monmouthshire and the extreme south-east of Glamorganshire, where the Old Red Sandstone occurs, the red marls have been extensively used for making bricks, e.g. near St. Julian's, north of Gold Tops, south of Malpas, and near Cwmbran, all in Monmouthshire[2] and at Llanishen and Whitchurch in the Cardiff area of Glamorganshire.[3] It should be remembered too that as far west as the Pontypool area, there was noted in Monmouthshire as late as the last quarter of the 18th century a liberal use of timber in house construction. In the parish of Aberystruth in 1779, 'all the houses, in number about 150, are built of *stones and timber, not of earthen sides and timber* as in some parts of Wales'[4]-which may be looked upon as a Welsh variant of the brick and timber houses of Herefordshire.

South Pembrokeshire, with its Old Red Sandstone, Carboniferous Limestone and Coal Measures may be conveniently discussed here. Building stone for local purposes has been obtained from all the harder rocks of the Milford district and thick roofing slates, often of peculiar colours, have come from the Old Red Marls on Skokolm Island: they were worked in the past for slating farm buildings.[5] At Milford Haven itself the Old Red Sandstone has provided marls for houses. Some grits occurring near the base of the Ordovician strata furnished some of the material used in Whitland Abbey, while mudstones ('rab') have been used for domestic buildings of some local importance, such as Cottesmore near Haverfordwest built of Redhill Quarry stone. Most of the buildings in Whitland itself are of Silurian sandstones, a close-grained grey rock from such local quarries as Pen-y-back. Some of the sandstones in the red marls of the Old Red Sandstone have been wrought for building south of Whitland. The green flaggy micaceous sandstone forms one of the best local building-stones and has been quarried in many localities here. It has yielded most of the stone from which Neyland is built.[6] In the Tenby district on the other hand, the Carboniferous Limestone has been the chief source of building-stone, where it was used locally, only small quantities having been exported.[7]

---

[1] *Ibid. (Ammanford),* pp. 221-3.

[2] *Ibid. (Newport), p. 17.*

[3] *Ibid. (Cardiff),* p. 16.

[4] Jones, Edmund : *A Geographical, Historical and Religious Account of the parish of Aberystruth* (1779), p. 50.

[5] *Memoirs of the Geographical Survey (Milford),* p. 166.

[6] *Ibid. (Haverfordwest),* p 227.

[7] *Ibid. (Tenby),* p. 206.

4 (*b*). The Vale of Clwyd. This piece of Cheshire-like scenery let down into Wales, a wedge of New Red Sandstone in a broad fertile valley may be looked upon in many respects as an extension of the Cheshire Plain isolated within the Silurian system. Here the half-timbered styles of the Cheshire type are predominant, in the Denbigh-Ruthin district for instance, but this feature is completely absent from the foothills of the Clwydian range on the one side and the edge of Mynydd Hiraethog on the other. In the Vale of Clwyd too there is a natural and extensive use of brick. Bricks were made .from the red Boulder Clay in the Vale of Clwyd and at Colwyn Bay and near Rhyl from the marsh clay.[1] Lime-stone too has been an important building material here. The grey and white crystalline limestones exposed in the sides of Moel Hiraddug have been largely worked for building purposes. The white limestone of the well-known 'marble church' of Bodelwyddan was quarried in the hills south of Abergele.[2]

5 (*a*). The south Wales Coalfield. The Coal Measures with their-band of millstone grit on north and south and their encircling rim of Carboniferous Limestone form a large area of south Wales. With them we must consider the Vale of Glamorgan with its diversity of recent rocks. For a full discussion of the geological significance of this region, the writings of Dr. F. J. North should be consulted.[3]

Over the whole of the coalfield the Pennant sandstone has been used for building and, due to the abnormal development of the district during the last one hundred years, when cheap transport became effective, its use has 'overflowed' to districts such as Cardiff. The stone however was used even in Roman times as 'the Pennant-grit walls of the Roman fort at Gelligaer' testify.[4] It has been used in the north in the Merthyr area[5] (together with stone from the Old Red Sandstone, Carboniferous Lime-stone and Millstone Grit); in the west in the Aman Valley, where it has been quarried 'over the whole outcrop but none of the quarries are used for other than local purposes,'[6] and in the heart of the coalfield in the whole of the Pontypridd-Maesteg area. 'The Pennant rock in a fresh form has a greyish-blue tint which changes on exposure to air, the prevailing tint of a building . . . being grey with a tendency to brown or yellow in parts.'[7] Some beds of this

---

[1] *Memoirs of the Geological Survey (Rhyl, Abergele and Colwyn Bay)*, p. 57.

[2] *Ibid.*, p. 10.

[3] North, F. J.: *Coal, and the Coalfields in Wales* (1931). North, F. J.: *The Evolution of the Bristol Channel* (1929).

[4] Ward, J.: *Romano-British Buildings and Earthworks* (1911), p. 255.

[5] *Memoirs of the Geological Survey (Merthyr)*, p. 224.

[6] *Ibid. (Ammanford)*, p. 222.

[7] *Ibid. (Pontypridd and Maesteg)*, p. 129.

sandstone split readily and it has been used extensively for paving farmhouse floors and such purposes.

Another sandstone, the Llynfi Rock, is harder and less fissile than the Pennant and where obtainable ('in the upper part of the Lower Coal series, especially in the west[1]) is preferred for building purposes. In the extreme west of the coalfield, the sandstones corresponding to this Llynfi Rock elsewhere have been used as well. Carboniferous Limestone indeed has been used for building and walling in all districts where it outcrops.[2]

Reference has already been made to the use of sandstones from the Coal Measures for paving houses. The more fissile were also used for roofing. On the western edge of the coalfield in Carmarthenshire the highly micaceous and fissile sandstones from the Ludlow Rocks (Silurian) -on the Llandeilo edge of the coalfield-were worked on a large scale for tile-stones, e.g. at Cil-maen-llwyd, Trap, Carmarthenshire. These may still be seen on old buildings in the neighbourhood but their use has now been wholly relinquished in favour of slates. The rock was split into slabs about half-an-inch thick and then dressed and pierced for a wooden peg.[3] Fissile sandstones were similarly used throughout the coalfield (see Chapter VIII). An 18th-century commentator describes the houses of the southern edge of the coalfield from Cardiff to Swansea as 'mostly covered with tile.'[4]

For the Llandybie district on the edge of the coalfield I am indebted to the Reverend Gomer Roberts for the following information. Local stone has been used for house-walls, together with river pebbles (called locally *popyls*) and pebbles from the fields. There were formerly several quarries in the district (Ffynnon Gollen, Cil-y-rhedyn, Cwm-nant-arw, etc.). Limestone is used in some of the farmhouses, particularly as cornerstones, lintels, etc. In the old cottages, the walls were built of inner and outer facings of large stones, the space between filled with small stone and a mortar of mud mixed with lime. Aberthaw lime was considered best for making this mortar although Llandybie itself produced a large quantity of lime. Interior walls were made (about 1800) of wattle daubed with mud, clay or lime mixed with cow-hair and -dung. The cottages were straw thatched without exception as were many of the farmhouses- broom, heather and fern forming the under-thatch. Today it is difficult to obtain adequate supplies of straw; rushes have consequently been used but the rush-thatch is much

---

[1] North, F. J.: *Coal, and the Coalfields in Wales*, p. 164.

[2] See for instance *Memoirs of the Geological Survey (Ammanford)*, p. 222.

[3] *Ibid.*, p. 223.

[4] Mathews, W.: *The Miscellaneous Companions* (1786), I, p. 76.

inferior. The tiles were obtained from Cil-maen-llwyd quarry (see above) and Llandybie church is tiled with the same stone.

The Vale of Glamorgan with its Mesozoic rocks is in many respects an individual area of considerable interest. One of its marked features is the orderly grouping of the cottages in neat villages. In many, straw thatch-because of the formerly extensive corn-growing-has predominated. Blue Lias Limestone, a Triassic conglomerate known as Radyr Stone and Rhaetic sandstone have been extensively used for building of various kinds. In the Cowbridge district in the 19th century, the Lias limestone was normally used[1] while the fact that limestone from Cwrt-yr-ala, near Cardiff, was used for the construction of Barry Docks[2] and for the new walls surrounding Cardiff Castle is indicative of its quality as a building material. It may also be mentioned that for the carved work. in the Norman ecclesiastical buildings of the Vale, Sutton stone (Lias) from near Bridgend was frequently employed. In the Early English period, stone was imported from Bristol but in the 15th century this was succeeded by the Rhaetic sandstones of Quarella and Pyle. For such buildings in later times Lias limestone and Radyr stone have been extensively used locally.[3] The Lias limestones, being separated from each other by shales, could be easily extracted in blocks of suitable size. The Quarella [? presumably *Chwarelau*] sandstone-white or pale green- was in fact a rock used extensively for building purposes-it belonged to the Rhaetic Sandstone series referred to above.

A feature invariably noticed by travellers in the Vale of Glamorgan in all ages is, to quote Gwallter Mechain, 'the universal custom of white-washing.' It may be the reason why Malkin maintained that 'a stronger contrast cannot be conceived than between a cottage in the vale of Glamorgan and a cottage in the vale of Aberdare or Ystradyvodwg'.[4] The custom however was widespread in Wales, as the literature testifies. In 1803, Oystermouth was 'a whitened town'.[5] In 1798, Machynlleth church had 'a fault common with many of the Welsh churches, in being whitewashed',[6] and in 1770, in Brecknockshire, 'the Welsh gentlemen in these parts seem fond of whitening their houses which gives them a disagreeable glare'.[7] The custom however may have been more thoroughly practised in the Vale, for it consisted of 'not only the inside and outside of houses, but barns and

[1] Thomas, [Sir] D. Lleufer: The Agricultural Labourer in Wales, p. 51.

[2] *Memoirs of the Geological Survey (Cardiff)*, p. 23.

[3] *Ibid.*, p. 92.

[4] Malkin, B. H.: *The Scenery, Antiquities and Biography of South Wales* . . . in 1803,1, p. 256.

[5] Barber, J. T.: *Tour throughout South Wales and Monmouthshire* (1803), p. 21.

[6] Bingley, W.: *Tour round North Wales in 1798*, I, p. 471.

[7] Gilpin, W.: *Observations on the River Wye . . . in . . . 1770* (2nd edit.), p. 94.

stables also, walls of yards and gardens, the stone banks of quickset fences, and even [large] solitary stones . . . [and is] said to have been repeated monthly, or at least several times in the year'.[1] It is mentioned here since it gave to the limestone buildings of the Vale as distinct a character as that of the half-timbered buildings of the eastern border or the stone buildings of the Harlech district.

5 (b). The northern Coalfield. The carboniferous rocks extend from the Point of Ayr in Flintshire south-east to Hawarden and Broughton and south to the Oswestry district. In the northern half of the coalfield most of the sandstones in the Cefn-y-Fedw Sandstone (of Millstone Grit type) have been used for local building purposes. As in the southern coalfield the sandstones of the Coal Measures have been similarly used at several places such as Flint Mountain, Mold and in the Buckley area.[2] The southern half of the coalfield-the Wrexham-Ruabon area-has many kinds of stone used in the past for building, the principal being Cefn stone (Middle Coal Measures), the Coed-yr-allt stone and the Abenbury pink freestone. Carboniferous limestone has been used extensively for houses and village churches.[3] The Cefn stone is a light-drab or buff fine-grained sandstone. Wrexham parish church and that of Ruabon are built of it. It has been used further afield in modern times, notably in the University College building, Bangor.[4] The whitish or greenish-white fine-grained quartzose Coed-yr-allt rock was obtained in the neighbourhood of Ruabon and in several other localities.

In the neighbourhood of both the north and south Wales coalfields, as we have indicated, brick making has long been an important industry. In the coalfields the rocks in which the coal seams actually occur include shales and other relatively soft argillaceous rocks which are suitable for brick-making. In the north Wales coalfield, the Upper Coal Measures include a great development of clay and marls with few workable coal seams, providing therefore for extensive brick-making. In the 19th century we find, for example, that brick was principally used in the farm buildings of Flintshire,[5] the 'good, country bricks' being made on the landowner's estate. In both Flintshire and east Denbighshire, most of 'the old [farm]

[1] Davies, W.: *General View of the Agriculture and Domestic Economy of South Wales* (1814), p. 137.

[2] *Memoirs of the Geological Survey (Flint, Hawarden and Caergwrle)*, pp. 171 ff.

[3] *Ibid. (Wrexham)*, pp. 176-8.

[4] Watson, J.: *British and Foreign Building Stones* (1911), p. 134.

[5] *Royal Commission on Land in Wales: Minutes of Evidence*, IV, p. 128.

houses were built of brick and timber'.[1] Brickworks occur throughout the
north Wales coalfield area and have influenced building in that region. This
is also true of Monmouthshire and east Glamorganshire in the south.

From the above survey it will be seen how closely building materials
in Wales have been associated with the geological map. Indeed it may be
said that geology has been the dominant factor, for the materials constantly
in demand throughout Wales have been stone, mud or timber. In the
absence of adequate stone supplies, recourse was made to the other
materials of which the supply depended ultimately upon conditions con-
trolled to a high degree by climate, geology and configuration.

The use of timber for building has undoubtedly been less in modem
times than at any other period. It has been suggested that stone came into
general use in Wales 'as building material for ordinary dwelling-houses ...
some time in the course of the Edwardian period' of the middle ages.[2]
Whatever the truth of this statement, it is a fact that cruck-construction,
which entailed an adequate supply of large oak trees of the requisite shape,
seems to have ceased in Wales by the 17th century, if not earlier. In the
same way, the 17th century marks the end of timber-framed building in the
west generally.[3] The number of later houses in this technique is small.[4] In
that part of south-east Wales where there was an adequate timber-supply,
the smelting of iron, and, later, the demand for pit wood for the coal mines,
caused woodland destruction on a large scale,[5] while it should always be
remembered that the 'damp' oakwood dominated by the common oak was
restricted to the lowlands, where now only remnants of the type exist owing
to agricultural development, felling and re-planting.[6] But in an analysis of
Welsh building-materials, the fact that the country was formerly more
extensively wooded than it is now should be borne in mind.

---

[1] *Ibid., Report*, p. 706.

[2] *Ibid.*, p. 692.

[3] Parkinson, J. and Ould, E. A.: *Old Cottages, Farm-Houses and other Half-Timber Buildings in Shropshire, Herefordshire and Cheshire* (1904), p. 31.

[4] See for instance *Royal Commission on Historical Monuments, England: Herefordshire, II, East* (1932), pp. xxviii-ix.

[5] Hyde, H. A.: *Welsh Timber Trees* (1935), p. 9.

[6] Hyde, H. A.: *Welsh Timber Trees* (1935), p. 9.

CHAPTER III

The Circular House

THE earliest known human habitations in Wales are chiefly circular in character and it is for that reason only that this form is considered at this stage. It is not suggested that the circular house is necessarily older typologically wherever it is found or that, in the evolution of house-types, it can be considered without relation to other forms.

In Wales, hut-circles have been found in many areas but unfortunately few of them have been adequately excavated. It appears probable- in the absence however of any great corpus of Welsh evidence- that this type of habitation was introduced in the Early Iron Age, although those excavated belong to the Romano-British period or to the Dark Ages. They have been recorded in Anglesey,[1] Caernarvonshire,[2] Denbighshire,[3] Merionethshire,[4] Montgomeryshire,[5] Cardiganshire,[6] Carmarthenshire,[7] Pembrokeshire,[8] Glamorganshire[9] and Monmouthshire.[10] In Anglesey we are told[11] that three main types exist: 'the simplest form is represented by the hut (fig. 2) excavated at Parc Dinmor, Penmon. The wall faced on both sides with blocks of stone, enclosed an area 25 ft. in diameter. A rectangular socket carried the central post of a conical roof of poles thatched with heather. On one side an enclosure of slabs set on edge formed a bed. There was no hearth within the hut, but the discovery of pot-boilers suggested that cooking was done in a leather bag, the stones being heated in a fire outside the door. The hut is a purely native type with no traces of Roman influence, though it does not necessarily belong to a pre-Roman period.'

This description in the Anglesey *Inventory* of what purport to be facts considered objectively contains two details which deserve comment in

---

[1] *An Inventory of the Ancient Monuments in Anglesey* (R.C.A.M. 1937), pp. lxxviii *et passim.*

[2] *Arch. Camb.,* 1922, pp. 335-45; 1923, pp. 87-113, 243-68 ; *Antiq. Journ.,* 1936, pp. 295-320.

[3] Davies, EUis : *The Prehistoric and Roman Remains of Denbighshire* (1929), pp. 97, 386.

[4] *An Inventory of the Ancient Monuments in . . . Merionethshire* (R.C.A.M. 1921), *passim.*

[5] *Arch. Camb.,* 1880, pp. 25-30 ; 1935, pp. 161-2 ; 1937, pp. 86-128.

[6] *Trans. Hon. Soc. Cymmrod.,* 1920-1, p. 118. See also for a general treatment of Welsh hill-forts by R. E. M. Wheeler and R. U. Sayce.

[7] *An Inventory of the Ancient Monuments in . Carmarthenshire* (R.C.A.M. 1917), pp. 393, 701.

[8] *Arch. Camb.,* 1910, pp. 271ff.; 1900, pp. 189ff.

[9] *Bulletin of the Board of Celtic Studies,* I, 1921-3, p. 70.

[10] *Arch. Camb.,* 1936, p. 314.

[11] See (¹) above.

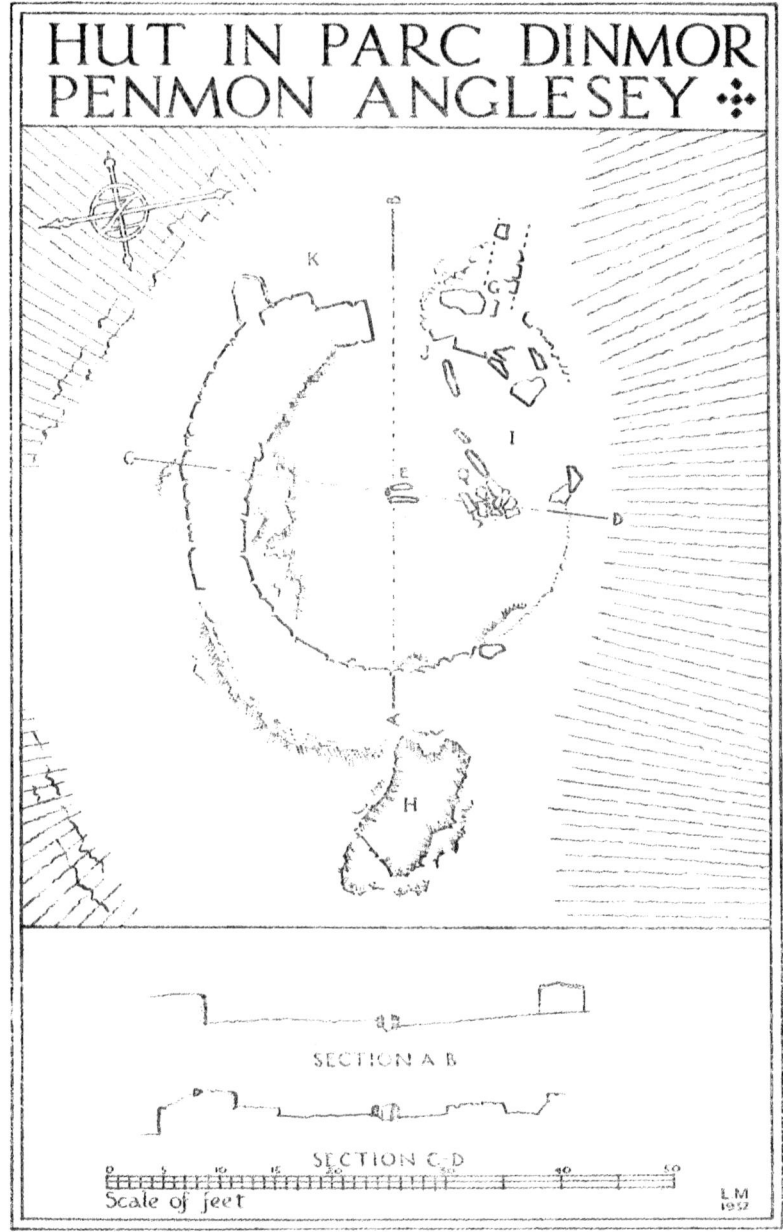

Fig. 2. Plan of circular hut at Parc Dinmor, Penmon, Anglesey.

passing. It refers (*a*) to 'the central post of a conical roof of poles thatched with heather', (*b*) to 'an enclosure of slabs set on edge [to] form ... a bed'. The excavation report by Mr. C. W. Phillips[1] however notes only 'a rectangular post socket' and 'a number of large slabs standing on edge to form an alcove or "bed".' The dogmatic assertion of the existence of a 'conical roof of poles thatched with heather' and the presence of a 'bed'—while I have no quarrel with it as *an interpretation* of the evidence—is wholly hypothetical, although recorded in the *Inventory* as fact! There is, for instance, no tittle of evidence for the use of 'heather'.

The second type is circular, but with a small annexe. These huts often have central hearths, drains under the floors and passages leading ' to the doors. The third type is a form known as a 'homestead group' and consists of a circular chamber with one or more annexes, the whole being arranged round an open courtyard. In such houses, circles of post-holes have often been found concentric with the outer wall[2] and a row of beds at the side of the room. Another feature of several of the circular dwellings in Wales is a raised platform, generally formed of stone slabs.[3]

Hut dwellings conforming to one or other of the above types have been found on all the sites in Wales enumerated above. In some cases too the dwellings are oval or rectangular in form (e.g. on Gateholm, Pembrokeshire). It is beyond the scope of the present enquiry to deal in detail with either the distribution of these sites or several problems—of date, etc.—which arise and which are the archaeologist's concern. But a study of some of the features of these dwellings is essential to our present purpose.

One fact which has emerged is the comparatively large number of such dwellings in the stony and comparatively soil-less western regions of Wales and the paucity of evidence for their existence in the eastern region of the country. It would appear that one reason for this distribution is the character of the country. Where wood was abundant it is likely to have been used in the construction of such huts and their traces have consequently disappeared to a high degree, or can only be found after careful investigation. 'Many camps yield no trace of any dwellings until they are excavated. Then remains often come to light of lightly constructed huts built of wattle. Occasionally all that is found is pieces of hardened clay with the impress of the wattle on them. As an example may be quoted the wattle dwellings of Hunsbury. The tribesmen were probably governed in their choice of building material by the local supply just as is the case today.

---

[1] *Arch. Camb.*, 1932, p. 250.

[2] See, for instance, for Caernarvonshire, *Antiq. Journ.*, 1936, pp. 305-6.

[3] *Arch. Camb.*, 1872, p. 242.

Thus, on the uplands of Caernarvonshire, where stone is plentiful and easily obtained, nearly every enclosure contains hut circles, whereas, in other areas, the local supply of willow twigs or hazel boughs was used to make good the deficiency in the stone supply.[1]

The construction of these huts can be studied from the details available from certain sites which have been adequately excavated in recent years. From the evidence from such sites as in Anglesey, Caernarvonshire and Glamorganshire, the stone walls were thick (2½ ft. in the Blaenrhondda huts) and consisted of earth and stones with rough facings of uncoursed stonework without and within. The Parc Dinmor hut mentioned above had a rectangular post socket, which presupposes a roof supported by a central post. The Blaenrhondda hut walls 'suggest that the stonework extended to a height of only 3 or 4 feet, above which tree branches and turves doubtless formed a conical roof. The definite evidence of a central pole was observed, although in a few of the huts small heaps of stone in the middle of the floor may have formed a basis for a roof post.'[2]

At Caerau, Clynnog, Caernarvonshire (fig. 3) there was in Room A of House I 'a central (or almost central) post-hole, marking the position of a single wooden upright, which carried the roof. The hole was 13 in. deep and somewhat irregular, but was certainly intended for this purpose.'[3] In Room B 'there was no central post-hole for the roof. Instead there is a small patch of hard yellow clay, 15 in. in diameter and 3 in. thick, almost in the centre of the floor. . . . Clay of this nature ... is certainly not natural in the present position. Three feet to the north-east a small flat stone was encountered. It is probable that it originally rested on the clay and formed the support for a central post.

'Such an arrangement occurs in House II, Room A, and probably also in House II, Room B. Between this clay deposit and the wall of the room there is a series of six post-holes. . . . Four of these holes are disposed with fair accuracy equidistant from one another and midway between the clay deposit and the wall. Post-holes 5 and 6 are, however, irregular and their position must be due to the presence of hearths. Just within the room at the entrance there is a double post-hole of the same type. It is clear from these indications that the room had a thatched roof supported on a series of six posts surrounding a central pole. This was necessary on account of the size of the room and the probable difficulty in obtaining timber of sufficient

[1] Sayce, R, U.: 'Hill Top Camps with special reference to those of north Cardiganshire' in *Trans. Hon. Soc. Cymmrod.*, 1920-1, p. 118.

[2] Wheeler, R. E. M., in *Rhondda MSS.* (in typescript in the National Museum of Wales).

[3] O'Neil, B. H. St. J., in *Antiq. Journ.*, 1936, p. 303.

length to reach from the centre to the wall without additional support. The double hole indicates that the entrance was covered in a similar manner.'[1]

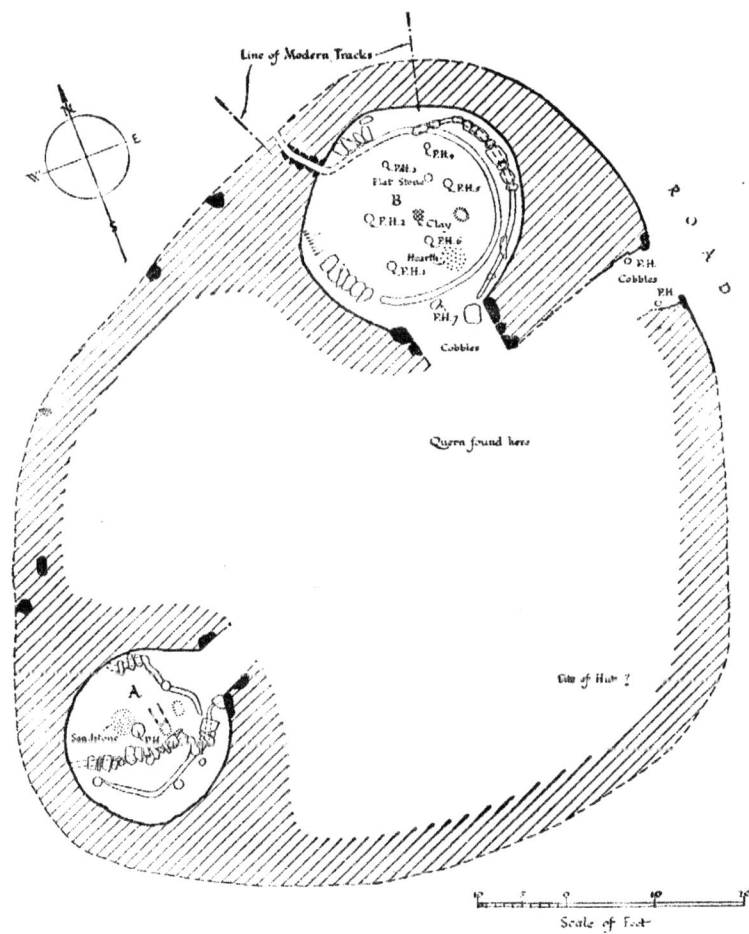

Fig. 3. Plan of House I, Caerau, Clynnog, Caernarvonshire.

From these facts it seems likely that a roof of poles covered with thatch and supported by a central pole (and in some dwellings by a series of poles arranged in a circle) seems to have been a normal feature of these houses.

---

[1] O'Neil, B. H. St. J.: *op. cit.*, pp. 305-6.

This was not however always the method of roofing adopted. Elias Owen[1] refers to a corbelled stone roof at Gerlan, Bethesda : 'the walls were of stone, the roof was formed of stones overlapping each other and the whole building resembled a large beehive. The entrance was four feet high and three broad.' This type will be considered later in this chapter.

The internal arrangement of the huts presents several features of importance. Hearths have been found in the centre, sometimes built up as in an example at Ty-mawr, Holyhead, or enclosed by orthostatic slabs as at Blaenrhondda. At Caerau, Clynnog, some of the hearths consisted of oval hollows in the floor, lined with yellow clay. In one of the rooms this was close to a post-hole, the post presumably being protected from the fire by a stone discovered there in its original position. In many instances, hearths were found against the wall while in several other cases, such as at Parc Dinmor, no hearth of any kind was found but quantities of pot-boilers suggested that the cooking was done by their use, the fire being probably outside.

In several cases, a raised shelf is a feature of the huts. At Ty-mawr, Holyhead, such a shelf was formed of a single stone and was flanked by hearths.[2] At Pant-y-saer, a raised platform two feet high and up to four feet wide passes eccentrically round the inside of the hut.[3] At Blaen-rhondda, Wheeler writes of one of the huts as 'apparently unique in the possession of a stone-built bench or sideboard which projected for a" distance of two feet from the west wall'.[4] This feature conforms to the *tyle* discussed below (p. 79). It is found also in some of the Portuguese huts, where stone 'benches' run round the whole of the interior.

Some of the huts are divided into irregular compartments by lines of upright slabs set on edge. This is the case in an instance from Ty-mawr, Holyhead, and in another at Parc Dinmor—the 'alcove or "bed" ' referred to above. Some of the floors are partially paved. Another feature of certain of the huts is a drainage system and paved channels which may indicate Roman influence. At least one of the paved channels in Anglesey seems to have been used by a metal worker.[5]

The use of such channels may be further referred to by a feature which appeared in some Monmouthshire cottages in the 19th century. An

---

[1] Owen, Elias: 'On the Circular Huts sometimes called *Cyttiau'r Gwyddelod* and their Inhabitants' in *Y Cymmrodor*, 1888, p. 338.

[2] *An Inventory of the Ancient Monuments in Anglesey*, p. 27.

[3] *Arch. Camb.*, 1934, p. 10.

[4] *Op. cit.*

[5] *An Inventory of the Ancient Monuments in Anglesey, p. lxxviii; Antiq. Journ.y* 1936, pp. 300ff.

excavation[1] of a Romano-British site at Finchingfield, Essex, in 1936 revealed a trench 'which seems to have served ... as "an outside, underground kitchen".' The occupier of the site stated that in the second half of the 19th century in certain parts of Monmouthshire, so his aunt, who lived there, informed him, the cottages were so small and inconvenient that their occupants had to cook outside underground. A trench had to be dug and lined with stones, bits of pot, clay, etc.: at one end was a broad ledge of stones over which they raised a domed roof with, below, a 'back-door', through which was inserted the bread for baking. The trench might serve several families and was divided up accordingly as required. 'The parallel,' writes the excavator, 'is extraordinarily close but our trench may also have been used in part for the minor metallurgical operations of our (hypothetical) worker in iron, bone and horn.' This possibility of underground cooking should always be considered in dealing with the Welsh sites : in many, as Stanley points out, 'it would have been impossible for the inmates, without suffocating, to have made a fire inside of wood, heath or gorse. We may therefore conclude that the larger animals were cooked in pits outside.'[2]

Finally, it may be suggested tentatively that the types of hut-circles recorded (a simple circle, a more elaborate dwelling with annexes and passages and the homestead groups) may represent social gradation. If we bear in mind that the Welsh Laws contain much material of great antiquity, it can be argued that the homestead-group may well represent some such habitation as the nine-chambered palace which was always the chieftain's right ('naw tei adyly ytayogeu y gwneuthur yr brenhin'[3]) while the simpler types represented inferior social status. It may be of interest to note here that Llywelyn ap y Moel (? 1395-1400-1440) in a poem[4] refers specially to one type of tacog's house as having a to *tyweirch* (turf roof).

We have now to consider the later history of the circular dwelling in Wales. Unfortunately the evidence is meagre. In a settled society, the circular house would be discarded : its size was limited by its mode of construction which made subsequent enlargement impossible. The development of the ridge-piece house of rectangular or sub-rectangular form outmoded the round house with its problems of roofing, lighting and heating. Consequently it is not strange that the evidence for circular houses is slight. They were probably set up mainly as habitations of a temporary

---

[1] *Trans. Essex Archaeological Society,* XXII (1939), p. 312.

[2] *Antiq. Journ.,* XXIV (1867), p. 237.

[3] Wade-Evans, A. W.: *Welsh Medieval Law* (1909), p. 57.

[4] *'I dy taeog do tyweirch,* in Lewis and others : *Iolo Goch ac Eraill* (1925), p. 119.

character. It is therefore, in this connexion, of interest to note that Wheeler,[1] in discussing the Blaenrhondda hut circles, suggests that the evidence there 'is only sufficient to enable us to conjecture that the village may have been the *hafod* of a pastoral people and . . . that its primitive type is not necessarily incompatible with a comparatively recent date.'

Giraldus Cambrensis in the 12th century refers to temporary dwellings, 'for service for a year' and his description of the Welshmen's dwellings may well be of circular huts (see note p. 114). The custom of the Welsh, he writes, is to raise dwellings of plaited rods, on the outskirts of the woods, enough to be of service for a year, and that with as little labour and expense as possible.[2] A poem,[3] attributed to both Dafydd ap Gwilym and Gronw Ddu o Fôn (14th-15th centuries), refers to the same custom of plaiting rods : 'Clymu brig . . . coed a'u blaen yn bleth . . . caban o ddail. . . capel crwn'. [Tying the ends . . . trees with their ends plaited ... a cabin of leaves ... a circular chapel]. The references to the *clymu brig* and the *blaen yn bleth* are very suggestive of a round dwelling, as will be seen when the circular-house technique in western Europe is considered below. The evidence is however inconclusive. Richards[4] indeed has argued that Giraldus referred to the practice of wattle-and-daub work and even suggests that the temporary houses could have been made in *bangorau* (wattle framing) for transport, but any one who has had ex-perience in transporting wattle-and-daub work will realize how impossible it is. If there were such movable houses the bangorau must have been of wattle only, which may have been the type in Richards's mind.

A reference in Peniarth MS. 96 (late 16th century) should also be considered.[5] Here in a Trystan and Esyllt episode is found the phrase 'gwnaethbwyd gwely o ddail yddynt a *ffebyll or koed ar dail*' [a bed of leaves was made for them and a tent of the trees and leaves]. Loth com-pares the *pebyll* with Dafydd ap Gwilym's often-mentioned *deildy*. Both were probably circular. I am reminded (by Mr. Tom Parry) of a couplet by Dafydd ap Gwilym describing a *deildy* made of nine trees :

> *I waered, yn grwn gwmpas,*
> *I fyny yn glochty glas.*
> [Below a circle, above a green belfry.]

---

[1] *Op. cit.*

[2] See his *Descriptio Kambriae*, cap. XVII.

[3] Cardiff MS. 26, p. 79.

[4] Richards, R.: *Cymru'r Oesau Canol* (1933), p. 126.

[5] Bulletin of the Board of Celtic Studies, V (1929-31), p. 121.

Mr. Parry adds that the description may be of the trees themselves and not of the *deildy.*,[1]

Further evidence of houses of a circular and temporary character in Wales brings us to comparatively recent times, to the period when squatters set up their houses on common waste lands. Such 'squatting' seems to have been common from the 17th to the 19th century[2] and in 1845 a Select Committee on Commons' Inclosure reported on the subject. The method generally adopted was to erect a *ty unnos*, a house built in one night and enclose around it a small area of ground. To accomplish this feat, the squatter 'gets his hut up with clods to begin with'.[3] These houses were sometimes round but often rectangular. 'The intending proprietor and his friends proceeded to [the building site] at nightfall and with great activity cut clods or square pieces of the green sward. When a quantity of the turf had been cut, a part of the company commenced building up the walls with the clods, which, having been raised sufficiently high, the previously prepared roof was put on and thatched with straw or rushes with all proper speed, so that the roof should be completed and smoke ascend through the chimney ere the sun rose. All this having been done, the active builder could say "My house is my castle" and bid defiance to all previous rights of lord of manor or owner of soil. The quantity of land that the proprietor of clod hall could lay claim to was decided by his throwing an axe from the door of the *caban* in various directions, the hedge being planted along this line.'[4]

It was to this kind of dwelling that the Education Commissioners doubtless referred in 1847 when they stated that the poor "inhabitants [of the Rhayader, Radnorshire, district] chiefly occupy clod houses without a window or aperture but the doorway and chimney and the roof covered with ashes, not watertight, only one room.'[5]

There is no doubt that a large number of these *tai unnos* must have been rectangular in character. But there is also evidence of circular—or at least sub-rectangular—houses of this type. Sir Lleufer Thomas reports in 1893[6] on 'the "ink-bottle" houses of squatter districts in Merioneth and Montgomeryshire. In these, the chimney is in the centre of the house and the roof tends to be of a circular shape, hence the name. They are generally

---

[1] *Revue Celtique*, XXXIV (1913), p. 378. For the *deildy* see Williams, Ifor and -Roberts, Thomas : *Dafydd ap Gwilym a'i Gyfoeswyr* (1935), pp. 36-7.

[2] *Royal Commission on Land in Wales : Report*, p. 589.

[3] *Select Committee on Commons' Inclosure, 1845 : Minutes*, p. 216.

[4] *Bye-Gones*, 19th May, 1875.

[5] Reports of the Commissioners of Inquiry into the State of Education in Wales, 1847, p.265.

[6] Thomas, [Sir] D. Lleufer : *The Agricultural Labourer in Wales*, p. 22.

made of mud or earth with wattle partitions and are straw thatched but they are not very numerous.'

Numerous indeed they could not have been for the present writer, forty-five years after this report was published, scoured the countryside without avail for traces of them, and failed to discover any local inhabitants who could describe them. Sir Lleufer in his *Report* describes these houses in considerable detail: 'There are still in the hilly districts of Garth-beibio, Llangadfan, etc., many old-fashioned cottages and even farm-houses, which present a wretched appearance, being often built of mud and wattling and thatched with rushes or heather, partly owing to the inconvenience and expense of procuring lime, timber and other material, and partly owing to the fact that at least some of them have been built by the occupiers themselves in the capacity of squatters on the wastes of the manor. . . A tapering aperture in the roof serves for a chimney, but quite as often as not the smoke escapes by the door, or oozes through the partitions after mellowing every article of furniture as well as the complexions of the inmates. Many of the older houses of this type have their fires of peat . . . *on the floor in the centre of the dwelling* and owing to the corresponding position of the chimney they were formerly known as "ink-bottle houses".'[1] The Merionethshire examples are cited in the neighbouring mountainous districts of that county.[2] In the absence of further evidence, it is impossible to discuss these dwellings more in detail, except to say that the presence of an open-hearth fire 'in the centre of the dwelling' is a feature to be noted. A friend informs me (1943) that he saw a circular dwelling with a central hearth near Llanfihangel Aberarth (Cardiganshire) about 1911.

It has been said that 'old and humble buildings have descended in the social scale in the course of their existence'.[3] One can certainly observe the persistence with which forms and methods of construction continue in use in Wales, and 'the strange persistence with which the characteristics extend from the earliest times to the present day'.[4] We have therefore to mention at this juncture the circular pigsties still to be found in parts of south Wales. Malkin writing[5] of the village of Welsh St. Donats at the beginning of the 19th century, states : 'In this village are several specimens of the genuine Welsh pigsty, .the conical form and solid fabric of which give an air of architectural dignity to these edifices.' This type of pigsty, now to be

---

[1] *Ibid.*, pp. 84-5.

[2] *Ibid.*, p. 101.

[3] Innocent, C. F.: *op. cit.*, p. 1.

[4] Henning, R. : *Deutsche Haus*, p. 163, quoted by Innocent, C. F.: *op. cit.*, p. 2.

[5] Malkin, B. H.: *op. cit.*, pp. 115-6.

described, still survives and examples are illustrated (plates 2-7).[1] Thirty-five examples—of which thirty-one survive, the others having been destroyed in recent years—are known in Brecknockshire, Cardiganshire, Carmarthenshire, Glamorganshire and Monmouthshire.[2] All these pigsties are circular. With two or three exceptions which have thatched roofs they are constructed entirely of stone, the stonework being identical in technique with the beehive-huts *(clocháns)* of Ireland and Scotland. The corbelling technique is illustrated in plate 6, which shows the interior of the Llantwit Major (Glamorganshire) example. The term 'beehive' is indeed apt, for the Llanover example, the exterior of which has been rough-cast, appears, as you approach it, like a large inverted wasps' nest.

A number of these pigsties was examined : they are all approximately of the same size. Their external height ranges from 10 to 13 ft., their internal diameter from 5 ft. to 6¾ ft. In one or two cases (e.g. at Bedlinog) there is a small 'window'. All the examples have small entrances, that at Llanover, for example, being 3 ft. by 2½ ft. wide. The walls are all thick, ranging up to two feet.

Why should these 'edifices' have been built as pigsties ? What is their date ? Do they represent human habitations which have so 'descended in the social scale' that they have been given over to pigs ? These are questions which cannot all be answered. None of the examples examined has any datable feature. In size none of them bears comparison with the early huts, most of which were well over 20 ft. in diameter. While all the examples are related to the lay-out of the farm buildings of which they now form a part some of them could possibly be earlier than those lay-outs. The Llanover example, for instance, is built on a roadside and the containing wall of the farm on which it is found does not encompass it: indeed even the later wall forming the sty-yard leaves a part of the building outside the farm area. The

---

[1] I am indebted to Sir Cyril Fox for the photograph and details of the Bedlinog (Glamorganshire) pigsty.

[2] Examples still surviving or—in the case of four examples—known to be in existence within the last fifty years, occur in the following districts : Blackwood, Blaina, Llanover, and Machen in Monmouthshire ; Aberdare, Bargoed, Bedlinog, Church Village, Cowbridge, Landore, Llanmadog, Llantwit Major, Neath Valley, Pentyrch, Pontardulais, Pontypridd, Rhiwfawr, St. Hilary, Skewen and Watford in Glamorganshire; Ammanford, Cil-y-cwm, Llanarthney, Llandybie, Pencader and Trimsaran in Carmarthenshire; Trecastle in Brecknockshire; and Llangrannog and Ystumtuen in Cardiganshire. I am indebted to over fifty correspondents for supplying me with information, drawings and photographs of many of these pigsties : their number precludes individual references but their willing co-operation—in several cases at much personal inconvenience—is gratefully acknowledged here. A map of the distribution of these circular structures would be illuminating but in view of the known fact that many of them have disappeared and the probability that many exist of which we are ignorant, such a map prepared on the present available evidence would be misleading.

Bedlinog example is earlier than the neighbouring buildings. In the same way the thatched example at Creigiau is not in a position where one would expect a pigsty. In short, the possibility in certain instances that these are buildings adapted as pig-sties cannot be ignored although it is not argued here.

The case for considering the buildings as survivals of the hut type must be dealt with. Although the sties are much smaller than the early hut circles known in Wales, they correspond to the size of the Irish *clochán* and the Scottish *bothan*. 'The normal, and I presume the most modern form of a beehive house' in Uig, Lewis, writes F. W. L. Thomas[1] in 1860 'is ... six or seven feet in diameter'. This can be compared with the measurements quoted for the Welsh pigsties. In the Lewis huts there were doors 2½ ft. high by 2 ft. wide which can be compared with the Welsh examples. Thomas draws attention to a hole left in the apex of the roof and closed with turf or a stone. This may be compared with the Bedlinog and Skewen sties, which have a similar feature. Macalister in his description of the Irish *clochán* writes[2]: 'At last the sides of the building approximated together so that the hole in the top of the chamber could be closed with a single flagstone.' This is the method employed in most of the pigsties, the Llanover example having an apex built above the stone.

Some of the Scottish beehive huts were inhabited in the 19th century but as we have seen the south Wales examples were described in the early years of that century as 'the genuine Welsh pigsty'. It is worth notice too that in the Irish Gaeltacht the beehive huts are now used 'not as dwellings, so far as I know, but as milk-houses or for storing turf etc. In ... Co. Kerry, beehive houses are still being built as outhouses.'[3] In view of this parallel, it can be argued with great probability that the Welsh circular pigsty represents a survival of the type and technique of the beehive hut as found in Ireland and Scotland.[4] The adaptation of the technique to pigsties is

---

[1] Thomas, F. W. L.: *'Description of Beehive Houses in Uig, Lewis . . .'* in *JProc. Soc. Antiq. Scot.*, Ill (1860), p. 136.

[2] Macalister, R. A. S.: *The Archaeology of Ireland* (1928), p. 242.

[3] Campbell, Åke: 'Notes on the Irish House. II', *in Folk-Liv*, 1938, p. 179.

[4] Since this chapter was written, Mr. W. F. Grimes, M.A., F.S.A., has ex-cavated the Saltway Barn Long Cairn near Bibury, Gloucestershire. He informs me that a chamber there (which may be described as a 'house for the dead' for it is an integral part of the plan and structure of the long cairn) took the form of a circular hut with forecourt or entrance passage, the whole built of dry stone-walling. The chamber had a corbelled roof of domical type and had a diameter of 5½ ft., the overall height being also about 5½ ft. Bonded into the wall of the hut, all around it and on one side of the passage was a stone 'seat', while the hut had also two niches. It is established therefore that the circular hut with a corbelled domical roof and of dimensions comparable with our 'pigsties', i.e. considerably smaller than the huts of the Early Iron Age-Dark Ages period was known in western Britain in Neolithic times.

easily explicable. The pig is the only domestic animal which could be accommodated in such a beehive hut, indeed for which such a hut is peculiarly suitable. Consequently with the abandonment of such structures for human habitation, the tradition and technique were applied to house the one domestic animal for which the beehive hut was suited. An analogy is to be found in the history of the medieval English hall. Halls continued to be built as barns for many centuries after they had ceased to be built for their original purpose. If this be the case, the circular pigsty constitutes the survival of a type which may well be the starting-point for any discussion of the Welsh house. The circular huts already discussed, similar constructions in Cornwall,[1] France,[2] Spain[3] and Portugal,[4] in Italy and Greece and in Denmark, Norway and the Swedish provinces of Oland and Gotland[5] must all be considered as parallels. It is of interest to note, too, that the domical corbelling technique is to be found in Iceland.[6]

The argument against considering these pigsties as such survivals can be stated briefly. They are found in a region which is comparatively poor in circular stone huts of an early date. The Blaenrhondda site is the only known instance in Glamorganshire and its date may be fairly late. Its presence however is an indication of the existence in this area of the hut tradition. But in those areas of Wales rich in stone hut-circles (e.g. Anglesey and Caernarvonshire) the survival of the technique does not appear to be known. With one exception : it must not be overlooked that the hut described above (p. 36) by Elias Owen, at Bethesda, Caernarvonshire, answers in every respect to the description of the south Wales 'pigsty'. Furthermore—although I do not attach much importance to this suggestion—it is possible that in a normanized region such as south Wales, the technique of the circular pigsty may represent a reflection for humbler purposes of the characteristics of the circular manorial columbaria so well-known in France and not unknown in the Vale of Glamorgan. But the weight of the evidence, it seems to me, although the matter must still be left open, favours the consideration of 'the genuine Welsh pigsty' as a survival

---

[1] Radford, C. A; R. : 'The Culture of South-western Britain in the Early Iron Age' in *Homenagem a Martins Sarmento* (1933), p. 326.

[2] Delamarre, M. J.-B. : 'Contribution a l'etude de l'habitat rudimentaire: les cabanes en pierre seche des environs de Gordes (Vaucluse)' in *Comptes Rendus du Congres International de Geographie Paris 1931*, III, pp. 293-8.

[3] Bosch-Gimpera, P. : *Etnologia de la Peninsula Iberica* (1932), pp. 490ff.

[4] Cardozo, Mario : *Citânia e Sabroso* (1938). I am indebted to Dr. H. N. Savory for this reference.

[5] Campbell: *op. cit.*, p. 174.

[6] Bruun, D. : *Fortidsminder og Nutidshjem paa Island* (1928), pp. 194-6.

of the domical *clochán* type, with a prehistoric prototype known from the Welsh Marches.

We must now deal with some circular-house types further afield in Europe since only by such comparisons can the Welsh problem be elucidated. The simplest form which is still widespread throughout most European countries is the conical hut now generally used by charcoal-burners and woodworkers (plate 8) e.g. in England, France, Germany and Switzerland and found also in Spain and the Mediterranean countries. It is found too in the Lapp *riskåtor* (twig-huts)[1] and in Sweden, Finland and the Baltic states and among the Arctic peoples as well as amongst primitive peoples in all parts of the globe. It is obvious that it is a type of high antiquity: its very nature makes its survival from early times difficult, but excavations in Germany and Finland have revealed its presence in the Stone Age.[2] Such huts in England 'are built of a number of thin poles laid together in the form of a cone; the feet are placed about 9 in. apart and they are, interlaced with brushwood. A doorway is formed by laying a lintel from fork to fork, and the whole is covered with sods laid with the grass towards the inside so that the soil may not fall from them into the hut. A "lair" of grass and brushwood is formed upon one side.'[3] In most cases the ends of the poles are tied together or held by the notches of their twigs. This type indeed seems to be illustrated in Wales by the *pebyll* and the *'clymu brig'* described above (pp. 38-39), the 'lair' corresponding to the *'gwely o ddail'*.

Some of the Gaulish huts shown on the Antonine column are round (others are rectangular) but the forms shown, as Addy has stressed,[4] show a higher stage of development than that of the conical hut, for the walls are vertical and the roof domical, although made of thatch. The walls are shown to be of wattle (fig. 4). Similar houses were found in ancient Ireland : 'a cylindrical house, made of wicker-work and having a cup-shaped or hemispherical roof'.[5]

O'Curry describes their construction[6]: 'The plan of the round house was precisely that of the ordinary tent or pavilion, with one exception in detail, however. While the usual canvas tent rises tapering ... to the top of a central upright pole, the round wicker–house was built by setting up

---

[1] Erixon, Sigurd : *Kulturhistoriska avdelningen* (1925), p. 101.

[2] Erixon, Sigurd : 'Some primitive constructions and types of lay-out, with their relation to European rural building practice' in *Folkliv,* 1937, p. 133.

[3] Innocent, C. F. : *op. cit.,* p. 8.

[4] Addy, Sidney 0. : *The Evolution of the English House* (1910), p. 3.

[5] Sullivan, W. K. : Introduction to O'Curry, E.: *On the Manners and Customs of the Ancient Irish* (1873), I, p. ccxcvii.

[6] O'Curry, E., *supra.* 111, pp. 31-2.

perpendicularly a number of poles or posts . . . ranged in a circle . . . and at equal distances from each other. The interstices between these poles or posts were then filled up with stout hazel and other rods in the form of wicker or basket-work . . . There was firmly set up, in the centre within, a stout post called a *tuireadh* . . . into which were inserted by mortices or otherwise attached a certain number of rafters which descended slantingly all round to the tops of the upright posts of the wall into which they were received . . . Cross-beams or pieces were inserted between them . . . until at last a regular shield roof with a sharp pitch was formed above: across the

Fig. 4. Gaulish houses on the Antonine column.

rafters. . were then laid bands or laths which were fastened with pegs or ... twisted withes ... On these again were laid what may be called a sheeting of rods and thin branches of trees.' The shell of the house being finished it was thatched with straw, rushes or sedge and the walls staunched, probably with clay, moss or skins. An account of the building of such a house is given in the *Life of Saint Colman Ela of LauEla* in which Saint Baoithin speaks :—

> *Of drops a pond is filled ,*
> *Of rods a round-house is built,*

and reference to the type are numerous in the Ancient Irish Laws. Some of the creel houses—which correspond to the Welsh *hafotai*—of Scotland seem to have been constructed in the same way.[1] Nor should the circular dwellings of the Glastonbury Lake Village be overlooked.[2]

Circular buildings illustrating typologically a higher stage of development are to be found in the Roman Campagna. They have been discussed at length by Professor Erixon.[3] On the Campagna, as he points out, within earshot of the Eternal City, the herdsmen live probably in much the same way as their forefathers did before Rome was built. They live in huts which are sometimes circular, sometimes oval or rectangular. These are known as *capanna*. The term itself is of interest since in the *cywydd* (p. 38) attributed to Gronw Ddu, the 'capel crwn' (round 'chapel') is described as

caban o ddail mân ym yw

[It is for me a *caban* of small leaves].

Caban is actually derived from *capanna* through Middle English and Old French *cabane*, and seems to have been used to connote amongst other types structures similar in several respects to the *capanna*.

In the Campagnan *capanna.*, the walls and the roof are, unlike those of the conical hut, constructionally independent. Three or four or more poles are set in pyramid fashion, their ends tied together at the top with strips of bark, as suggested in the description of the *caban*. A circle is then marked out, whose centre is the hearth-place and whose periphery is marked inside the circle of slanting posts. This is the wall-line and into it are driven posts which intersect the main supports some distance above their bases. A coarse rope of twisted osier is run along the tops of these posts to join them and to fasten them to the slanting posts at their line of intersection. These main supports are then cut off at that line, which now forms the wall-plate. The whole building is plaited with osiers and covered with canna stalks or coarse twigs and again with dry grass until the resultant structure appears to be in one piece with no separate vertical walls. The central hearth consists merely of the smooth earth floor but generally with a circle or rectangle of small protecting stones. There is no chimney.

Erixon points out that in the largest of all Stone Age huts discovered in Finland a similar technique was employed. In this case there was an outer ring of poles and an inner circle of vertical piles, together with a separate porch (fig. 5). 'The construction was therefore identical with [that of] the Roman *capanna,* with the sole deviation that the outer sloping posts in the

---

[1] *Proc. Sac. Antiq. Scot.,* VII (1866-8), p. 177.

[2] Bulleid, A. and Gray, H. St. George : *The Glastonbury Lake Village* (1911), I, pp. 55-7.

[3] In *Folkliv,* 1937 : See note (2), p. 44.

conic wall would appear to have been retained in the Finnish Stone Age and not cut away as on the Campagna.' Similar evidence is obtainable from south Germany and 'the double combination of outer sloping support and inner vertical wall, or outer sloping roof wall and inner support as found in the *capanna* was not an isolated phenomenon but is a transition type or intermediate form between roof house and wall house, which may have been more widespread and more numerous than can at present be shown'.[1]

Fig. 5. Framework of Stone Age hut, Raisala, Finland.

It appears to me that Room B in House I at Caerau, Clynnog (above, p. 33) and the huts at Ty-mawr, Holyhead (the same construction is suggested[2] to explain the central hearths) may well represent this type in Wales, adapted to stone-country technique. O'Neil's suggestion that the inner circle of posts was due to 'the probable difficulty in obtaining timber of sufficient length to reach from the centre to the wall' appears unsatisfactory. There would have been no such difficulty. It should be considered whether the significant absence of a central post-hole[3] and the presence of an inner circle of posts represent in Wales a variant of a wide-spread building-technique still to be found on the Italian Campagna.

To sum up : from the meagre evidence available in Wales, we have proof of *(a)* circular houses, principally in stone, of types paralleled in many parts of western and northern Europe and the Mediterranean region. These

---

[1] *Ibid.*, p. 134.

[2] *An Inventory . . . Anglesey*, p. lxxix.

[3] But see (p. 35 above) the reference to the 'patch of hard yellow clay' at Clynnog.

existed from the Early Iron Age to at least the Dark Ages. They have developed walls, while some of them may possibly represent the transitional stage of construction exemplified in the Italian *capanna*. *(b)* Circular huts of a temporary character, of wood, seem to have existed in medieval times. Some of these appear to have been of the conical form widespread throughout Europe, *(c)* In later times, the squatters' 'ink-bottle' houses represent a circular or sub-rectangular form with a central hearth, but so poorly built that they have now disappeared completely. *(d)* The circular pigsties of south and west Wales, together with isolated structures in north Wales similar constructionally, point to the persistence to modem times in Wales of a building-technique comparable with that found in Ireland and western Scotland, and probably belonging to the same culture.

CHAPTER IV

The Rectangular House: The Long-House

THE essential difference between circular houses and houses of a rectangular character is in their construction, although Erixon has shown[1] that a transitional type is known where rectangular houses have developed from the adoption of the tripod technique of the circular house in duplicate or triplicate, joined together however by a ridge-piece. Innocent has illustrated a similar construction from Yorkshire.[2] But even in such houses the ridge-piece is a necessity, and it is this which marks the fundamental difference between round and rectangular houses.

The ridge-piece, ridge-pole, ridge-tree, or roof-tree called first in Old and Middle English and *nenbren* in Welsh, is of great antiquity. It is the horizontal pole set at the ridge of the roof to support the slanting poles on each side which form the framework of the roof. 'The construction of wooden roofs has never progressed beyond this stage and the majority of modern roofs are formed of rafters leaned against a ridge-piece. The role of the ridge-piece in gabled buildings is merely that of a convenience in the fixing and fastening of the rafters, but this has only been understood in recent times, and as the old builders believed that the ridge-tree bore the weight of the roof, they endeavoured to make it sufficiently large and strong to carry that weight and they took pains to give it adequate support.'[3]

Åke Campbell in his studies of Irish houses[4] refers to two types of rectangular dwellings, namely, the gable-chimney house where the chimney is in the gable-wall and the central-chimney house which has the chimney 'not at either gable but somewhere in the middle-distance, space being thus allowed for a room between the chimney and the gable-wall. The central-chimney type allows for the possible presence of the sloping thatched gable.' Campbell concludes that this latter type stands in close relationship to the 'beehive' houses of a circular or sub-rectangular character.

Such houses are known in Wales and must be referred to here since they represent a link between the circular and rectangular forms. It seems likely that the 'ink-bottle' houses described by Lleufer Thomas (above, pp. 39 - 40) approximated to this type. In the same area in which these houses

---

[1] *Op. cit.,* pp. 134-5.

[2] *Op. cit.,* p. 12.

[3] *Ibid.,* p. 11.

[4] Campbell, Ake : 'Irish Fields and Houses : a study of rural culture', in *Bealoideas,* V (1935), p. 74.

were found lies Abemodwydd, a house described by M. F. H. Lloyd in 1935[1] and photographed (plate 9) by the present writer in 1937. The house is now uninhabited and falling into ruins. Abemodwydd is of central-chimney type. It has a 'hip' or sloping thatched gable and a room (see fig. 6) between the chimney and the gable-wall. The house is situated in the eastern part of the central-Wales moorland and is a good example of the intrusion of the lowland half-timbered technique into the moorland. It will be noticed that the western gable end (the weather end) and part of the north wall are built of local stone in the normal technique of the moorland. The remainder of the house however is timber-framed with lath-and-plaster fillings. In plan, Abemodwydd is the Welsh counterpart of a widespread Irish type. (Fig. 30 shows another example).

A house similar in plan but with slate roof and no sloping gable was surveyed and planned (fig. 31) in the Rhostryfan area of Caernarvonshire and will be described in the next chapter.

But the central-chimney type is to be found widespread in Wales in another form—in the houses where both men and cattle are found under the same roof, a type which we shall call the 'long-house.' Since Welsh long-houses include instances both of central and gable chimneys, both will be discussed in this chapter.

The fundamental issue which determined the lay-out of this type was the need for shelter under the family roof for man and animal in conditions where easy access to the cattle in all weathers was a necessity. Consequently the housing of man and his cattle under the same roof is found widespread throughout Europe where primitive conditions and environmental causes have demanded it. It is found, for example, in Holland ('the Dutch farm-house is nearly always under one roof, along with the bam and the cowhouse : you walk out of the kitchen straight upon tethered and munching cows').[2] In Friesland and Saxony, Schleswig, Hanover and Westphalia a similar arrangement is found.[3] Vitruvius in dealing with the plan of a Roman country house, writes of ox-stalls and stables 'placed in the warmest places' near the fire. Galen, describing the Greek peasant's house as it existed in Asia Minor in the 2nd century A.D. speaks of 'a single big room with the hearth in the middle and the cattle stalls on the right and left'.[4] Similar houses are found in the High Alps and the well-known 'Saterland

---

[1] *Montgomeryshire Collections,* XLIV, 1935-6, p. 84-5.

[2] Powell, A. H.: 'Country Building and Handicraft in Ancient Cottages and Farmhouses', in *The Studio Yearbook* 1920, pp. 34-5.

[3] Addy, S. 0. : *op. cit.,* pp. 79ff.

[4] Lange, Konrad: *Haus und Halle : Studien zur Geschichte des antiken Wohnhauses und der Basilika* (1885), p. 32.

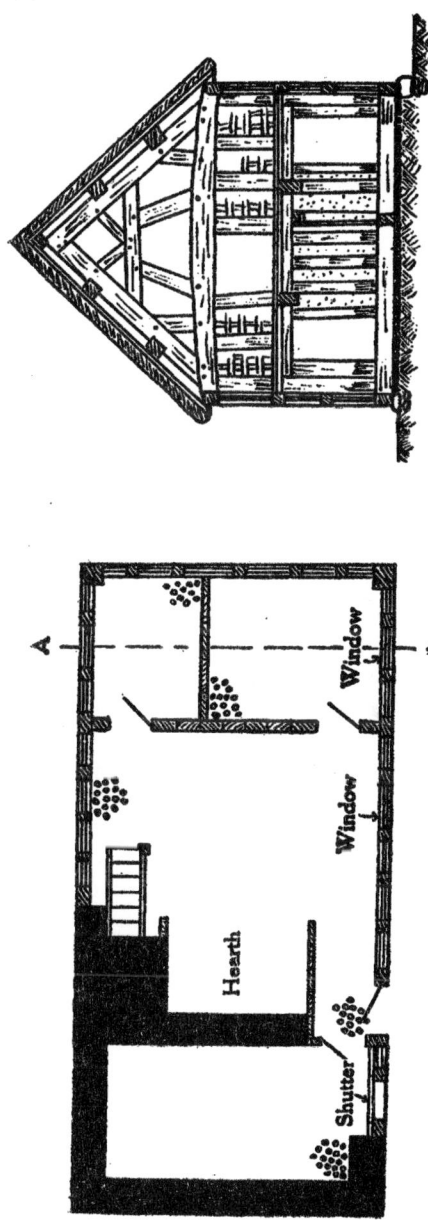

Fig. 6. Abernodwydd, Llangadfan, Montgomeryshire: ground plan and cross-section (lenght 38 ft.).

house' was also of this type, where the main floor was reserved for family use while the smaller partitioned rooms on both sides served for cattle stalls. Houses of a similar character are known from Yorkshire: Addy describes such a house, almost square in character, in that county. Denmark provides examples[1] and also the neighbouring parts of south Sweden[2] where the type

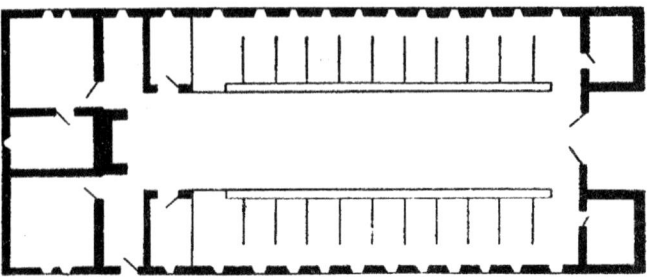

Fig. 7. The 'Saxon' house: ground plan.

'forms a clear and firm tradition, probably from prehistoric times'. The type occurs 'as an archaic one in some parts of western Norway'.[3] Finally, examples are known from all the Keltic lands—Scotland, Ireland, Cumberland, Brittany and Wales.

One fact of importance which emerges from an examination of the evidence for this distribution is that we are here dealing with two types of house-cum-byre, and those types greatly different. As far as I can judge, no detailed comparison is possible between the 'Saxon' house and the Welsh long-house. The ground plan of the 'Saxon' house—which is characteristic in various modified forms of central and southern Europe is basilical with nave and aisles (fig. 7). The middle always forms the floor *(diele)* 'which is entered at the gable end through a large gate and which goes through the whole house as far as the dwelling rooms at the end. . . In the forms of the Frisian and Saxon house generally in use,. the horses and cows are always so placed on both sides of the "floor" that they are foddered from it. Over the "floor", over the cattle stalls and over all the other rooms up to the ridge of the roof the corn harvest and hay harvest are stored on boards and poles laid between the joists. In the Saxon house the background of the "floor" ends in a low hearth on both sides of which .are the bedsteads of the family

---

[1] Zangenberg, H. : *Danske Bondergaarde : Grundplaner og Konstruktioner* (1925).

[2] Erixon, S. : in a letter to the author. See also his *'Svenska gardstyper'*, in. *Foreningens for svensk kulturhistoria tidskvift, Rig,* 1919, pp. 1-39.

[3] Sommerfelt, Alf: in a letter to the author.

arranged in a kind of narrow and rather high cupboards, whilst over against them and near them, the men-servants sleep over the horses and the maids over the cows. To the right and left of the hearth extends the space used for the household which is uninterrupted as far as the two opposite side walls of the house. This part of the house is lighted by high and broad windows, and on either side a glass door forms an exit into the open air. Usually too the well is inside the house at the side of the hearth.[1] Thus the master of the house can superintend the whole management of the household from the hearth and his bedstead.[2] In the Saterland house a similar arrangement is found, the cattle being housed at the sides behind pillars. This may be compared with houses in the High Alps (plate 10). The Yorkshire 'house and shippon' as described and illustrated by Addy seems to be a greatly simplified modification of the same type.

In no detail can this type be compared with the long-house, which is. characteristic of the western European regions and parts of Scandinavia in particular. In the long-house, as we shall see, the cows are housed *under the family roof itself* and Åke Campbell does not preclude the possibility that 'this custom, which was once prevalent over north-western Europe ... was not a *purely Celtic one*'.[3] As he points out, the custom cannot be ascribed to poverty as it is still commonly met with among people who could easily afford separate accommodation for the domestic animals but who prefer to cling to the old tradition.

In Wales the long-house has a wide distribution. It was once, as far as can be judged the predominant type over large areas of the moorland plateau (Region 3, Chapter II) from the Hiraethog moors in the north through Merionethshire, Montgomeryshire, Cardiganshire, Radnorshire and Carmarthenshire, to north Pembrokeshire in the south-west and Glamorganshire and Monmouthshire in the south-east. I have found no surviving example of it in Caernarvonshire but I have been informed by older men in that county, that it was formerly known there also.[4] Since this work has been in the press, I have been informed of three surviving examples at Gwalchmai, Bodffordd and Trefdraeth in Anglesey : these I have had no opportunity of examining: a photograph of one example reveals that it is a typical Anglesey *croglofft* cottage with a cow-house adjoining,

---

[1] See page 126.

[2] Meitzen, A. : *Das deutsche Haus in seinen volksthumlichen Formen* (1882), p. 10. Quoted by Addy, op. cit., pp. 79-81. With this type of house should be compared the lay-out of the Late Bronze Age farmsteads at Wasserburg Buchau (second phase), illustrated in dark, Graham: *Archaeology and Society* (1939), p. 67.

[3] In Bealoideas, 1935, p. 68.

[4] See also O. Gethin Jones : *Gweithiau Gethin.* 1884.

and internal access from house to byre—a modification to be expected in Anglesey.

As the term implies, the long-house is a single, long, low, oblong building which houses both the family and its cattle. The dwelling itself is always at one end, generally called the 'upper end' *(pen uchaf)* though this depends upon the situation of the house—in some cases the dwelling is the 'lower end' *(pen isaf)*. The other end (generally *pen isaf*, occasionally *pen uchaf*) is the cow-house. Between the two is the door. In most cases this opens into a passage called penllawr (literally, the head of the floor) or *bing*, with another door at its further end. This passage dividing the house into its two parts, dwelling-house and cow-house, generally serves as a feeding-walk. There are however many instances *(a)* where the feeding-walk does not exist and *(b)* where it has been modified by the insertion, between cow-house and dwelling, of a dairy, store-room or calf-box. It is obvious from the houses examined, most of which have been greatly altered and reconstructed during the last one hundred years that originally the Welsh long-house consisted only of these two parts, dwelling-house and cow-house, upper end and lower end. The upper end, without exception, was always paved, the paving terminating in the passage, the cow-house floor being of earth. The name *penllawr*, 'head of the floor', is therefore significantly descriptive. At a later date in several of the houses examined, the dwelling part was partitioned off into two, three or even four rooms, parlour, dairy and bedroom(s). On the other hand, several houses examined were built with provision made for these separate rooms.

One of the features characteristic of the modem renovation of these houses is that of raising the roof of the dwelling end to make possible a second storey. Consequently from the outside, many long-houses appear as modern dwellings of 19th-century type with a central 'front' door, two ground-floor windows (one on each side of the door) and two or three above, with a low-roofed out-building attached (see plates 14, 23, 32). This is the case, for instance, at Dinas Isaf, Pen-y-graig, Rhondda, Glamorganshire, a house with a fireplace beam dated 1638, but which is itself possibly earlier in date. About 1880 the dwelling-end was raised in the manner described and during recent years the dwelling-end has been so altered by the insertion of a new fireplace, the blocking-up of the 1638 fireplace and various other reconstructions, including an asbestos corrugated roof to replace the original stone-tiled roof, that the complete appearance of the building has been radically changed.

But despite these reconstructions, the essential feature—that of internal access to the cow-house—has been retained and is an excellent example of the tenacious clinging to the old tradition, referred to by Campbell, by people who, if they so desired, could easily afford separate accommodation for their domestic animals. In the unrestored examples, there is a loft *(towlod, taflod)* for storing wool, cheese and corn and sometimes used as a bedroom for the servants, which is entered in some instances by a staircase from without but generally by a stone staircase from within. The floor of the loft is usually on a level with the wall-plate.

In all the houses examined, the walls are of great thickness, averaging from two to three feet. Throughout the moorland plateau they are generally of mud and stone, but of stone only where a good supply (e.g. Dinas Isaf, Pen-y-graig) was available.

In all the houses examined the living room or kitchen adjoins the cow-house. With a few exceptions, the main (in several cases, the only) fireplace is against the transverse wall which separates the dwelling from the cow-house. This is the normal placing of the hearth, which is therefore, in relation to the whole building, in a central position (see figs. 8-19). Another feature of interest is that in every case the floor level of the cow-house is considerably lower than that of the dwelling. In some instances, one or two steps lead up from the cow-house to the kitchen : in others it is the far end of the dwelling itself which is above the level of the kitchen and cow-house. This feature occurred persistently in the houses examined and its significance will be discussed later in this chapter.

Before dealing in greater detail with the various examples, we must now examine the literary references to the type. The earliest description is to be found in *Breuddwyd Rhonabwy*, one of the Mabinogion tales probably committed to writing in the early 14th-century, much of it (as with many Welsh folk tales) being probably considerably older than the manuscript in which it is found. To quote from it in translation: 'And Rhonabwy and Kynfrig Frychgoch, a man of Mawddwy, and Cadw-gan Fras, a man of Moelfre in Cynllaith, came together to the house of Heilyn Goch the son of Cadwgan the son of Iddon. And when they came to the house, they saw an old hall, very black and lofty, whence issued a great smoke, and on entering, they found the floor uneven and full of puddles and where it sloped it was difficult to stand thereon, so slippery was it with the mire of cattle. And where the puddles were, a man might go up to his ankles in water and the urine of cattle. And there were boughs of holly spread over the floor, whereof the cattle had browsed the sprigs. . . And being weary with their journey, they sought to sleep. And when they looked at the raised platform *(tyle)* there was on it only a little short straw full of dust and fleas with the stems of boughs frequent in it for the cattle had eaten all the straw

from head and foot.' This is obviously a description of a building which
housed both men and animals.[1] But the absence of a bower should be noted.

Llawdden, a 15th-century poet, referring in a poem to the dangers of
the *gwylliaid* (bandits) speaks of

> *Gwely'r amaeth a'r geilwad*
> *Wrth y côr*[2]

[the bed of the husbandman and the oxen-driver near the stall].

The 'Depositions taken the 21st April, 1607, concerning the setting
on fire of a barn in Machynlleth, Montgomeryshire'[3] provides us with an
early 17th-century reference to the type. The evidence was given before
justices at Mathafarn. 'The said David' testifies a witness 'brought in his
hand into his house fire in a cowsherd . . . with which he fired some straw
that he held in his hand and then delivered the same straw kindled to his
wife and she went to look at some kine that were tied up in *the lower end of
the house.'* Another witness 'thought to have the fire whereby she might
have light to go to the *lower end of the house* to look to certain kine of hers
that one of her children had that evening before tied up. A third witness
speaks of 'a cow he had sick *in the lower end of his house'.* From these
depositions it seems that the long-house with its *pen uchaf* and *pen isaf* was
a normal type in that area in the 17th century. The date of several existing
long-houses throughout Wales points to its widespread distribution at that
time.

---

[1] In Chaucer's England ('Ful sooty was hir bour and eek hir halle*—The Nonne Preestes Tale,
l. 12), the use made of the house may have been somewhat similar. But here there was a
second room (the bower), see p. 106. Morris and Skeat (Chaucer: The Prologue, The Knightes
Tale, The Nonne Preestes Tale from the Canterbury Tales [1931 Impression], p. 195) write:
'Whilst the widow and her "daughters two" slept in the bower. Chanticleer and his seven wives
roosted on a perch in the hall, and the swine ensconced themselves on the floor . . . Cf.

> *"At his beds fete feeden his stalled teme*
> *His swine beneath, his pullen ore the beame."*

Hall's Satires, bk. v. sat. 1 ; v. 1. p. 56, ed. 1599.'
I am indebted to Mr. Ffransis G. Payne for this reference.

[2] Llanstephan MS. 128, p. 197. I am indebted to Mr. Ffransis G. Payne for this reference.

[3] Public Record Office MS. Wales 4-141-3. I am indebted to the late Professor E. A. Lewis,
University College, Aberystwyth, for this reference and to Miss Amy ' Foster for a transcript of
the manuscript.

A late 17th-century publication,[1] while it is in great part a lampoon, shows that in some instances at least houses had not at that time been partitioned off. 'We found no *Apartments* in these their Habitations, every edifice being a *Noah's Arc*, where a *Promiscuous Family*, a Miscellaneous Heap of all kind of Creatures did converse together in one Room, the Pigs and the Pullen and other Brutes either truckling under, or lying at the Bed's-feet of the little more *refin'd* yet their *Brother* Animals'. In the same way, sixty years later we hear that 'their Houses generally consist but of one Room but that plentifully stocked with Inhabitants : for besides the Proprietors . . . you shall have two or three swine and Black Cattle . . . under the same roof'.[2] In Caernarvonshire in 1797, 'men, women and children,—cows, sheep and pigs—pig promiscuously together'.[3] At Corwen, Merionethshire, in the same year, 'the people, cows, asses, hogs and poultry all live in one apartment'.[4] In the early 19th century, Cardiganshire farm-houses were 'of a miserable description. The dwelling house is generally a wretched hovel divided into two apartments on the ground floor with sometimes two or three small chambers above stairs or on a loft which is accessible only by a ladder : and the whole is so blackened by peat smoke and by filth as to be hardly tenantable for human beings. The . . . beast houses ... are in unison with the principal buildings'.[5]

When we come to the 19th century, the long-house type had become so singular in a countryside where extensive rebuilding had altered the character of the houses that it inspired several descriptions. Notable amongst these is the detailed study of the type in Carmarthenshire by the Land Commissioners to which we shall refer below. Thomas Pryce, in his 'History of the Parish of Llandysilio', Montgomeryshire, has a detailed description of great value of an eastern-Montgomeryshire long-house. 'In the early part of the [19th] century many of the farm houses and smaller cottages were taken down and replaced by more substantial buildings of brick. . . I will mention a house belonging to a little farm of a few acres of pasture-land which has recently been converted into an outbuilding. . . This was a low building about 36 feet by 18 feet under one long thatched roof. It had a single entrance door, the framework of which reached to the eaves, which were about 7 feet from the ground, and two small windows in front of unequal sizes, one 2½ feet by 2⅓ feet and the other 3 feet by 2 feet. The

[1] [Richards], W. : *Wallography or The Britton Described* (1682), pp. 110-11.

[2] *A Trip to North-Wales* (1742), p. 64.

[3] *A Trip to North-Wales* (1742), p. 64.

[4] Wigstead, H. : *Remarks on a Tour to North and South Wales in the year 1797* (1800), pp. 21, 36.

[5] Rees, T. : *The Beauties of England and Wales*, XVIII (1815), p. 407.

kitchen entered directly by the door was 15 feet by 7 feet and contained an open hearth, the only fireplace in the house and had a small brick oven, apparently of more modern construction, built out to the outside, in a semi-circle. A small bedroom, half the size of the kitchen and lighted by the first mentioned window, was the only other room on the ground floor. At the back of this room was the hay bin of the same size as the room in front and open to the roof. The kitchen and small room were planked over : above the kitchen was the principal bedroom, reached by a ladder and the hay loft was over the small room. This bedroom had one little window in the gable end but no ceiling,, the thatched roof reaching to the floor at both sides. The cow-house under the same roof occupied the other end of the building. The house was built of timber framework and brick. . . The large chimneys *in the centre of the buildings* with their roomy hearths and comfortable inglenooks were an important feature in the old houses.'[1]

In a description of a Mynydd Hiraethog farm, we are told[2] that 'rhyw un adeilad hir oedd, yr anifeiliaid a'r rhai oedd yn gofalu amdanynt yn byw yn un a'i gilydd, yn lle tebyca i arch Noah y gellid meddwl amdano" [it was a single long building, the animals and those who cared for them living together, a place as like Noah's Ark as any one could think of].

The *Report* and *Minutes of Evidence* of the Royal Commission on Land in Wales have an exhaustive study of a number of long-houses particularly in Carmarthenshire[3] but much information is also given about housing throughout Wales. For instance, we are told that at Pen-y-coed uchaf on the Rug estate, near Corwen, 'there was merely a wooden partition: between the cowhouse and the house'.[4] The Commission's descriptions of various Carmarthenshire examples may be referred to here and will provide a convenient starting-point for the discussion of individual houses.

Lan, Llandeilo (fig. 8 and plate 11) had only one entrance into the dwelling-end, that through the feeding-walk. The feeding-walk however had no opposite doors. The dwelling-end was partitioned into a living room and a parlour-bedroom. There was a step up from the living room into the parlour-bedroom, and a stone staircase in the living-room up to the loft. The chimney was of wattle-and-daub. There was no dairy.

Tŷ'r celyn, Llandeilo (fig. 11 and plate 12) was a house of the same plan with a later lean-to addition forming a dairy. 'The loft' stated a witness,[5]

[1] *Montgomeryshire Collections,* XXXII (1902), pp. 257-8.

[2] *Cymru,* 1916, II, pp. 77-8.

[3] *Royal Commission on Land in Wales : Report,* pp. 690-713.

[4] *Ibid. : Minutes,* IV, p. 247.

[5] *Ibid.,* III, p. 250.

'was only one room in which men and women had to sleep without any partition between them'. Two neighbouring farmhouses, Cefn-hendre and Ffynnon Deilo were stated to have been similarly built.

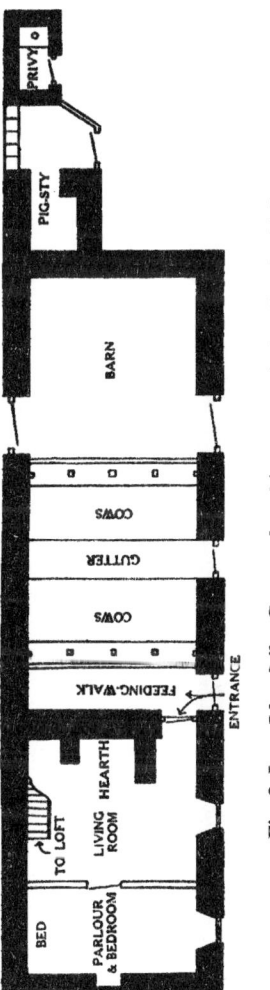

Fig. 8. Lan, Llandeilo, Carmarthenshire : ground plan (lenght 90 ft.).

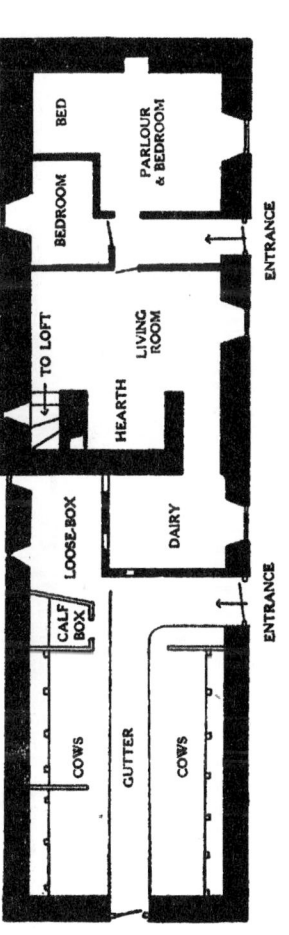

Fig. 9. Cwmneilath, Llansadwrn, Carmarthenshire : groundplan (lenght 75 ft.).

Blaenwaun, Llansadwrn (fig. 10 and plate 13) was again of similar type, with an added lean-to store. At the time when the *Report* was prepared the feeding-walk had been converted into a dairy. This was also the case at Esgair, Llansadwrn (fig. 12). At Nant-y-ffin, Llandeilo (fig. 13 and plate 17) the feeding-walk had two opposite doors. The dwelling-end consisted of three rooms (and a small store-room which had been made by partitioning off a part of the middle room). In this case too the steps leading up from the living-room to the bedrooms should be noted.

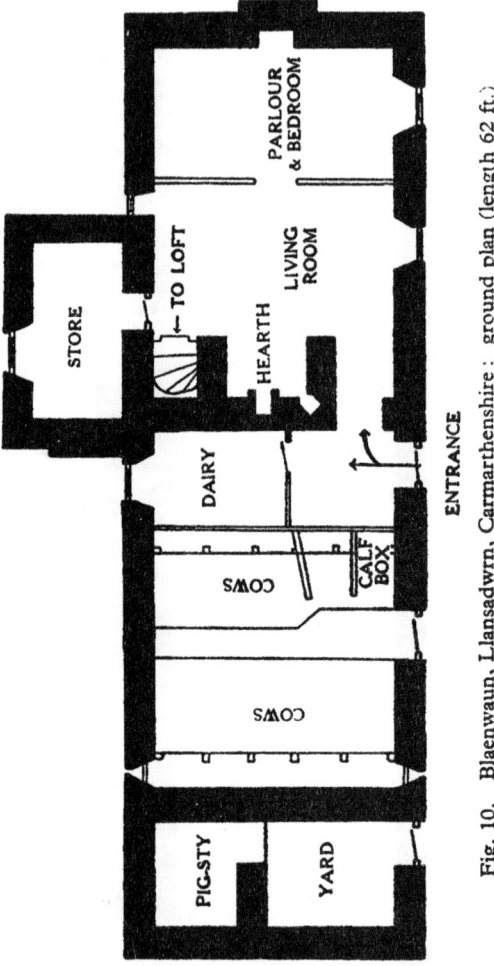

Fig. 10. Blaenwaun, Llansadwrn, Carmarthenshire : ground plan (length 62 ft.)

The *Report* cites three other houses—Cwmeilath, Maes-y-rhiw and Bwlch-y-gwynt, all in the parish of Llansadwrn, as illustrating the first stage in modernizing the type (but see p. 67). Of these, Cwmeilath is here illustrated (fig. 9 and plate 14). In this instance a dairy has been inserted between the dwelling-end and the cow-house, a front entrance

made into the house between the living-room and parlour and the walls of
the dwelling - end carried to a higher elevation than those of the cow -house

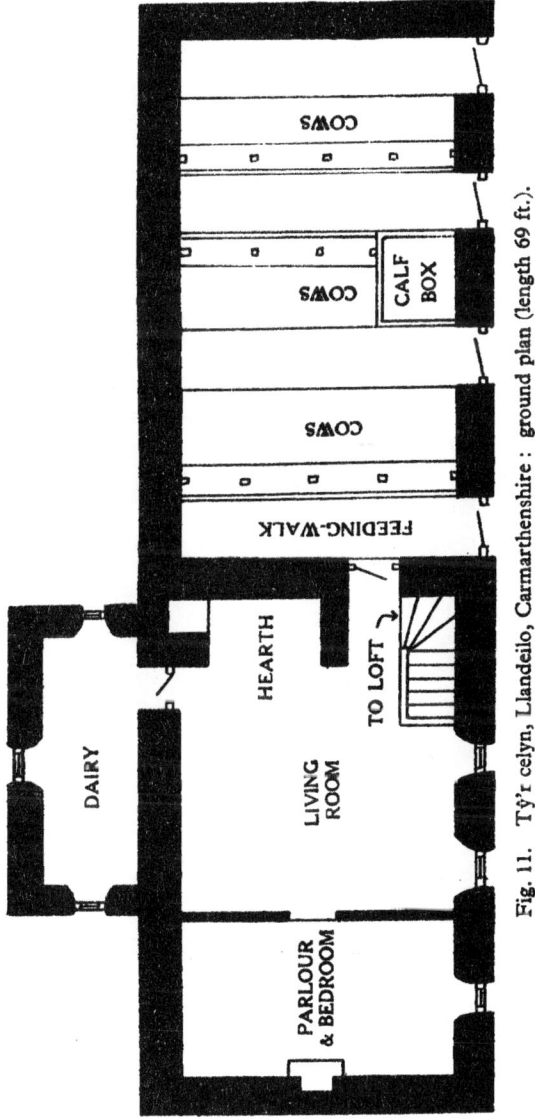

Fig. 11. Tŷ'r celyn, Llandeilo, Carmarthenshire : ground plan (length 69 ft.).

end. It should be noted too that there is an exterior staircase leading to the loft from the gable end as well as an interior staircase of the more normal type.

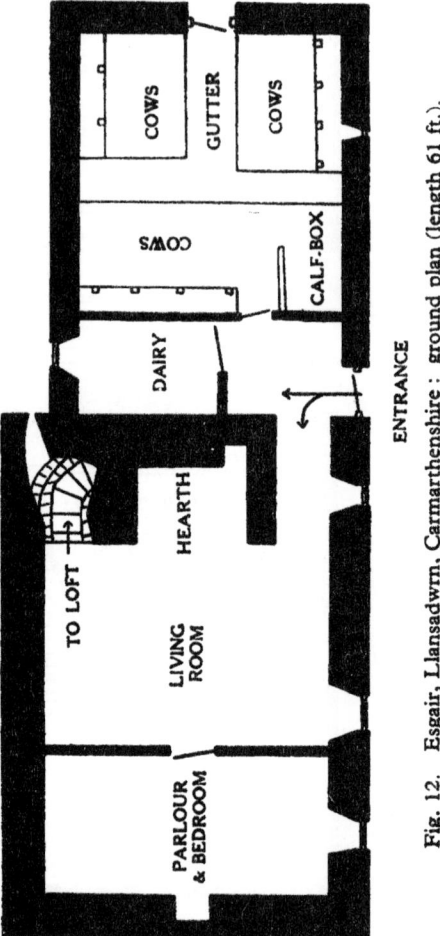

Fig. 12. Esgair, Llansadwrn, Carmarthenshire : ground plan (length 61 ft.).

Ystradaman in the parish of Betws (fig. 14) is another example cited in the *Report* of a house with a feeding-walk with opposite entrances, an additional front entrance and the dwelling-end walls raised above the elevation of those of the cow-house end.

The present survey was carried out forty years after the preparation of the Land Commission's *Report*: it was therefore to be expected that the surviving examples of this type had diminished in number. Many have been so reconditioned as to be to all purposes new buildings. For instance, the Medical Officer of Health for the Dolgelley Union in 1896 wrote in that

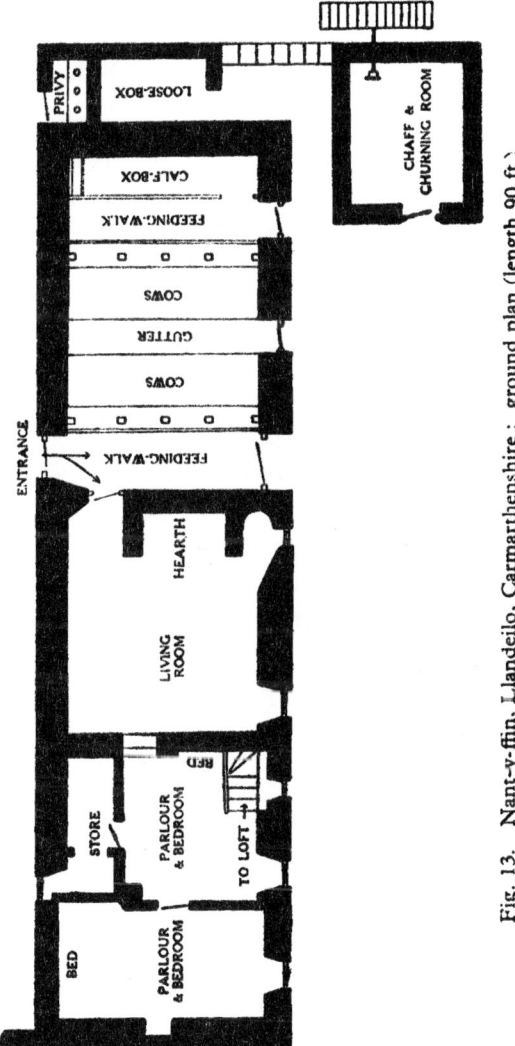

Fig. 13. Nant-y-ffin, Llandeilo, Carmarthenshire : ground plan (length 90 ft.).

year : 'The ordinary form of farmhouses [in this district] was an oblong building under one roof—one part used as the house and the other as a byre . . . But I am glad to say that much improvement has been made in many

farmhouses in this district since [1893]'.[1] In the same way, there were many
long-houses in Glamorganshire at the end of the 19th century, but the great

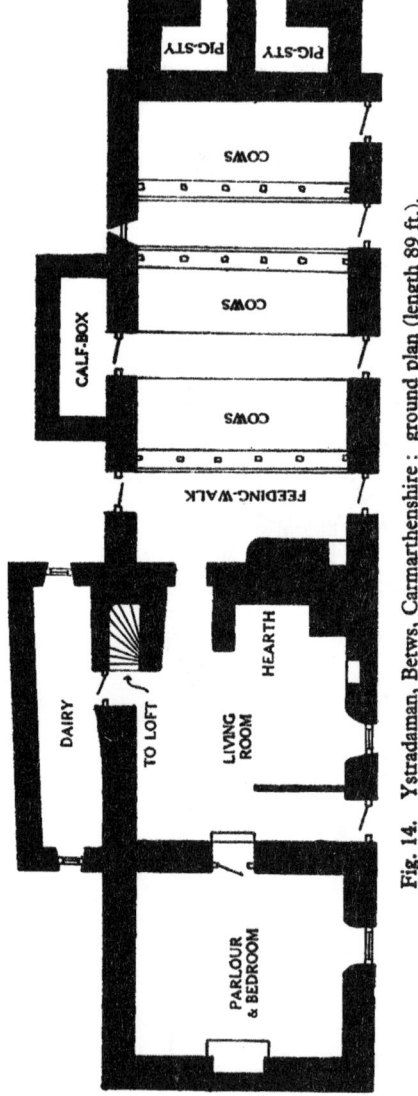

Fig. 14.   Ystradaman, Betws, Carmarthenshire : ground plan (length 89 ft.).

[1] *Ibid., Report,* p. 697 note.

majority of them have either been abandoned or so reconditioned that their original features have been lost. Most of the houses described in the Report are now substantially altered.

We shall now consider 'samples' of long-houses from various other areas in Wales. With a few exceptions these were examined and photo-graphed during the last few years.

There is still a fair number of long-houses in Cardiganshire. Several have been visited in the course of the present survey. The only method of obtaining a record of all the examples would be to visit every farmhouse in each parish. This was of course impossible and since much of the countryside is remote and inaccessible, I had to depend to a great degree upon information from individuals, before visiting various sites. Unfor-tunately such information was often withheld. An example may be quoted. A friend, a Nonconformist minister, described to me how, in a funeral at which he officiated, the coffin was brought out of the house 'past the heads of the cattle, the only doorway in the house', but he refused to divulge the name of the house or its precise locality 'since the family would not like a stranger to see the kind of house in which they lived'. This strange outlook was characteristic of many otherwise cultured individuals in several districts and contributed much to the difficulties of the survey. On the other hand I record with gratitude the ready co-operation of many well-informed people in the various localities. Mr. S. M. Powell, M.A., head master of Tregaron County School, with the aid of his staff and pupils, provided me with a list of over forty houses which had been known to be long-houses and some of which still retained their original features.

Llwyn-rhys, Llanbadarn Odwyn, was a house of great historical interest.[1] It was photographed before the Great War (plate 15) and a second time when its roof had been 'restored' (plate 16). When visited during the course of the present survey it was found to have disappeared completely. The house was of 16th-century date—possibly indeed of the 15th-century — the roof resting on oak principals (crucks) set on large stones at the floor level (plate 72). The house originally consisted of a dwelling-end and cow-house under the same roof, the doorway from the upper to the lower end being on one side of the open fireplace, in the manner normal to the central-chimney type. The house is referred to in the State Papers for 1672 when Morgan Howell was licensed on the 28th October to preach at 'the house of John Jones' under the Indulgence of that year.[2] To make his house more sui-

[1] I am indebted to Mr. W. J. Hemp, M.A., F.S.A., for a copy of the notes made by him when he visited Llwyn-rhys about 1915. For two views of the house, see also *Cymru*, 1901, II, pp. 245, 271.

[2] Richards, Thomas : *Wales under the Indulgence, 1672-1675* (1928), p. 156.

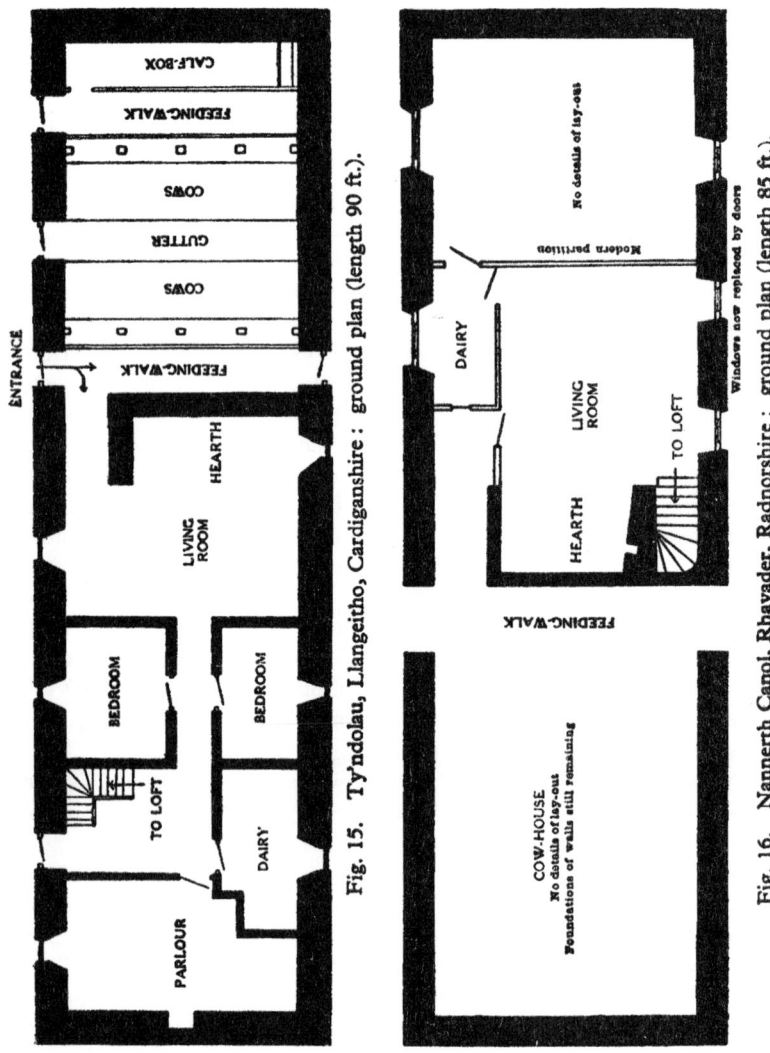

Fig. 15. Ty'ndolau, Llangeitho, Cardiganshire : ground plan (length 90 ft.).

Fig. 16. Nannerth Canol, Rhayader, Radnorshire : ground plan (length 85 ft.).

table for religious services, John Jones added a small wing to his house : this can be seen in the foreground of the illustration. It represents a popular method of extension and may be the origin of the house-name, *Ty Croes.* The lean-to, also in the foreground, was still later.

Ty'ndolau, Llangeitho (fig. 15 and plate 18) has been considerably altered in recent times, the lower end being now used as a cart-house. The transverse passage with its opposite doors, however, still remains. It is of interest to note that the practice of building the walls of the dwelling-end at an elevation slightly higher than those of the cow-house is not a wholly modern development. In this instance the difference in the roofing is contemporary with the building itself, which seems to be of 17th-century date. The main chimney is central, a small fireplace having been inserted later in the gable-end.

Ty'n-coed uchaf, Blaencaron (plates 19-20) has now been abandoned as a dwelling-house and is used as an outbuilding. It still retains most of its original features. Like many of these houses in mid-Cardiganshire its thatch has been covered with corrugated-iron sheeting. But the illustration (plate 19) shows that its original thatch, which still remains, was held down by ropes : the pegs can be seen fixed in the wall above the doors and windows. Ty'n-coed again conforms to the normal type. It is a building of great length, with a stable as well as the cow-house at one end. The only fireplace is central between cow-house and dwelling but there is a second door in the dwelling-end.

Gwastad Gwrda[1], Abermeurig (plate 21) is another example of a 17th-century house so restored as to make impossible the detailed reconstruction of its original plan. In this instance the dwelling is known as *neuodd (neuadd)*, the rooms in the gable-end—there are as in many other instances steps up from the living-room to these rooms—being the *pen uchaf.* Dr. Ifor Williams has explained[2] how the *neuadd* (hall) was divided into two parts, the *uwch gyntedd* ('in anteriori parte aule') and the *is gyntedd* ('in inferiori parte aule'). There was also a third part, as Dr. Williams points out, *y tâl isaf,* where the *penteulu* sat. The tradition may have persisted in this instance, the dwelling-end being the *neuadd*, the kitchen the *is-gyntedd* and the parlour-bedroom end the *uwch-gyntedd*. These two terms do not however appear to be in use there. A further note on the connotation of the word *neuadd* may be of value. In the Martianus Capella glosses (9th century), *nouodou* appears as a gloss on *palatia* and therefore in that context means 'palaces'.[3] Dr. John Davies's dictionary (1632) equates it with *aula.* Gwastad, it should be added is of cruck-construction—as would be expected (see Chapter VI) in a *neuadd* form.

---

[1] See *Journal of the Welsh Bibliographical Society,* VI (1943), p. 14.

[2] Williams, Ifor : *Pedeir Keincy Mabinogi* (1930), p. 131.

[3] Dr Henry Lewis in a letter, 2nd December, 1939. He points out too that in the *Book of Taliesin* (p 63, line 5) the form *neuodd* (not *neuadd*) is presupposed since it rhymes with *o'th vodd.* Dr. Ifor Williams kindly supplied me with an exhaustive note on the word *neuadd.*

Gwarfigyn, Blaenpennal and Nantylles, Blaencaron are two instances of Cardiganshire long-houses now converted to other uses. Gwarfigyn is now used as a cow-house and the details of its original lay-out difficult to trace. At Nantylles the dwelling-end has been reconstructed and the entrance from the feeding-walk to the house blocked up. Its original plan is however easy to follow, the cow-house end retaining all its chief features. Another long-house in the same county which has now become a cow-house is Ty'n-pwll, in the parish of Ysgubor-y-coed in the north of the county. Gwarcwm, Llanwnnen, old Blaen-pant, Neuadd-lwyd, and Rhiwsiôn Isaf, Drefach, Llan-y-bydder, at the other end of the county may also be mentioned.

Several good examples of long-houses survive in Carmarthenshire. Pant-mawr, New Inn, could not be photographed owing to its position and the proximity of the outbuildings. It is a central-chimney house of cruck construction and a long-house of normal type. Gwndwn, Pencader (fig. 17 and plate 22) was abandoned as a dwelling at the end of the 19th century when a new house was built. The old house retains its original features and is practically untouched. The illustration shows that it has only one (central) chimney and that the walls of the dwelling-end are at a higher elevation than those of the cattle-end. The dwelling-end has two rooms, a kitchen and parlour-bedroom, two steps leading up to the latter from the kitchen. The *penllawr* has two opposite doors, but a later dairy has been added on the south-eastern side of the house and is entered from the feeding-walk. An interesting feature is an external wall built at right-angles to the house between the dwelling-end and the cow-house to separate the cattle-yard from the domestic area. This now forms one of the walls of a later outbuilding : its whitewashed end can be seen in plate 22.

Coedlannau, Pencader (plate 23) has been reconstructed. The original feeding-walk door can however be seen. The house is of the usual type. Another reconstructed house is Whithen, Pencader. Its doorway (plate 24) is a good example of the normal feeding-walk type.. Maes-y-bidiau, Abergorlech (plate 25) is another example of the two-roomed dwelling-end, with a large central chimney, while Erw Domi, Porth-y-rhyd (plate 26) illustrates the same type—still occupied—-in an advanced stage of disrepair. Cefn-hirfryn, Cynghordy (plate 32) is a departure from the normal type. Here is a kiln-room between the kitchen and cow-house, communication with the cow-house being by means of a staircase and through the kiln loft to the dwelling-end. The wooden ventilator of the kiln-room is shown in the photograph. In Brecknockshire, Hepste Fawr, Penderyn (fig. 18 and plate 27) represents an interesting example of the type. The front door leads into a 'vestibule' directly behind which is a bull-stall and a calf-box. The cow-house is entered from the 'vestibule' by a door on the left. The open drain behind the cows *(llaesodren)* here runs through the wall.[1] On the right, three steps lead up into the kitchen.

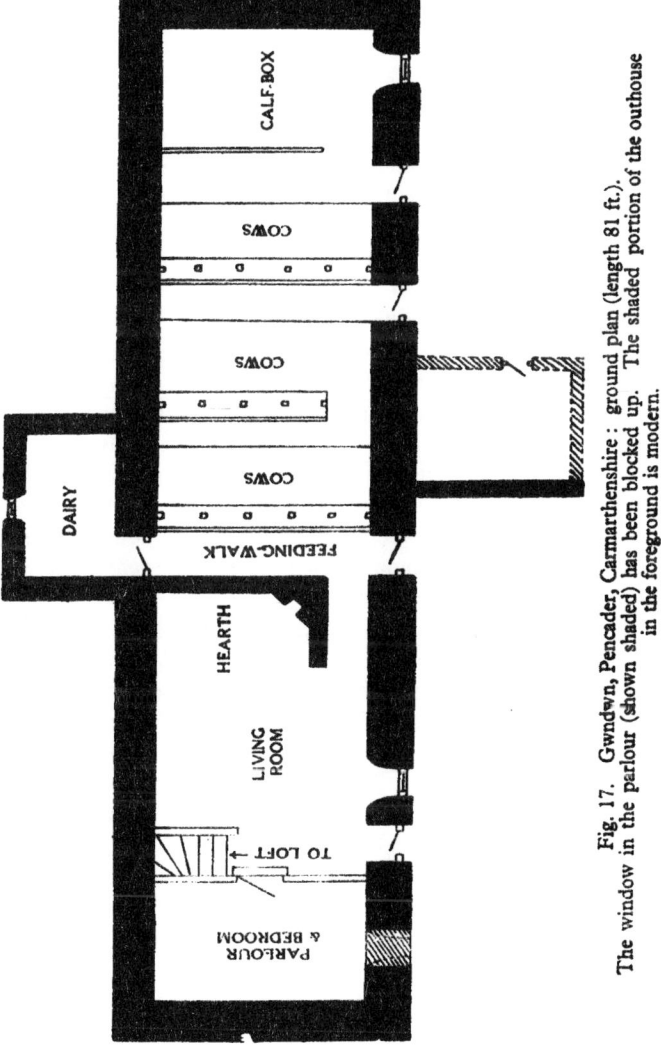

Fig. 17. Gwndwn, Pencader, Carmarthenshire : ground plan (length 81 ft.). The shaded portion of the outhouse in the foreground is modern. The window in the parlour (shown shaded) has been blocked up.

---

[1] Cf. Evans, E. E. : 'Donegal Survivals', in *Antiquity*, 1939, fig. 3, p. 213.

Plate 28 shows the view from the kitchen-doorway into the cow-house.

The long-house was formerly well-known in Glamorganshire, but, as one native of the Rhondda Valley informed me, 'they have disappeared during my lifetime because of the sanitary laws'. T. C. Evans *(Cadrawd)*[1] defines *penllawr* as a term known in his parish which is situated in the Llynfi Valley: 'a passage', he writes, 'in the very old farmhouses between the place the cattle were kept and the dwelling-house'. Dinas Isaf, Pen-y-graig (plate 29) is a surviving example of the type. The dwelling-end, as has been mentioned, has been altered in recent years, a fireplace inserted in the gable-end, the roof raised and covered with asbestos sheeting. But the internal access to the cow-house has been maintained and the unrestored parts of the building point to a medieval date. Plate 30 shows a view of the cow-house from the entrance to the living-room.

Such houses were also to be found in the Vale of Glamorgan: the inspection of a much restored and converted house in the village of St. Hilary showed that formerly it was of this type. Other examples, all restored, are Argoed Edwin, Llanharran and several in the Tawe, Neath, Rhondda, Cynon and Rhymney valleys. Hendre, Pontypridd, a house probably of 17th-century date, has a stone staircase on the left of the central fireplace leading to a loft above the cow-house but there appears to have been no communication between dwelling and cow-house on the ground floor. Ynys-llwchwr isaf is another Glamorganshire example (near Pant-y-ffynnon on the Carmarthenshire border).

Three examples may be cited from Radnorshire. Nannerth Canol, near Rhayader (fig. 16) is now an out-house and no details of the lower end arc available. The plan however shows that it conformed to the normal type. Llannerch-y-cawr, Cwm Elan (fig. 19 and plate 34), a house of cruck construction has no transverse feeding-walk, the stalls being placed longitudinally as in Dinas Isaf, Pen-y-graig, and Cwmeilath, Llansadwrn—without, however, an entrance in the gable-end. The upper end of the dwelling (the parlour and dairy) is approached by stone steps up from the kitchen. This house, with its foundations dug into the valley-side with a screen of trees around, is a good example of the method by which the peasant builder obtained shelter from the prevailing winds.

Ciloerwynt, Dyffryn Claerwen (fig. 20 and plate 31) in the same county is different from the examples discussed. It is of gable-chimney type and originally had only one room in the dwelling-end. It has the usual loft above, lighted by a dormer window in the stone-tiled roof. This house formerly had opposite doors, one of which has now been blocked up but the

---

[1] *History of Llangynwyd* (1887), pp. 146-7.

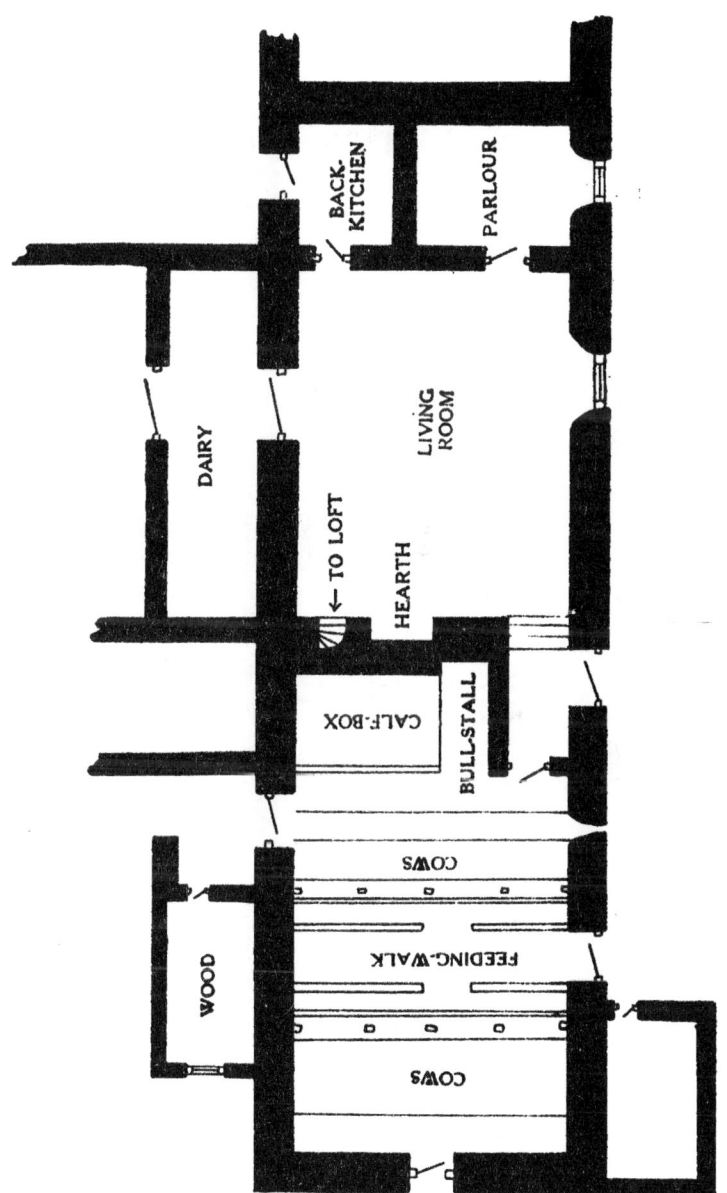

Fig. 18. Hepste Fawr, Penderyn, Brecknockshire : ground plan (length 69 ft.).

feeding-walk did not extend across the building (see plan). The house is of cruck construction and the door-lintel is dated 1734.

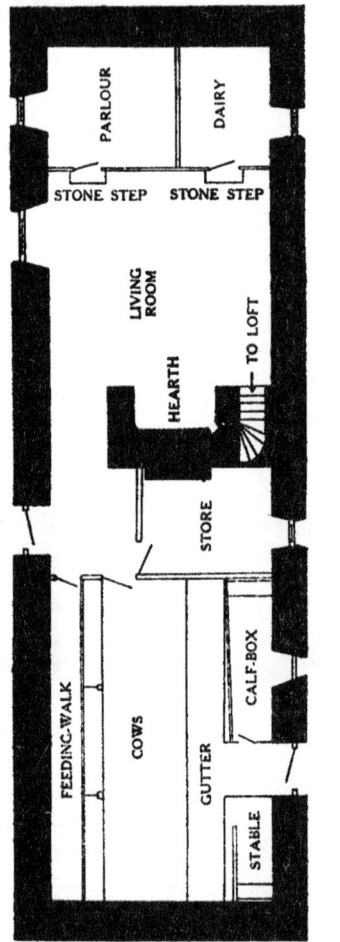

Fig. 19. Llannerch-y-cawr, Cwm Elan, Radnorshire : ground plan (length 75 ft.).

Montgomeryshire provides another example of the same nature Pant-y-drain, Kerry, a gable-chimney house. Here again the floor-level of the dwelling is higher than that of the cow-house (fig. 21). The house is in the half - timbering area of the county and the gable and front walls of the cow-house are of wood. It is a good example of the adaptation of the long-house to valley conditions in an oak-growing area. The house is however much 'restored' and the present access from the dwelling-end to the cow - house is

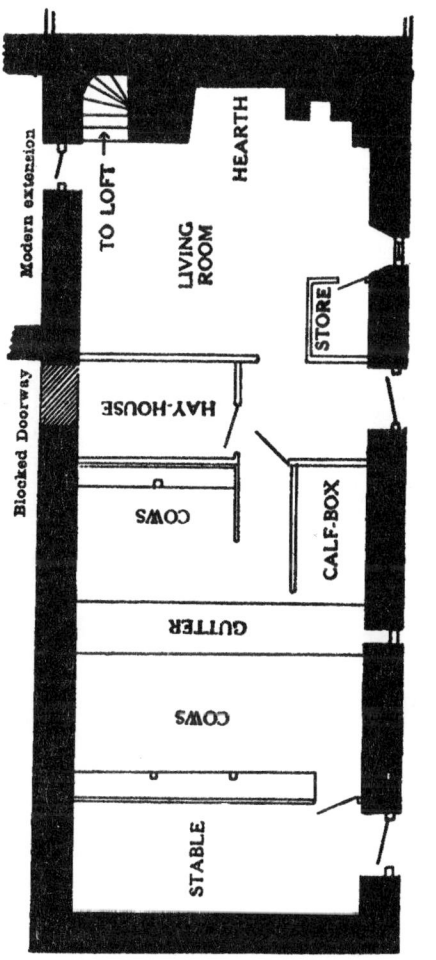

Fig. 20. Ciloerwynt, Dyffryn Claerwen, Radnorshire : ground plan (length 57 ft.).

through the loft, a 'modernization' also apparent in other instances. At Dolhelfa, Llangurig, access from the house to the granary is possible. In Glamorganshire, Hendre, Pontypridd (above), shows a similar development.

We have already referred to the manuscript references to houses of this type in Montgomeryshire in the early 17th century. The type was

formerly widespread through the county. Richards[1] figures a typical
example dated 1665 from Pennant Melangell in the north-east of the county.

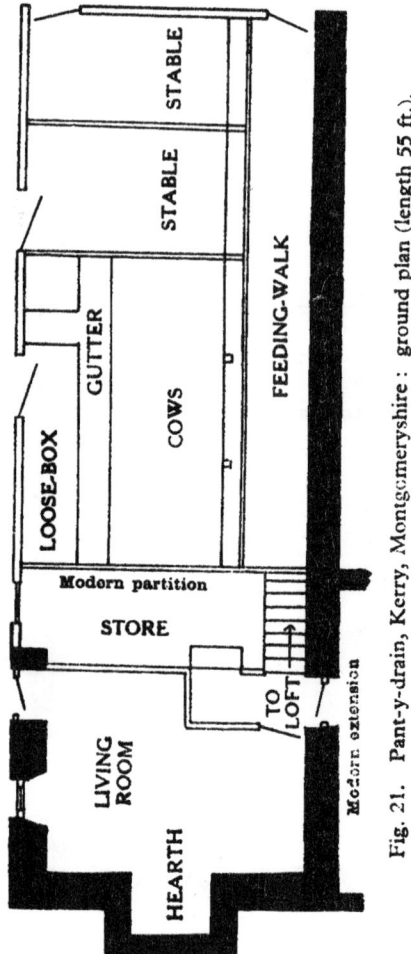

Fig. 21.   Pant-y-drain, Kerry, Montgomeryshire :   ground plan (length 55 ft.).

[1] Richards, R.: *op. cit.*, p. 127.

In the south, Bryn-du, Llanidloes, now much altered, is of long-house type with a two-feet drop from the dwelling-end to the cow-house.

In Merionethshire, while there was much evidence of the former existence of long-houses, no surviving example was discovered. Nant-llwyn-gwedd and Meriafael Bellaf near Abergynolwyn were both formerly long-houses. The former, now altered is still inhabited but the latter—which is of gable-chimney type—is used as an out-house. Wenallt Fawr, Cae'r ceiliog, north-east of Bala, is now not a farmhouse. It has a date-stone inscribed 1719 but there are traces that the original house was much earlier. Mr. W. F. Irvine, who adapted it for stable purposes in 1913 informs me that it was of good long-house type. Nant-y-clawdd hen, Llanfor, inhabited about seventy years a'go, now a cow-house, is a gable-chimney long-house with one room at the dwelling-end and a drop of 1½ in. from the *penllawr* to the cow-house floor.

In Caernarvonshire, no surviving long-houses were examined but, as has been mentioned above, several inhabitants knew of their former existence there. Mr. Evan Rowlands, Llanllyfhi, tells me 'Mac hen dy eto yn Penrhiwiau, Clynnog, yr anifeiliaid o dan yr un to a'r teulu'. [There is still an old house at Penrhiwiau, Clynnog, with the animals and the family under the same roof.] Hughes and North[1] figure a plan of Derwen deg, near Conwy, which had a hatch in the partition wall between the house and cow-house, but this does not seem to be a modification of the normal long-house plan. An example from the literature has already been cited from Denbighshire where the type was also well-known, but where in many parts, rebuilding and restoration have completely eliminated the ancient types.

It seems probable that a form of farmhouse widespread throughout the whole moorland area is a typological descendant of the long-house. In this type (plate 33) the dwelling-house, cow-house and stable are generally under the same roof but each is entered by a separate door from the outside and there is no internal communication of any kind. Several long-houses have been reconstructed in this form and the prevalence of the type throughout the area suggests that it originated as a modification of the earlier form.

We have now examined 'samples' of long-houses from all the moorland area. In plan, all consist of dwelling-house and cow-house with internal access from the one to the other. In the majority of cases the fireplace is more or less central to the whole building, near the junction of cow-house and dwelling. Only in a small number of examples is the fireplace at the gable-end. In several of the houses, the dwelling ends in a transverse passage (with a door at each end) which serves as a feeding-walk

---

[1] *Op. cit.,* p. 35.

for the cattle. This passage and the dwelling itself is paved. In almost all instances all the dwelling-end or the 'best' part of it (then known as *pen uchaf*) is above the level of the cow-house and approached by one or more stone steps. These facts must now be considered in detail.

It is justifiable to suppose that the long-house in its earliest form was a simple shelter for man and his animals, the family occupying one end, the cattle the other and an open-hearth fire in the centre between them.

Even though it has been traditionally held that the cows must see the fire and that 'warmth increases the yield of milk'[1] it is probable that the convenience of housing the complete stock under one roof had much to commend it to our ancestors. In some other Keltic countries, this primitive form has existed down to recent times. Campbell[2] describes a one-roomed dwelling in Co. Kerry, Eire, with opposite doors. 'Either door is used as occasion requires in order to prevent the changeable winds from entering the kitchen'. He describes how today in summer in houses with two opposite doors, the cows are driven in turn through one door into the kitchen, milked and then driven out through the other, to make place for the next.

Aage Roussell[3] has described long-houses of a similar primitive kind on the Isle of Lewis. 'Coming in from the road you bend your head and step in at the door in the middle of the long side, and find yourself in a gloomy byre. Just inside the door a pavement runs right across the house [cf. the Welsh *penllawr*] but immediately on its left is a step . . . down to an earth floor. This is where the cattle are kept on a layer of manure that grows steadily throughout the winter. . . A crude partition of boards reaching only to the height of the walls separates the byre from the "fire room", where the peat fire burns on the middle of the clay floor'. Here in the Scottish Isles is the prototype of the Welsh long-house. The raised pavement might at first sight appear to be functional: by raising the floor above the level of that of the cow-house, it would be possible to prevent the liquid manure and urine from running into the dwelling-end to cause the conditions described in the house ofHeilyn Goch (above). Such conditions were not however unknown in the Isles.

'There is no doubt' writes Roussell, 'that the original arrangement was the undivided house so that the cattle in the lower end and inhabitants in the upper end lived in one room'. Thomas indeed describes such an arrangement on the Isle of Lewis : 'A door leads into the main building

---

[1] See for instance, Evans, E. Estyn: *op. cit.*, p. 210, and Thomas, F.L.W.: 'On the Primitive Dwellings and Hypogea of the Outer Hebrides', in *Proc. Soc. Antiq. Scot.*, VII (1866-8), p. 157.

[2] *Béaloideas*, V. pp. 68-9.

[3] Roussell, Aage : *Norse Building Customs in the Scottish Isles* (1934), p. 16.

which is entirely open through its whole length. About two-thirds of the lower end is occupied by the cows ; the upper or fire end is marked off by a row of stones. The fire which never goes out is about the middle of the floor'. With the undying fire of the Scottish Isles should be compared to the Welsh practice of covering up the fire each night (*anhuddo*). For the fire to be allowed to bum out was a great misfortune which might have serious consequences for the family. On many hearths fire was said to have been kept burning without break for generations. This custom is mentioned in the Welsh Laws. The term *benthyg tân*, "to borrow fire" shows that, for the rekindling of fire, or in the case of new hearths, fire was obtained from what was known as *tân byw*, "living fire".[1] We are here dealing with related cultures.

The long-house was known not only in the Scottish Isles but on the mainland as well. In Perthshire, for instance, at the end of the 18th century, a commentator writes : 'I must add with regret that in several places, the houses ... are still mean; the farmer and his cattle lodge under the same roof. . .'[2] Robert Burns writes :—

> *The Sowpe their only hawkie does afford*
> *That 'yont the hallan snugly chowse her cood.*[3]

In Cumberland, too, states Dickinson, writing in 1875, 'a century ago many sets of farm buildings consisted of oblong blocks adjoining the farm yards. The dwelling at one end of the block was separated from the out-buildings by a covered passage. There was an inner door opening out of the passage into the kitchen or living room and another on the opposite side into the byre ; and the passage was a common thoroughfare for men and dogs, horses, cattle, wheelbarrow, poultry, etc.'[4] In brief, the housing of the cattle under the family-roof is an arrangement characteristic of the Keltic Highland Zone of Wales, Ireland, Cumberland and Scotland.

Roussell,[5] Stenberger,[6] Campbell[7] and others have drawn attention to a wider distribution of the type over north-western Europe. Several of the

---

[1] Jones, T. Gwynn : *Welsh Folklore and Folk Custom* (1930), p. 179.

[2] *General View of the Agriculture in the County of Perth* (1799), p. 52.

[3] *The Cotter's Saturday Night*, II, 93-4. I am indebted to Principal J. F. Rees, University College, Cardiff, for this reference.

[4] [Dickinson, W.]: *Cumbriana* (1875), p. 197.

[5] *Op. cit.*

[6] Stenberger, Marten: 'Remnants of Iron Age Houses on Oland', in Acta Archaeologica, II (1931), pp. 93-104. See also his Oland under aldre Jamaldem (1933).

[7] See note (2), p. 76.

houses on Öland Island, dated about 300-500 A.D., are as Roussell stresses, 'pronounced long houses' and Roussell argues with much probability that some of them contained byres. In Jutland an Iron Age house was divided 'into a living room . . . and an outhouse and stable' with a hearth set centrally between the two ends.[1] At Ginderup in Thy is 'an ancient settlement which has been used for several centuries, beginning almost with the Christian era' where the hearth is 'in the middle of one half of the house. Household utensils also mark this part of the house as the living room. Just as certainly is the other half the byre.. . At the long wall there are stalls .. . numerous tethering posts [and] a halter which has been cut through when the people were endeavouring to save the animals during the conflagration that destroyed the house. That they were not entirely successful is shown by the fact that the byre contained the charred remains of two sheep and a cow. No trace of a partition was found in the house.'[2] In the same way, Gudmund Hatt's excavation of a late Iron Age house at Solbjerg on the island ofMors revealed an un-partitioned long-house containing the bones of three oxen and a horse.[3] The three-roomed *gamme* of the Finnmark Lapps of Norway are also parallel in type. They consist of a living-room, passage-way and cow-shed.[4]

There is therefore no doubt that the long-house, with man and cattle under the family roof (as distinct from the basilical type widespread over the continent) was formerly found throughout north-western Europe from the early centuries of the Christian era onwards. Its strong persistence in the Keltic lands may point to its origin there but this can only be determined by further research.

We have stressed the importance of the step separating the dwelling-end from the cow-house or in many instances separating the bedroom end of the dwelling from the rest of the house. In the Hebridean houses this step corresponds to the edge of the *penllawr* but, in view of the fact that the layer of manure in the cow-house 'grows steadily throughout the winter' it cannot be explained there as a simple method of preventing the liquid manure from running to the upper end. Instances are actually known where, due to the accumulation of manure in the lower end, the occupiers of the upper end have to keep their boots on until they are on their beds!

A similar raised platform was found in some of the Iron Age houses of Scandinavia. It is a matter of conjecture whether the raised platforms of

---

[1] Roussell, A.: *op. cit.,* p. 40.

[2] *Ibid.,* p. 42.

[3] *Ibid.,* p. 42.

[4] Vreim, Halvor : 'The Ancient Settlements in Finnmark, Norway', in *Folkliv,* 1937, p. 188.

some of the Welsh circular huts belong to the same tradition (see p. 36). What appears to be a similar arrangement is described above in the house of Heilyn Goch. There the raised platform accommodated the bed and corresponded to the 'platform' across the ends of so many Welsh long-houses, accommodating principally the bedroom but in later times often the dairy too. Professor W. J. Gruffydd draws my attention to a feature which has persisted to this day in most Caernarvonshire cottages. In his own home, for instance, in Bethel, Caernarvonshire— a house built about 1850—with four bedrooms and a tiled kitchen, the tradition persisted of building on one side of the kitchen a raised platform of slate, six inches above the kitchen floor and about two and a half feet wide. On this was placed without exception the long-case clock and the dresser, i.e., the valuables of the family tradition.

The word used in *Breuddwyd Rhonabwy* for the raised bed-platform is *tyle*. This is translated by Lady Charlotte Guest as 'couch' but it can best be interpreted as 'raised platform'. Its gender in the tale is feminine whereas generally it is masculine. Over a large area of Wales its one meaning is 'hill, raised ground, mound'. With this should be compared Irish *tulach*, 'hill', which seems to be related (for -*ach* = -*e*, cf. *imbarach* =*bore*). Timothy Lewis's *tyle* = Irish *tolg* 'bed' must be rejected. Irish colg, bolg, correspond with Welsh *col, coly* and *bol, boly* not with **cyle* and **byle*. But *tolg-* + *lle* i.e. 'the place of a bed' would not only give the form tyie but also account for the gender of the noun in this tale, since lie used to be feminine. *Safle*, literally 'place to stand' and *tyle,* 'place to lie', would then be antithetical nouns. In the Welsh Laws,[1] reference is made to a *sow ar y thyle and partus suis dum sit ar e thele* with the explanation '[*in suili*]'. It is noteworthy that the sty is generally raised above the sty-yard in the same way that the 'raised platform' of the house is above the remainder of the floor. It seems likely therefore that the *tyle* referred to a raised platform (in house and pigsty alike) on which bedding was generally laid. This might be the shelf of the circular hut or the *pen uchaf* (in later times) of the long-house. It may also be that *tyle*, 'hill' (masculine) and *tyle,* 'raised platform' (feminine) are two different words, derived, as suggested, from different sources : but this is a philological problem which need not be further discussed here.[2]

Finally, a brief reference must be made to the fireplace in the Welsh long-house. We have already remarked upon the practice of maintaining a continuous fire, common alike to Wales and the Hebrides amongst other areas. In the Welsh houses—except where modernity has introduced the

---

[1] Owen, A. : *Ancient Laws and Institutes of Wales* (1841), I, p. 454, and II, p. 77.

[2] For much of the material in my treatment of the word *tyle* I am indebted to Dr. Ifor Williams, who is, however, not responsible for the conclusion which I have reached.

built-up grate—the fire was always on the floor, generally against the partition wall separating the two parts of the house. All the cooking was done by means of this fire. The normal method (still not completely demoded) was by means of the baking-pot with a flat lid, which for the baking of bread or the roasting of meat was encased in burning peat. This is still known in some parts of Wales as the *ffwrn* (oven). The built-in oven was not known in large areas of the Welsh moorland until a comparatively recent date although it appeared earlier in some lowland areas of Wales which had been long under Norman and English influence : in the Vale of Glamorgan for instance, where examples from Tudor times are known,[1] and where the tradition of the built-in earthen oven persisted down to modern times. But such an oven of early 19th-century date recently removed to the National Museum from a house at Llandow, bore a Bideford maker's mark. Typologically, it is a true descendant of the Tudor ovens known in the Vale and the probability is that the tradition represents cultural influence from south-western England.

Built-in ovens are shown however in most of the plans figured in this book. They are all of 19th-century date. In the description given above (p. 57) of a Llandysilio (Montgomeryshire) house the brick oven is noted as 'apparently of more modern construction' than that of the house itself—and this on the eastern fringe of the Welsh moorland. An observer in west Montgomeryshire, writing in 1887[2] and describing the normal house of the district states : 'Weithiau gwneid ffwrn hefyd ond y rhan amlaf crasid y bara yn y crochan pobi' [sometimes an oven was built but generally the bread was baked in the baking pot]. In some parts of west Wales, the bread was baked outside the house, often on a rock surface under an inverted pot, the fire over it being kindled from the straw from which came the grain for making the flour used in the bread baked. The *gradell* 'griddle', also has a long history in Wales.

For all domestic purposes therefore the open-hearth fire (with its bar, or crane, chain and tilter, together with its cauldron and pot) was adequate. Campbell has shown[3] that in Ireland too this 'pure hearth-type' is usual: 'it stands in direct contrast with the Middle-and, especially, the East-European tradition, where the stone-built oven completely dominates the fireplace, indeed, even the whole kitchen. Thus Ireland is in this respect the antithesis to Finland and Russia'. The same appears to be true of Wales[4] until comparatively modern times, when we find a convergence of the built-in

---

[1] Peate, Iorwerth C.: *Guide to the Collection of Welsh Bygones* (1929), p. 81.

[2] Peate, David : *op. cit.* (MSS.).

[3] *Bealoideas,* V, p. 70.

[4] Feate, Iorwerth C.: 'The Pot-Oven in Wales' in *Man.*, XLIII (1943), 3.

oven culture with that of the open-hearth, the built-in oven being an importation from the English lowland. It should be noted too that in a large number of instances, the built-in oven is a feature not of the kitchen but of the back-kitchen, which is often a late lean-to addition.

CHAPTER V

The Rectangular House: The Cottage

IT is no part of the purpose of this work to consider the social organization of the Welsh nation but a digression is necessary here to enable us to understand the reason for the presence throughout the countryside of a large number of small houses (many of them now abandoned) of the cottage type which were occupied by small farmers completely dependent upon the land or by labourers or craftsmen who supplemented their earnings by farming on a small scale. These small steadings have long been known in Wales by the term *tyddyn* (plural *tyddynnod*) and the *tyddynwyr*—crofters as they may be called—formed in a very real sense the essential nucleus of the Welsh nation. Several of the long-houses referred to in the previous chapter belonged to this class but owing to their individual type they have been considered separately.

The term *tyddyn* in the sense of 'homestead' appears in the old Welsh Laws. There it is stated in the Venedotian Code that four *erwau* constitute each *tyddyn*. In the Demetian *Code*, the youngest son is to have the principal *tyddyn* and eight *erwau* of land, while a similar rule is laid down in the 'Gwentian' Code.[1] We are not here concerned with the legal or even the social significance of the term. It need only be remarked that the holding was small: Ellis explains that an *erw* was theoretically 4,320 square yards in area. In brief, the small steading was a basic principle of ancient land holding in Wales. The union of Wales with England resulted in what Thomas E. Ellis has described[2] as 'the grafting of the manorial system upon the old Celtic tenures' and as far as any generalization is possible, this statement holds good, though it has been pointed out[3] that certain legislation (e.g. 31 Eliz. cap. 7 [1589]) encouraged the development of cottages with four acres of land. The practice of consolidation however, once the Keltic system had been officially over-thrown, proceeded to reach its culmination with the enclosure movement of the 19th century and the social organization and farming practice of the present century. We have already referred to this in general terms (p. 2).

The Royal Commission on Land was given a large number of instances of this consolidation of which a few examples may be quoted. In fifty years of the 19th century about 120 houses fell into ruins in the parish

---

[1] Ellis, T. P. : *Welsh Tribal Law and Custom in the Middle Ages* (1926), I, pp. 229-30.

[2] *Royal Commission on Land in Wales : Minutes*, I, p. 785.

[3] *Ibid.*, p. 822.

of Llanycil, Merionethshire, only fifteen houses being built in that period. In
the neighbouring parish of Llandrillo, forty-two farms were reduced to half
that number in a generation. At Trawsfynydd in the same county fifty-one
cottages, occupied by agricultural workers, fell into ruins and twenty-six
farms were consolidated to form only thirteen holdings ;[1] it was not that 'the
croft system has broken down', as Sir Cyril Fox has suggested: a large part
of the social system traditional to the Welsh countryside was deliberately
destroyed. The results were calamitous. They have been ably described by
Hugh Evans in a notable Welsh work.[2]

A partial desertion of the countryside followed. Hundreds of the
small steadings were eliminated: the houses fell into ruin and only isolated
clumps of trees around stone heaps now mark the position of many of them
(plate 35). The 'croft system' did not break down of itself—it was broken by
a system superior in strength but which was alien to the whole Welsh
tradition. Remnants of the old system have remained into the 20th century
but, as Sir Cyril Fox's paper[3] has shown, the *tyddynnwr* today is fighting a
losing battle. 'The life is too hard, the rewards too slight, the inconveniences
of isolation too manifest' in a machine age which caters principally for
industrial and urban organization only, the Welsh rural community being
left mainly to fend for itself. As a result, agriculture and the country life
have suffered : there has been a steady trek to the towns and the *tyddyn* is in
danger of complete extinction.

This brief statement is necessary to understand the nature and distribution of many of the cottages of Wales. The statement of Giraldus
Cambrensis that the Welsh 'live not in towns or villages or forts but as
hermits they frequent the woods' is well known. Except in certain low-land
areas such as the Vale of Glamorgan and eastern Montgomeryshire which
have long been under English influence, the neat nucleated village with its
aggregation of old cottages is completely unknown. A characteris-tic Welsh
community may be studied on the accompanying map (fig. 22) of a small
area of north Pembrokeshire, where the local church is not (as is generally
to be found in south Pembrokeshire or the Vale of Glamorgan) the centre of
a nucleated village.

The simplest type of rectangular cottage found in Wales is the
single-roomed gable-chimneyed structure, where the occupants live and
sleep in the same room. A 17th - century observer speaks of a Welsh cottage

---

[1] *Ibid., Report,* pp. 348-9.
[2] Evans, Hugh : *Cwm Eithin* (1931).
[3] Fox, Sir Cyril: *op. cit.,* p. 439.

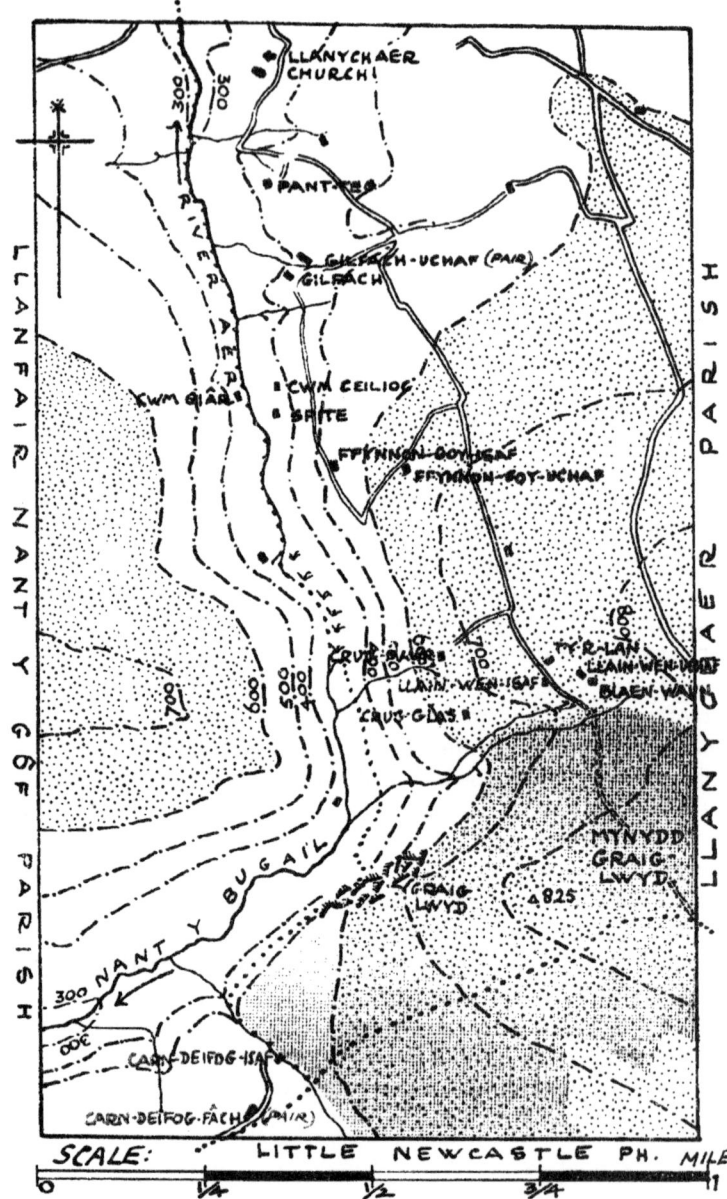

Fig. 22. A north-Pembrokeshire moorland area. The open moorland is stippled dark in the Graig Lwyd and Mynydd Graig-lwd area; other place-names, exept rivers and Llanychaer church refer to *tyddynnod*

as 'a Dunghill modell'd into the shape of a cottage, whose outward surface was so all to be negro'd with such swarthy plaister that it appear'd not unlike a great blot of Cow-turd. This Structure stradled over about eight Ells of ground, above the surface whereof the Eves were advanc'd about two Yards, and the Chimney peep'd about a Foot above the Eves : the light flow'd in through the *old circumference* of a bottomless *Peck*; which being stuck in the Thatch, supply'd the place of an Orbicular Casement. The Door-way was a breach in the wall toward one end, which being of a dwarfish size, i.e. two Foot lower in stature than an ordinary Man, we were forc'd to abridge our Dimensions and to creep in. The Parlour, Hall, Kitchin, i.e. one Room.'[1] In 1800, at Ponterwyd, Cardiganshire, 'one' apartment served for the inhabitants of every description, with one small hole to admit the light: the entrance unprotected by a door, but with a blanket as a substitute'.[2] Hutton, in 1803, describes a cottage at Mallwyd, Merionethshire, as 'a miserable hut, consisting of one small and black room, the floor native earth and the sole light admitted by the door',[3] and at Dinas Mawddwy in the same county, he remarks that 'the inhabitants could not injure themselves by falling downstairs'.[4]

Describing Caernarvonshire cottages at the end of the 18th century, John Evans writes : 'The dark mud wall, rocky floor, and a few brown rushes, the family bed, suggested the idea of a den : the parents and their numerous progeny were assembled round a small fire of peat'.[5] At Llanberis, Caernarvonshire, in 1806, the same type was evident: 'Dol-tŷ-du, tŷ lled fychan un corn wedi ei doi â llechi: gwellt-glas ar y grib a rhanau o'r to. Yr oedd yn rhy isel i gynwys llofft.'[6] [A somewhat small one-chimneyed house, slated; grass on the ridge and parts of the roof. It was too low to contain a loft],

The Commissioners on Education (1847) give several descriptions of the one-roomed cottage. At Strata Florida, Cardiganshire, 'the hut where the schoolmaster lived . . consisted of a single room 12 feet square, without any other chimney than a hole in the roof'.[7] At Tal-y-llyn, Merionethshire, 'the house accommodation is wretched. The cottages are formed of a few loose fragments of rock and shale, piled together without mortar or whitewash.

---

[1] R[ichards], W. : *Wallography or The Britton Describ'd*, pp. 17-18.

[2] *The Cambrian Directory* (1800), p. 78.

[3] *The Cambrian Directory* (1800), p. 78.

[4] Hutton, W. : *Remarks upon North Wales* (1803), pp. 12.. 18-19.

[5] Evans, John : *Letters written during a Tour through North Wales in the year 1798* (1804), p.162.

[6] Williams, W. : *Hynafiaethau . . . Plwyf Llanberis* (1892), p. 70.

[7] *Report*, p. 147.

The floors are of earth : the roofs are wattled and many of these houses have no window. They comprise one room in which all the family sleep'.[1] At Rhos-llannerch-rugog in Denbighshire, there were 'cottages of one room only, built by the poor people themselves, -an acknowledgement of from 7/- to 15/- per annum to the landlord as ground rent'.[2] The clod houses of Rhayader, Radnorshire, 'without a window or aperture but the doorway and chimney' comprised 'only one room'.[3] At Cynwyl Gaeo, Carmarthenshire, they write of 'a wretched hovel containing only a single room ... and a floor of bare earth'.[4] Of the cottages of Brecknockshire, Radnorshire and Cardiganshire generally, they pronounce 'the cottages to be very little, if at all superior to the Irish huts in the country districts. . . In very few cottages is there more than one room, which serves the purpose of living and sleeping'.[5] At Raglan, in Monmouthshire, in 1893, a cottage is described 'on the road to Llanishen . . . consisting of one room only. This room is 10 feet x 9 feet and the roof (thatched) rises at six feet from the ground. When the occupier came, the floor was simply a mud one'.[6]

Hugh Evans in his reminiscences of his early life in the Cerrig-y-drudion (Denbighshire) district shows how the one-roomed cottage persisted to within living memory : 'Un ystafell oedd y rhan fwyaf o dai y gweithwyr. . . Byddai'r simnai yn agored, y tân o fawn, carreg ar yr aelwyd, a'r llawr yn llawr pridd'.[7] [Most of the workers' houses were one-roomed. . . The chimney would be open, the fire of peat, a stone on the hearth, and the floor of earth], I have myself seen such a cottage (now demolished) in south Cardiganshire. They were to be seen too at the end of the last century in Flintshire: in the Mostyn district, 'some [cottages] contain only one room'.[8] Plate 36 shows such a cottage at Pont-rhyd-fendigaid,., north Cardiganshire, in 1910. It will be noticed that there is no window in the hearth-end.

But many of these single-roomed cottages were divided into two by the inhabitants themselves. This represents the next stage in their typology. Probably the Pont-rhyd-fendigaid example illustrated was so divided since there is a window in its further end, probably to light the bed place, the door lighting the living-end. The most usual method of such a division was by

---

[1] *Ibid.* p. 63.

[2] *Ibid.* p. 66.

[3] *Ibid.* p. 265.

[4] *Ibid.* p. 228.

[5] *Ibid.* p. 56.

[6] *Royal Commission on Labour : The Agricultural Labourer : England: Monmouthshire* (1893), p. 70.

[7] Evans, H. : *Cwm Eirhin* (1931),, p. 63.

[8] *Royal Commission on Land in Wales : Minutes of Evidence, IV*, p. 52.

arranging the furniture—the dresser in particular— to serve as a partition between the living and sleeping ends. In the Strata Florida example, cited above, 'a hurdle and an old chest of drawers' served as a partition 'between this and the adjoining cottage' but this was probably exceptional.

The Commissioners for Education (1847) in their general survey of Brecknockshire, Radnorshire and Cardiganshire state that 'a large dresser and shelves usually form the partition between the two [ends]: and where there are separate beds for the family a curtain or low board is (if it exist) the only division, with no regular partition'.[1] Hugh Evans states : 'rhoddid dreser a chwpwrdd *press* ar draws yn aml i wneud siamber'[2] [a dresser and a 'press' cupboard were often placed across to form a chamber]. Culley in 1867 had referred to a similar arrangement in south-west Wales : ' . . . partitions often formed by the back of a box bed or chest of drawers'.[3] F. H. Norman described (1867) cottages in Caernarvon and Anglesey 'of one room about 18 or 20 feet long by 14 or 15 broad. This room is unceiled and paved with stones and is used as a living and sleeping room. It is generally partially divided by two box beds (i.e. four-post beds boarded on three sides) which are placed nearly across the centre of the room, leaving only a narrow passage to connect the portions of the room which are used by day and by night respectively. Although only one room, the cottages, with the furniture thus disposed, have the appearance of having two rooms, the backs of the beds being fitted with shelves, on which the household crockery etc. is placed'.[4] A similar arrangement of box beds and furniture to form 'two rooms' in some Caernarvonshire cottages was noticed during the course of the present survey. 'In Tŷ Isa [Rhiw, Llŷn, Caernarvonshire] there was no *palis* [partition], but the backs or sides of the four-posters acted as such' writes Mr. Ll. 'Wyn Griffith.[5]

The next development from this stage was the cottage partitioned into two 'rooms'. In a mud cottage at Llithfaen, Pwllheli, Caernarvonshire, at the end of the 19th century, the partition was 'made of cloth'.[6] The Commissioners on Education (1847) in describing a cottage at Tal-y-llyn, Merionethshire, refer to the sleeping end as 'separated from the rest of the hut by wisps of Straw forming an imperfect screen'.[7] John Evans (1798)

---

[1] *Report*, p. 56.

[2] *Op. cit.*, p. 63.

[3] *Report of the Commission on the Employment of Children, Young Persons, and Women in Agriculture, 1867 : Pembroke and Carmarthen, p. 48.*

[4] *Ibid., Part III, North Wales*, p. 34

[5] In a letter to the author, 10th October, 1937.

[6] *Royal Commission on Land in Wales, Minutes of Evidence*, I, p. 528.

[7] *Report*, p 63.

describes a cottage near Barmouth, Merionethshire as a one-roomed hut 'divided by a partition of lath and reeds'.[1] I have myself examined similar partitions *between cottages* at Rumney, Monmouthshire, recently abandoned. Evans's further description is of value : 'The floor was the native soil rendered very hard and uneven from long and unequal pressure. At the farther end was a fire of turf, laid upon a few stones, near which stood a three-legged stool, a small cast-iron pot, some branches of broom tied up for a besom and a few bundles of rushes thrown down for a bed. These constitute the principal furniture'. In a cottage at Pendine, Carmarthenshire in 1847, the Commissioners for Education remark that the single room is divided by a 'partition of wattle covered with plaster'.[2] A partition 'about five feet high' is noted in 1893 in the Haverfordwest (Pembrokeshire) district.[3]

The single-roomed cottage divided into two 'rooms' by means of a partition became widespread throughout Wales and there are constant references to it. 'One smoky hearth', writes Gwallter Mechain[4] 'for it should not be styled a kitchen; and one damp litter-cell, for it cannot be called a bed-room' was the ordinary type of cottage in Anglesey, Caernarvonshire, Merionethshire and Montgomeryshire in the 18th century. Warner[5] describes a 'tenement. . . divided into two apartments' in Brecknockshire. Writing of Carmarthenshire cottages, the Commissioners for Education (1847) state : 'There are not usually more than two rooms. Cupboard beds are those most commonly used'.[6] Mr. John Davies,, County Surveyor's Office, Horeb, south Cardiganshire, tells me that such two-roomed cottages were numerous in his county: 'most of the two-roomed cottages that I knew

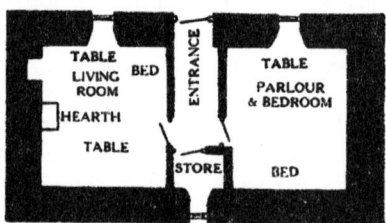

Fig. 23. Pensarn-mynach, Cribyn, Cardiganshire : ground plan (length 33 ft.).

[1] Op. cit., p. 115.

[2] *Report,* p. 229.

[3] Thomas, [Sir] D. Lleufer ; *The Agricultural Labourer in Wales,* p. 71.

[4] *Op. cit.* (North Wales), p. 82.

[5] Warner, R.; *A Walk through Wales in 1797,* p. 46.

[6] *Report,* p. 229.

had a bed in the kitchen and in the "parlour" (or *pen-isaf* as it was called)'.[1]

This reference to a *pen isaf* in cottage as in farmhouse should be noted, the *lower* end being the end not occupied for living purposes—the end furthest from the hearth. Plate 37 illustrates a surviving Cardiganshire two-roomed cottage : its plan is shown in fig. 23.

A further development in this type of cottage may be compared with the development of the lay-out of the long-house. A part of the sleeping-end was set aside for use as a dairy (in the *tyddyn* especially) or a pantry. Such an arrangement was found at Great Mains, a small *tyddyn* at Llaeth-dy, Radnorshire (fig. 24 and plate 38). This house, occupied within living memory, was visited in 1936. It is of dry walling, roughly pointed in places,

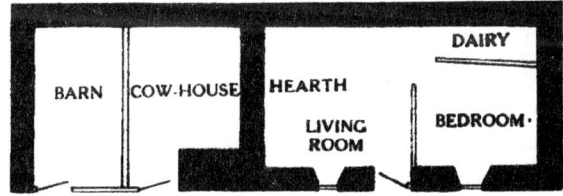

Fig. 24. Great Mains, Llaethdy, Radnorshire : ground plan (length 36 ft.).

with a rush thatch and a ridge of grass-grown clods. The purlins of the roof are of rough unhewn branches. The one room of the cottage is divided by low boards into three—living room, bedroom and 'dairy'. The fireplace is of open-hearth type with a wattle-and-daub canopied louvre above. Well-built cottages with a similar lay-out were examined at Glan-paith, near Aberystwyth, Cardiganshire, in 1939.

The two-roomed cottage, whether the rooms are formed by the arrangement of the furniture or by partitioning, and often with an extra dairy or pantry, was common to most parts of Wales at one period and has remained to the present day in several districts. In addition to the references already discussed, the type has been noted by Lleufer Thomas[2] in the English-speaking part of the Narberth Union, Pembrokeshire ('they consist, of two rooms only, each being from 10 to 12 feet square : there is generally no loft, the roof being open to sight, but there is a partition about 5 feet high to divide the rooms'), the Llanfyllin district of Montgomeryshire ('many consist of two rooms only, a kitchen and a bedroom — chamber, in colloq-

---

[1] Letter dated 1st November; 1937.

[2] *The Agricultural Labourer in Wales* (1893), pp. 85, 116.

uial Welsh *siamber* - both being on the ground floor'); and in the Ruthin
district of Denbighshire ('by far the greater majority of cottages in the dist-

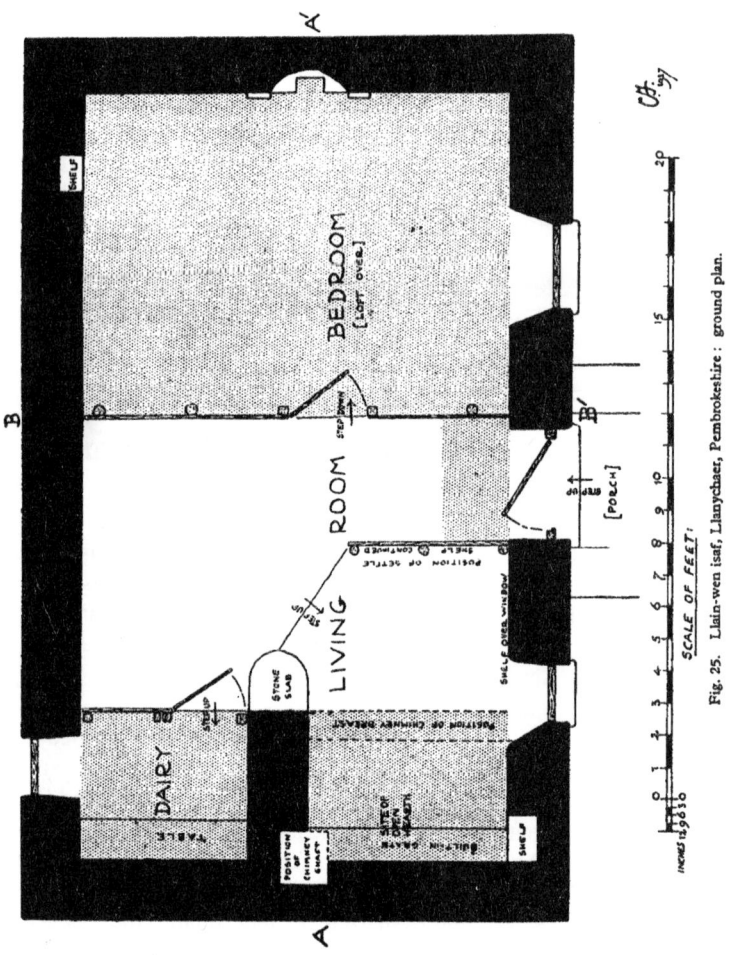

Fig. 25. Llain-wen isaf, Llanychaer, Pembrokeshire: ground plan.

rict have only two rooms'). *The Report of the Commissioners on the
Employment of Children, Young Persons, and Women in Agriculture* gives
many descriptions of these houses throughout Wales, e.g. at St. Issells,

Pembrokeshire (p. 111): 'built of mud and roofed with thatch . . . two rooms on the ground floor from 8 to 12 feet square'; Cellan, Cardiganshire (p.130): 'two rooms, many with only one'; Machynlleth, Montgomeryshire (p.133): 'most having only two rooms'.

Such two-roomed cottages inevitably created problems in accommodation. Rural families have always been large and in consequence, there were throughout Wales bad instances of over-crowding. The various Government reports of the 19th and 20th centuries all bear witness to this fact. 'Sleeping accommodation unsatisfactory', 'lamentable deficiency of bedroom accommodation', 'the gravest evil is the want of bedroom accommodation'—such strictures on the Welsh cottage appear throughout the many Blue Books. If these deficiencies were apparent to the outside observer, it is certain that they caused much concern too to the inhabitants themselves and the provision of extra sleeping accommodation gave rise to another development of the cottage-type which we have been discussing. This resulted in the *bwthyn croglofft* or cockloft cottage.

This cottage-type in its Pembrokeshire variation has been described fully by Sir Cyril Fox :[1] 'the living-room [see fig. 25] which is entered from the central doorway, through a short passage ceiled with boards, is open to the roof, the passage is formed by the bedroom partition on one side, and on the other by a fixed screen some 7 feet high which keeps the draught away from the house-place in front of the hearth. The fire of culm, a mixture of clay and coal-dust, formerly burned on the floor, but a small grate has as usual been built in at a later date. The chimney being central to the gable, the smoke is directed inwards diagonally up the back of the hearth, this renders the "chimney corner" on the further side in every respect a comfortable sitting-place. . . The recess at the other end of the gable is shut off from the kitchen by a wooden partition and ceiled "to keep away the dust". It is the dairy . . .In front of the dividing wall between dairy and hearth—indeed a projection from it—is a small semi-circular stone bench (*y fainc*) used as a stand for the washing bowl and for culinary purposes generally'.

The bedroom, as in all such two-roomed houses, occupies the other end. But here it is ceiled at a height of seven feet. Above it is a loft, a 'dark and airless triangular space' the floor of which is the ceiling of the bedroom. This constitutes the additional sleeping accommodation, which, by this simple expedient, is doubled without any actual addition to the house itself. The loft is reached by means of a movable ladder (figs. 26 and 27). Fox

---

[1] *Op. cit.,* p. 430.

points out that in some of the north-Pembrokeshire cottages which he
examined the loft is boarded up so partitioning its interior from a view of the

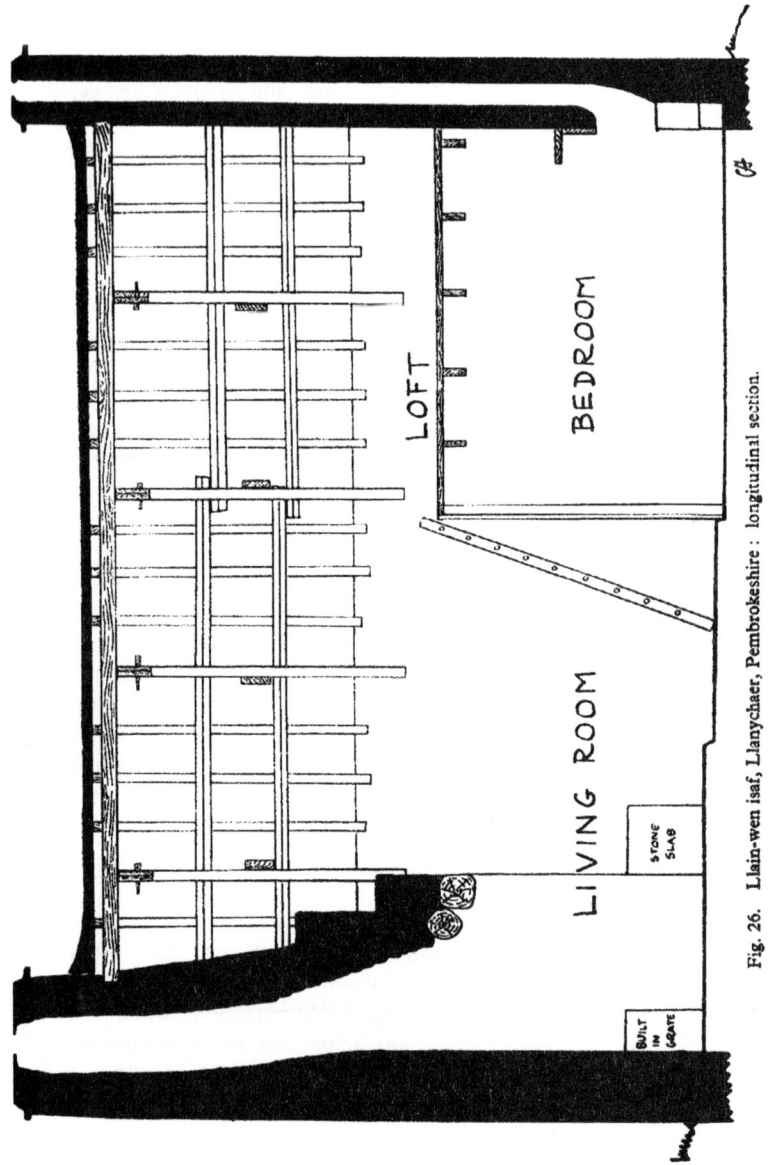

Fig. 26. Llain-wen isaf, Llanychaer, Pembrokeshire : longitudinal section.

kitchen (plate 39). The north-Pembrokeshire *croglofft* cottage is illustrated in plates 41-4. Fig. 28 is a plan of a typical *tyddyn.*[1]

I have indicated in this volume as elsewhere[2] that 'constructional technique is largely conditioned by environment' but Fox has maintained[3] that 'this is not the case with lay-out; such spatial relationships as that of dairy to hearth, so constant in our [Pembrokeshire] house series are, I suggest, not superficial or recent but ancient and fundamental, linked to customary procedure in the basic activities of human life. Differences in these relationships represent, on this view, very early cultural divergence. If this be true the Pembrokeshire cottages represent one of the many strands of culture which in the Dark Ages or earlier went to the making of the social and economic pattern of rural Wales'.

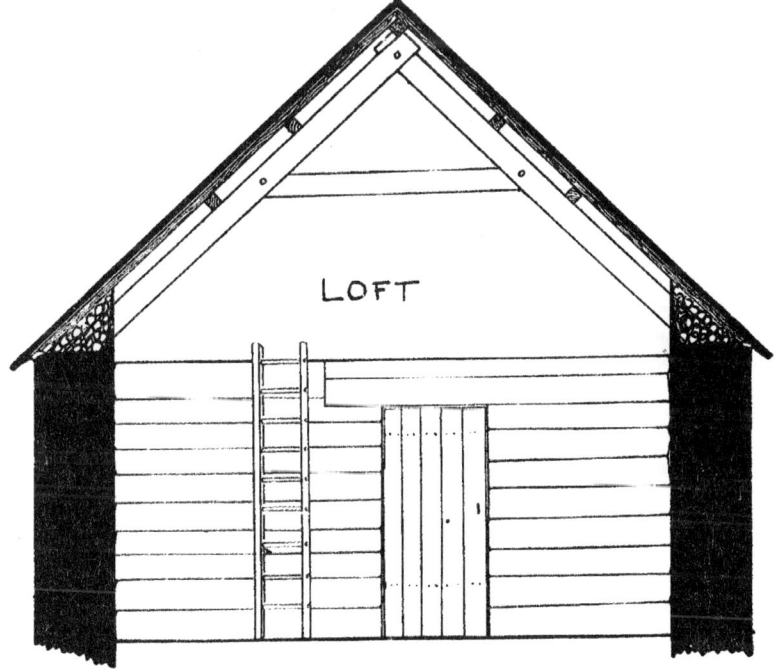

Fig. 27. Llain-wen isaf, Llanychaer, Pembrokeshire : cross-section.

---

[1] I acknowledge with gratitude the permission given by my Director, Sir Cyril Fox, to reproduce here his excellent drawings and photographs of the group of *croglofft* cottages examined by him.

[2] See Fox's paper, p. 438.

[3] *Ibid.*, pp. 438-9.

I am inclined to doubt one detail of this view—that of 'the spatial relationship' of dairy to hearth. It has already been shown above that in the simple two-roomed cottage (without loft), the dairy often occupied a small part of the sleeping end and was in no way related to the hearth. An important desideratum of the dairy has always been a position which would give it the maximum degree of coolness. This is probably why in so many farmhouses it occupies the far gable-end, facing north, north-east or east. But it is also true that when the living and sleeping accommodation is limited, it is the dairy's position which usually suffers. For example, in some of the long-houses illustrated, the dairy has even been relegated to a part of the feeding-walk, so as to free all possible living and sleeping space for man and animal.

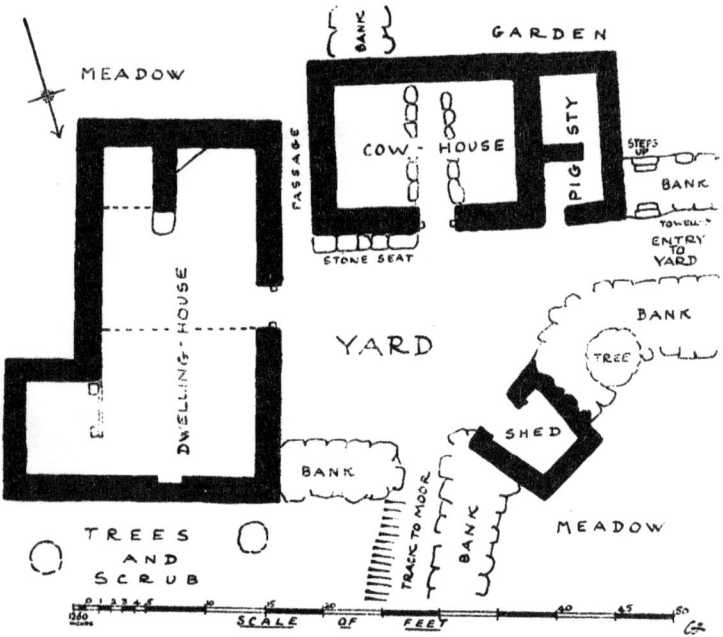

Fig. 28. Carn-deifog isaf, Llanychaer, Pembrokeshire : sketch plan of tyddyn.

The same feature is seen in the *croglofft* house. Here we have the problem of sleeping accommodation solved by doubling it through the introduction of a ceiling for the 'chamber'. Consequently the dairy's position in that end had to be sacrificed. It went into the one recess in the living-end which it could occupy without the serious disorganization of the household— that near the hearth. That this was not altogether a satisfactory solution is shown by the fact that in the Pembrokeshire examples it had to be ceiled 'to keep away the dust' which would naturally be a problem near the hearth. And to free the sleeping-end for its maximum use for that purpose, the dairy may be seen in fig. 28 not only near the hearth (the warmest part of the house) but also facing south !

It seems probable too that the *croglofft* development, with its ceiling and ladder 'stair', does not represent a 'strand of culture' from the 'Dark Ages or earlier' but a post-medieval development influenced (possibly though not necessarily) by the introduction into the normal Welsh rural economy of houses of more than one storey. In type and date, I believe the *croglofft* development to be comparatively recent. We shall see later one method by which it has evolved.

Fox suggests[1] that this type of two-roomed cottage 'has a much more limited spread' than has the simple form and adds that 'as far as my knowledge goes it is coastal, and west coastal at that'. He states however that on such a point further information is necessary.

The distribution of the *croglofft* cottage-form is not coastal or west coastal, although it so happens that it has survived in greater numbers in some coastal counties than in inland areas of Wales. No distributional significance should however be attached to this fact since it happens that those areas in which it has so survived have been less affected by rural rebuilding than most other parts of the country.

Anglesey used to have a large number of *croglofft* cottages, several of which have survived : some were visited during the course of this survey. They are referred to in 1867 by F. H. Norman[2] as one of the three normal types in the island (the others—already referred to—being (a) a single-roomed cottage divided by means of furniture into two, and (b) a single-roomed cottage divided into two by a thin partition): 'in a third class, this [sleeping] portion is divided into an upper and lower floor, access being obtained to the upper floor from that portion of the cottage which is used as a living room by means of a removable ladder. Although greater decency is thus obtained, the ventilation is probably worse in the cottages last described than in those in which there is no partition". Lleufer Thomas[3] adds to this description : 'There is a "cock-loft" over one-half of the house, and this is approached by a movable, or if fixed, very rickety ladder. Hardly ever is there any ceiling to be seen, a calico screen nailed to the rafters being found instead. . . According to a practical mason of much experience,

---

[1] *Ibid.*, p. 438.

[2] *Op. cit.*, p. 34.

[3] *Op. cit.*, p. 132.

the expense of building a cottage of the ordinary type with a half-loft and earthen floor would be about 50*l.*, and a rent of from 2*l.* to 2*l.* 12*s.* would be usually paid for it'. The cottages visited were not *tyddynnod* and the dairy (being therefore unnecessary) was not found. A Llanddaniel example visited (its exterior pebble-dashed) housed a family of nine !

A recent (1939) Government Report states : '[In Anglesey] many of the houses in the rural districts are in reality one-roomed cottages of the old-fashioned "Celtic" type. These are divided by light partitions into two—the kitchen and the "siamber" (chamber), and in some of these a so-called "grogloft" (*sic*) (from the Welsh "crogi"—to hang) reached by a ladder, is provided by means of boarding stretched across at about the level of the eaves. These lofts are generally over the "siamber" but are sometimes over the kitchen as well. Some . . . measure about six feet at the apex of the roof to the floor, while the roof slopes down on each side to meet the flooring. The only source of ventilation and of light to the "grog-loft" apart from the door is by means of a small skylight which seldom measures more than 18 ins. by 15 ins. and which does not always open. . . In one of these cottages . . . the "grog-loft" was over part of the "siamber" only'.[1]

Caernarvonshire has several examples. The *croglofft* cottage is well-known in the Llŷn peninsula and has been well-described in a recent novel by Llewelyn Wyn Griffith[2] which should be read for a faithful description of life in such a house. 'As you enter through the door, the kitchen is on your right: a small room with no ceiling between the floor and the roof. On the right of the door as you enter is a wooden partition, three feet wide and six feet high, to keep out the cold. On the left as you go in there is a wooden partition running up to the roof with two doors in it, one vertically above the other. Through the lower door you enter the bedroom: this has a wooden ceiling which serves as a floor to the attic above. To get to the attic bedroom you pull down a ladder which normally lies on the attic floor. These are the three rooms of the cottage'. Mr. Griffith informs me[3] that the cottage described is Tŷ Uchaf, Rhiw, Llŷn. He states that there was a 'buttery' in the recess near the hearth (cf. the Pembrokeshire examples), 'its floor raised about six inches above the floor' of the kitchen. He adds also: 'I presume that the *palis* [partition] is (comparatively) recent so as to give a *taflod* [loft] : in Ty Isa there was no *palis* but the backs or sides of the fourposters acted as such'. In Llŷn—and indeed in other parts of north Wales—the living room is known as *y llawr* (the floor), the bedroom as *y siambar* (the

[1] See the *Report of the Committee of Inquiry into the Anti-Tuberculosis Service* (1939), pp. 145-6.
[2] *The Wooden Spoon* (1937).
[3] Letter dated 10th October, 1937.

chamber), the loft as *y daflod* or *y groglofft* and the partition as *palis* (cf. French *palisse*).

Ty'n-rhosgadfa (fig. 29 and plate 45) in the Rhosgadfan district of Caernarvonshire shows one way in which the *croglofft* has developed. Here there are two cupboard beds placed in such a way in the sleeping-end that it is impossible to have a dairy in that end. The dairy is, therefore, as in the Pembrokeshire examples, in the recess near the hearth but here by forming a small outshut the dairy has been enlarged. Another hearth feature in all the Arfon examples is a cupboard set in the gable-wall near the fire itself. Above the two cupboard beds a *croglofft* has been formed by placing boards across : it is entered by means of the usual removable ladder. Two cupboard beds placed in this position seem to be a characteristic arrangement in this district. Several houses so arranged were examined and it is tempting to suggest that one method by which the *croglofft* evolved was by placing boards across the tops of two cupboard beds in such a position.

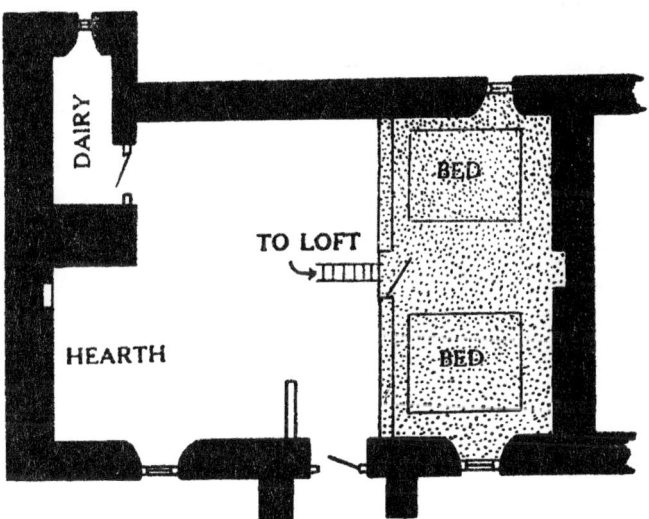

Fig. 29. Ty'n-rhosgadfa, Rhosgadfan, Caernarvonshire : ground plan (length 31 ft.).
The stippled portion indicates the extent of the *croglofft*.

If such be the case, this would help to fix the earliest date for the *croglofft* development in north Wales: the cupboard bed in Wales is not earlier than the 15th-16th centuries, a fact that corroborates the suggested dating of the *croglofft* in Wales to post-medieval times. This placing of two cupboard beds in the sleeping-end in the position shown in fig. 29 precludes also a dairy in the sleeping-end, so that such houses—even without the *croglofft* development—may have dairies in other positions. At Llainfadyn, Rhos-isaf (plate 46), the partition between the two ends is formed of furniture, but here too there is a loft above, boarded, with a door. This house is of 18th-century date. An interesting feature here is that the screen 'to keep out the cold' is formed of a slate slab, eight feet high by four feet wide, and one inch in thickness. This type of screen, in wood or stone was a normal feature of all the two-roomed houses examined in north Wales.

Hughes and North[1] describe a two-roomed house, Cymryd near Aberconwy, the earliest part of which, they state, dates 'from the late fifteenth or early sixteenth century'. This consists of a 'hall' about 18 ft. by 12½ ft. and a chamber about 7 ft. by 12½ ft. They think that the 'very small size of the latter seems to point to the fact of the comparatively recent intro-duction of a second room at that date'. Both rooms were originally open to the roof, 'but very soon after the house was built a loft was added above the chamber only, approached from the latter by a ladder and trap-door in the floor, the hall remaining open to the roof. At a later period the hall was half-covered by a loft and [later] was taken completely across'. Here therefore is an early example of a *croglofft* (approached this time from the bedroom). Hughes and North refer also to some other examples.

Miss S. M. Griffith, of Tregarth, Bangor, informs me that the *croglofft* type ('tŷ llawr a siambar') was a normal feature in the parish of Llandegai. Here too a cupboard in the gable-hearth wall was usual and the 'loft was entered by means of a ladder which could be drawn up'.[2] In the Pwllheli district, 'the majority of the cottages have two rooms downstairs, a kitchen and a "chamber" and a half-loft over the chamber. The newer cottages ... .have a complete loft over the whole house'.[3]

The *croglofft* development occurs also in Denbighshire, but at Foel Eryr, Bylchau, the half-loft is over the living-room and is approached by a ladder .from the bedroom-end. In the Cerrig-y-drudion district (Denbighshire - Merionethshire border) Hugh Evans describes a clod house (*'tŷ tywyrch'*): 'Yr oedd yno ryw fath o derfyn ar ei ganol i wneud dwy ystafell, ac yr oedd y tad wedi rhoi croglofft isel wrth ben y siamber i rai o'r plant gysgu ynddi'.[4] [There was some kind of a partition across its centre to make two rooms, and the father had made a low *croglofft* above the chamber for some of the children to sleep in], I have no evidence of it from Flintshire. The type is well-known also in Merionethshire. A number in

[1] *Op. cit.,* pp. 16-17.

[2] Letter dated 1st September, 1938.

[3] Thomas, [Sir] D. Lleufer : *The Agricultural Labourer in Wales,* p. 149.

[4] Evans, Hugh : *op. cit.,.*p. 68.

ruins was examined at Rhos-y-gwalia, east of Bala ; another example (not examined) was reported from Cefn-ddwysarn. A description[1] of Dolgelley houses in 1888 reads : 'Of many of the cottages the accommodation consists of a downstairs room, a bedroom, and a "half-loft" in the higher part of a sloping roof; the garret being often unventilated, and lighted only by a glass tile.' Lleufer Thomas states[2] that 'in the parish of Llangelynin (1893) there is a row of cottages at Y Friog [now better known as Fair-bourne] ... [with] a "half-loft" with sloping roof for a bedroom. "Wains-cot" [i.e. cupboard] beds are used so as to act as partitions'. There were similar houses at Llwyngwril.

An example of the *croglofft* development in the heart of the central-Wales moorland has fortunately been well-described.[3] This house was for some time the boyhood home of Sir Owen Morgan Edwards : 'Tŷ isel hen ffasiwn oedd Cae Rhys lle y trigent pan ddeuais i adnabod y mab a hwythau gyntaf. Y gegin fel ceginau hen dai Cymru a'r rhai a welid hyd yn ddiweddar yng Ngorllewin yr Iwerddon, a gwaith y lle yn olchi a chorddi (gyda buddai gnoc) yn cael ei gyflawni ynddi neu ynte ger y drws pan y byddai'n adeg i hynny. Yr enllyn a'r bara yn agos i law. Llofft uwchben y siambar dros un hanner i'r tŷ ac ysgol i'w symud a'i rhoi i ddringo iddi. Yr oedd y math yma ar dai i'w gweled yn fynych hyd yn lled ddiweddar mewn rhannau o Arfon'. [Cae Rhys where they lived when I came first to know their son and them was a low old-fashioned house. The kitchen like the kitchens of the old Welsh houses and those to be seen until lately in western Ireland, all the work, washing and churning (with a knocker churn) being performed in it or at the doorway when the time was favourable. The 'relish' and bread near at hand. A loft over the chamber, over one half of the house and a movable ladder to be placed to climb into it. This kind of house was often to be seen until lately in parts of Arfon]. Cae Rhys is now an outhouse. It is illustrated here (plate 47). The door on the right is a new insertion where a window used to be. The chimney has been removed.

In Montgomeryshire the type was also known. Wigstead, describing a visit to a Llan-y-mynech inn in 1797, writes : 'I was accommodated with the state room which was a cockloft at the very brink of a step-ladder staircase. The tiling of the roof came very near in contact with my head while recumbant'.[4] Llan-y-mynech is in the extreme east of Wales, on the Shropshire border. Bryn-mawr, Llanerfyl, with its sleeping-end now much altered, was also of related type (fig. 30 and plate 48 and frontispiece). This

---

[1] Thomas, [Sir] D. Lleufer : *op. cit.,* p. 101.

[2] Thomas, [Sir] D. Lleufer : *op. cit.,* p. 101.

[3] Gruffydd, W. J.: *Owen Morgan Edwards, Cofiant,* I (1937), p. 26.

[4] Wigstead, H.: *op. cit.,* p. 14.

house however is of central-chimney type. The fireplace is central between bed- and living-rooms. The house is of cruck-construction having one pair of crucks more or less central to the living-end. There is a loft over half the living-end reaching from the crucks to the far gable-wall, the entrance into it being formerly by a ladder from the cruck-end, facing the hearth.

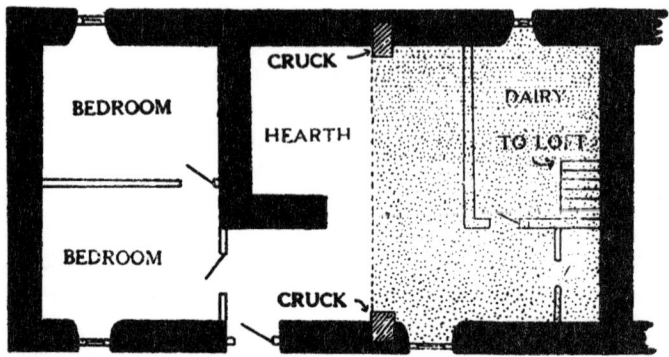

Fig. 30. Bryn-mawr, Llanerfyi, Montgomeryshire: ground plan (length 38 ft) The stippled portion indicates the extent of the *croglofft*. The dairy and stairs are modern

This is the only instance known to me of a central-chimney house with a half-loft. The house itself on the open moorland in one of the most inaccessible situations in the whole of Wales has the outward appearance of a long-house, the dwelling and outhouses being under the same roof. But there is no internal access from the one to the other. The screen of trees planted to shelter the house from the prevailing south-westerly winds should be noted and also the position of the building in relation to the slope of the moorland.

The normal *croglofft* type was known also in this moorland area. Mr. Sam Ellis, Utica, New York, who left the Garthbeibio district many years ago describes Ty'nsietin in that parish as having 'cegin, siambar a bwtri fechan ac un llofft—ysgol ac nid grisiau i ddringo iddi'[1] [kitchen, chamber, a small buttery and one loft—a ladder not a staircase to climb up to it]. Mr. Ellis adds that an opening had been made in the house-wall to gain access to the cow-house so that here as in Anglesey (p. 53) we find a convergence of the *croglofft* and house-byre types. There was also a screen 'to keep out the cold' ['i gadw'r oerni allan']. Mr. Ellis also mentions Bryn Chwilod uchaf,

---

[1] In a letter dated 22nd January, 1939.

Bryn Chwilod isaf and Y Wern-fach in the same district as of a similar lay-out.[1]

A *propos* of these moorland *tyddynnody* Mr. Ellis draws my attention[2] to details of the greatest interest showing the persistence of the open-field system in a part of the Garthbeibio moorland known as Y Waun Oer down to modern times. The Waun [lit. moorland] was divided between a number of farmers, each piece of land being known as a 'parcel' ('parseli'). No term such as acre ['acer neu gyfer'] was used, the land being measured in another way : the term used was 'the work of a scythe-man' ('gwaith gŵr a phladur'). The parcels varied from the 'work of two' to 'the work of ten men with scythes'. One parcel belonged to Rhiwfelen, Cwm Banw, the next to it to Llechog, Cwm Twrch, etc., i.e. the parcels did not belong to neighbouring farms. The 'boundary' between each parcel was formed by a narrow strip of unpared land. Mr. Ellis describes the Waun as 'tir oer mwsoglyd pislyd' [cold, mossy, watery land].

But to return to the *croglofft* houses, my attention was drawn by Dr. R. D. Thomas of Welshpool to Paradise Cottage in the parish of Leighton, on the Shropshire border. This is a half-timbered structure, consisting of two rooms. As in the Denbighshire example referred to, the living-end is ceiled but the bedroom-end is open to the roof. The half-loft is entered by a ladder from the bedroom (plate 40).

Cardiganshire and Carmarthenshire provide many examples of the *croglofft* development. Of the Llandybie district of Carmarthenshire, for instance, the Rev. Gomer M. Roberts writes[3] : 'Yn yr hen fythynnod y cofiaf amdanynt yn Llandybie, dwy ystafell oedd iddynt ar y llawr, a cheid croglofft iddynt yn ddieithriad, ac ysgol bren symudol yn arwain iddi o'r gegin. Nid oedd un drws i'r groglofft namyn y twll yr âi'r ysgol drwyddo'. [In the old cottages which I remember at Llandybïe, there were two rooms on the ground floor, and invariably a cockloft, with a movable wooden ladder leading to it from the kitchen. The loft had no door, only an opening for the ladder]. In Cardiganshire, 'there still exist. . . some small, damp houses ... two rooms on the ground floor . . . a room above . . . approached by a movable ladder'.[4] I know of no instances from Radnorshire although the two-roomed cottage was at one time common in the county, some of

[1] In a letter dated 19th February, 1939.

[2] In a letter dated 10th July, 1939.

[3] Letter dated 27th October, 1939.

[4] *Report . . . Anti-Tuberculosis Service*, p. 158.

them with a central fireplace that 'warms both the kitchen and the chamber'.[1]

A reference is however made in 1867, to cottages in the parish of Cwm-deuddwr, consisting of generally 'two rooms downstairs with a loft over-head to the roof[2] but whether this was a half-loft cannot be ascertained from the description. Evidence is also lacking from Brecknockshire but a reputed *croglofft* cottage is reported from the Talgarth district. In parts of this county much cottage-building was carried out in the 19th century.[3] In Glamorganshire the *croglofft* does not seem to have been a normal development. The type occurred however in Monmouthshire. 'At Raglan, one [cottage] had a very good living room 12 ft. x 10 ft. with a small back scullery. The bedroom was about 2 ft. lower than the living room [cf. *pen-isaf*] and 4 ft. x 10 ft. Over this was a small compartment in the roof. Here lived a man, his wife and six children ; the husband, wife and three children in the bedroom, the three remaining children in the roof. There were no stairs to the roof apartment, the ascent being made from the living room by chairbacks or a small ladder'.[4]

From this evidence, it will be seen that the one-roomed house, divided into two by means of furniture or permanent partitions and with a half-loft to provide extra sleeping-room, was formerly to be found throughout the greater part of Wales. It will be noticed that the normal position of the loft is over the chamber, but that it has been recorded over part only of the chamber, and in other instances over the kitchen. The tendency was noted in Anglesey to extend the loft over the kitchen as well as the chamber. This would be, of course, the logical development and the long rambling lofts over the long-houses would provide an analogy. The cottage partitioned on the ground floor and with a loft, sometimes divided into two, provided by ceiling both living-room and chamber, represents the final development of the single-roomed type. Once this stage was achieved, its typological successor was the upper-storeyed cottage with windows above and below.

The single-roomed cottage (sometimes partitioned) with a loft over all its area is well exemplified in Glamorganshire, a county which provides no surviving example of the half-loft type. In the mid-19th century, at Peterston-super-Ely, the 'cottage accommodation is deplorable. It consists of

---

[1] *Third Report of the Commissioners on the Employment of Children, Young Persons, and Women in Agriculture* (.1867), p. 164.

[2] *Ibid.*, p. 164.

[3] *Ibid.*, p. 84.

[4] *Royal Commission on Labour : The Agricultural Labourer : England : Monmouthshire* (1893), p. 70.

old thatched buildings, very low, with one living room, a portion of which is generally partitioned off for a pantry, and a general garret or sleeping room for the whole family'.[1] At Llantrithyd, 'most of them have one sitting [i.e. living] room with a pantry or lean-to attached. There is generally a good-sized upper bedroom under the thatched roof ,which is *sometimes divided*. A bed is often placed in the sitting room'.[2] At Penmark 'there is a sitting room from 12 to 16 feet square; in the better sort a small room on the same floor used as a bedroom, overhead is a loft, which is very rarely divided by a partition'.[3] Similar descriptions are given from the St. Athan district, Coychurch, Penrice, Llantwit Major, etc.

In 1893, Sir Lleufer Thomas[4] described the 'more common type of cottage' in the Bridgend-Cowbridge district as 'a low straw-thatched stone building with two rooms downstairs, one being a large, roomy kitchen where all the cooking, eating and washing is done, and where as a rule there is a bed as well. The other room is generally very small and almost always damp. Over these two rooms there is a loft, generally approached by a ladder with the roof coming down to the floor, and a window which cannot be opened let in to the roof. Too often this loft has no partition'. A feature of many of these cottages seems to be that the floors were sunk below the level of the ground surface. The type characteristic of Llantwit Major is described as a single-roomed cottage with a room above, 'approached by means of a wooden ladder'.[5] This type was examined (1939) at Rumney, near Cardiff. Here however the houses had an upper storey with a window. The single room measured 15 ft. by 12 ft. The walls, of mud and stone were 2 ft. thick. A ladder led from the living room to the bedroom above, and the houses which were in a row of three were separated only by lath-and-reed partitions.

This type seems to have been widespread in Monmouthshire in the 19th century: that is, the single-roomed cottage with a loft had developed into a cottage with an upper storey in that county—and in the Vale of Glamorgan—at an earlier date than in the uplands of Wales. This was a natural development since along this tongue of lowland, new ideas and new customs had spread quickly from the English plain from time immemorial. We are told that the colliery population of Blackwood, Monmouthshire, about 1840 retained the 'two rooms on the floor, one of them a bedroom' but

---

[1] *Third Report of the Commissioners on the Employment of Young Children*, etc pp. 71-2.

[2] *Ibid.*, p. 73.

[3] *Ibid.*, p. 74.

[4] *The Agricultural Labourer*, p. 47.

[5] *Ibid.*, p. 51.

there were also 'rooms above used as bedrooms'.[1] At the end of the century while some 'old mud-and-thatch cottages are found here and there' the average cottage in Monmouthshire had a living room and pantry on the ground floor and two bedrooms on the upper floor.[2]

In the same way, the two-roomed cottage with an upper storey had gained a firm hold in the Vale of Glamorgan (plate 49) although in many cases it was scarcely better than its lofted prototype. 'The general type of cottage' wrote the Medical Officer of Health for the Cowbridge (Glamorgan) district in 1893, 'consists of two rooms, a bedroom and living-room. The roof is thatch and very often out of repair. The only means of ventilation to the rooms upstairs is through the opening in the floor by which access is gained to the room, the windows being invariably fixed and not having a sash for opening. Downstairs the floor is generally made of mortar and is most uneven with large holes here and there, besides being very damp, and there being no thorough ventilation for any part of the house'.[3]

To return to the cottage with a loft over its complete floor space, this type was also well-known in Pembrokeshire and west Carmarthenshire. It is described as characteristic of the Poor Law Union of Narberth by Lleufer Thomas.[4] 'In this class of cottages there are generally two rooms downstairs, which provide all the accommodation of the cottage. Upstairs there is generally a long rambling unpartitioned loft, incapable of being utilized for any purpose except that of a lumber room as the roof which is neither ceiled nor rendered reaches to the floor and no light is admitted except occasionally through a window in the gable-end of the house. As there are therefore only two habitable rooms in most of these cottages, the greatest economy has to be exercised as to space and the beds in use are often such as can be converted in the daytime as to have the appearance of a cupboard or chest, with the bed-clothes folded inside.'

In the Vale of Clwyd, Denbighshire, as in Monmouthshire and parts of Glamorganshire, the cottage with bedroom on the upper floor had been introduced in the 19th century. But here again it was little better than the Pembrokeshire loft. The then rector of Llandyrnog, writing in 1893, states : 'Where there is a room upstairs, there are no partitions ; beds cannot be partitioned off so that even grown-up children who have left the district, when they return for a visit, have to sleep in the same common open

---

[1] *Royal Commission on the Employment of Children (1842)*, III, p. 490.

[2] *Royal Commission on Labour : The Agricultural Labourer : Monmouth*, p. 67.

[3] Thomas, [Sir] D. Lleufer : *The Agricultural Labourer*, p. 51.

[4] *Ibid.*, p. 63.

bedroom'.[1] A typical example of this kind in that parish had a bedroom 12 ft. by 13 ft.

An old type of cottage in the Radnorshire-Brecknockshire district was described by the medical officer of the Builth district at the end of the last century. While it had bedrooms upstairs, the upper floor was little more than a loft. At Pentre-llwyn-llwyd a cottage, built of mud and stone and tiled with shingle had a kitchen 12 ft. by 10 ft., height 6¼ ft. It had an earthen floor, an open fireplace and one window 15 in. square. A bedroom on the ground floor, about 7 ft. by 5 ft., had a window about a foot square : like the kitchen it had an earthen floor. Over these rooms were two bedrooms with 15 in. windows on the floor level. The walls were 18 in. high, the roof sloping up to about 9 ft.[2]

In parts of mid Wales, the single-roomed cottage developed horizontally not vertically, *i.e.* the building was lengthened to contain an extra bed-room, but in this development no upper storey was added. Peate[3] writes of the Llanbrynmair moorland : 'Ni byddai ystafelloedd ond ar y llawr, a gelwid yr ystafelloedd cysgu yn siamber, siamber bellaf etc.' [There were no rooms except on the ground floor and the bedrooms were called chamber, furthest chamber etc.]. But in such houses, the calls of the *tyddyn* sometimes necessitated the use of one of the rooms for other purposes. Hutton, describing a house in the Dinas Mawddwy district (1803) 'of three low rooms' accommodating a family of thirteen, states that they were used 'one for the day, one for the night, which held their whole stock of beds and one for lumber chiefly utensils for husbandry'.[4]

In Caernarvonshire we found a three-roomed cottage on a different plan. This was a central-chimney house with a room between the fire-place and the gable-wall (fig. 31). It also contained a *croglofft*, the ladder for reaching it however being within the chamber and not on the living room floor. The walls of this house were extraordinarily thick—three and a half feet. This lay-out should be compared with that of many Irish houses. Kevin Danaher,[5] Sean Mac Giolla Meidhre,[6] Åke Campbell[7] and others have described Irish examples in detail.

---

[1] *Ibid.,* p. 116.

[2] *Ibid.,* p. 170.

[3] *Op. cit.*

[4] Hutton, W. : *op. cit.,* p. 23.

[5] 'Old House Types in Oighreacht Ui Chonchubhair', in *Journal of the Royal Society of Antiquaries of Ireland,* LXVIII (1938), pp. 226-40.

[6] 'Some Notes on Irish Farm-houses', in *Bealoideas,* VIII (1938), pp. 196-200.

[7] (I) 'Irish Fields and Houses', in *Bealoideas,* V (1935), pp. 57-74, and (II) 'Notes on the Irish House', in *Folkliv,* 1937, pp. 207-34.

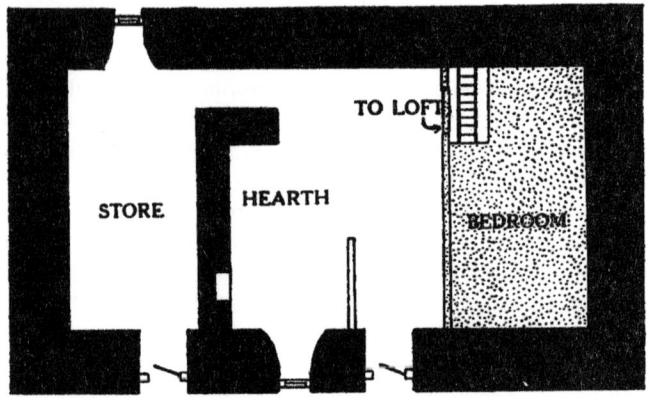

Fig. 31. Cottage, Rhos-isaf, Caernarvonshire : ground plan
(length 39 ft.). The stippled portion indicates the extent of the *croglofft*.

Welsh cottages therefore, throughout the whole country have belonged, until modern building introduced new types, to the single-room tradition. The variations and developments of that type can be traced in all the thirteen counties. Very often the simple form—a single room for living and sleeping—and a more developed variant, e.g. the *croglofft* stage, could be found at the same time in the same district: no chronological development can be traced except that the fully-developed upper-storey bedroom is everywhere a comparatively late feature. The cottages appear scattered throughout the countryside: 'congl rhyw gae, ochr rhyw ffordd, cesail rhyw fynydd, cysgod rhyw hen gelynen'[1] [in the corner of a field, on the side of a road, in the shelter of a hillside, under the shade of an old holly-tree] as one writer puts it. Often a large number would be found dug into a valley-side so that all the gable-wall or the back-wall up to the eaves would be in the earth.[2]

The Welsh cottage as described above in its partitioned form belongs to a well-known class of dwelling. It is the dwelling described in Chaucer's *Nun's Priest's Tale*, 'Ful sooty was hir bour and eek hir halle'. "The simple cottage of which he was writing was the traditional English house, familiar in examples great and small, with its two rooms. The larger room was the hall, the smaller the bower or chamber, the first the main room of the building entered directly from outside, the second an inner and private room

---

[1] Peate, D.: *op. cit.*

[2] See *Cymru*, 1907, I, pp. 141-3.

to which access was obtained from the hall'.[1] In its unpartitioned form the Welsh cottage belongs to a still earlier tradition, to a culture in which the privacy of a bower, well-developed in the English lowlands even in Chaucer's time, was not an essential feature. For parallels within the modern period, the cottages of England in general give us no clue :[2] we are dealing in Wales with a culture which is essentially different from that of (at least) the greater part of England and for close comparisons it is to a neighbouring Keltic land that we have to turn—to Ireland.

To deal first with the type least represented in this survey, the central-chimney house, as described on pages 50 and 100, this three-sectioned lay-out is characteristic both of an Irish and a Scottish type, where a bedroom is regularly found at the upper end of the house behind the fire. Abernodwydd (fig. 6 and plate 9) with its sloping gable belongs with certainty to this type and Bryn-mawr (fig. 30 and frontispiece) too belongs to this tradition, but in the case of the Rhostryfan cottage (fig. 31) it is probable that the room behind the fireplace has originated as a development of the gable-chimney house. Since only these few examples were discovered it is useless to attempt any further speculation.

The cottage in Wales corresponds closely to similar houses in Ireland in several respects. The gable-chimney house consisting of only one room was formerly as common in Ireland as it has been in Wales. 'The division of the room by means of the dresser may have been adopted at an early stage, the dresser being especially suitable as a kind of partition'.[3] We have seen that the dresser, cupboard bed and other furniture were used in the same way in the Welsh cottage. The disposition of the furniture in the Irish examples compares very closely with that found in Wales.[4] When the single-roomed Irish cottage was partitioned, this was done as in Wales by means of 'very thin wooden partitions, *séleâla'*. In Ireland too, additional accommodation was often provided by building lofts. While such half-lofts in Wales were built at one end only of the house, and that generally the sleeping-end, examples are found in Ireland of half-lofts at both ends of the cottage. Campbell compares this Irish feature with a well-known housetype in southern Sweden—Sydgotiska huset—which has the kitchen in the centre of the house without any loft and at both ends additional chambers with lofts. In Wales however such half-lofts are invariably found only at one end.

---

[1] Thompson, A. Hamilton : *The English House* (1936), p. 3.

[2] See for instance Oliver, Basil: *The Cottages of England of the 16th, 17th, and 18th centuries* (1929), Batsford, H. and Fry, C. : *The English Cottage* (1938).

[3] Campbell, A.: *op. cit.* (II), pp. 211-12.

[4] *Ibid.,* see for instance figs. 1 and 4, pp. 214, 225.

In the Irish house as in the Welsh, the loft is normally reached by a ladder from the kitchen.

Finally in Wales as in Ireland, the fireplace is of 'pure hearth' type. In Wales, the built-in oven is universally absent from the types described above as it was from the long-house. 'Owing to the absence of ovens', writes Lleufer Thomas,[1] ' "bake stone" bread is generally used' and he points out that even in modern (1893) cottages, ovens are not provided or suitable fireplaces built for their insertion. Indeed the cooking methods described by Campbell as characteristic of the Irish countryside used to be normal to Welsh rural districts too. When we come to consider the construction of the fireplace, the floor, roof and walls, we shall see how close in all details is the comparison between the cottages of Wales and Ireland. Undoubtedly the Welsh cottage belongs to a culture evident throughout the Keltic zone of the British Isles.

---

[1] *Op. cit.,* **p.** 85. I

CHAPTER VI

The House of the Welsh Laws

NOW that we have considered the early circular structures in Wales and the two most widespread forms of the traditional Welsh house—the long-house and the one-roomed cottage—it is necessary to discuss the house-form described in the Welsh manuscripts as characteristic of Wales during the Age of the Princes, that is, before the annexation of Wales by Edward I in the 13th century.

The principal references to the Welsh tribal house are to be found in the laws of Hywel Dda. Hywel,[1] the grandson of a famous prince, Rhodri Mawr, lived in the 10th century. He died in 950. He is known to have acknowledged Edward, son of Alfred and king of the English as overlord of Wales in 918 : by 942 Hywel had become 'king of all the Welsh'. He now undertook the formidable task of establishing Welsh law and embodying it in writing. These laws 'elucidate the working of the tribal system more completely than any other documents of European history'.[2]

The Welsh manuscripts fall into three distinct groups representing three recensions of the original law of Hywel: they are the Venedotian, the Demetian and the 'Gwentian' codes. 'No MS. in Welsh or Latin preserves for us the original code of Hywel. . . The nearest approach to evidence of what was contained in the first law-book is the consensus of all codes and versions, and there is, in point of fact, so much in common between them as to make this criterion not unserviceable'.[3] The Venedotian Code relates to the north-west province of Gwynedd, the Demetian Code to Dyfed, the south-west province. The 'Gwentian' Code has nothing to connect it with Gwent. Lloyd (p. 355) indicates that its reference to Dinefwr 'points rather to Deheubarth'—south Wales. Wade-Evans[4] however suggests a relationship with Powys, the province of north-east and central Wales, and favours dissociating the terms 'Demetian' and 'Gwentian' from the two codes concerned, substituting for them the names Book of Blegywryd and Book of Cyfnerth.

---

[1] For Hywel Dda see Lloyd, Sir J. E.: *Hywel Dda* (1928) and the same author's *History of Wales to the Edwardian Conquest* (new edition, 1939).

[2] Sir Paul Vinogradoff quoted in Ellis, T. P.: *Welsh Tribal Law and Custom in the Middle Ages* (1926), p. iv.

[3] Lloyd, Sir J. E.: *History of Wales,* p. 356.

[4] Wade-Evans, A. W.: *Welsh Medieval Law* (1909), p. xii.112

The oldest manuscript of the laws (Peniarth 28) is in Latin and is dated about 1180. The laws appear to have been translated into Latin for the benefit of foreign bishops and abbots who came into the country. The oldest Welsh text (Peniarth 29) known as the 'Black Book of Chirk' dates to about 1200. The earliest manuscripts of Hywel's laws extant were therefore written about two hundred and fifty years after his death and probably contain some elements introduced by the recensors. This is indeed likely but it is also certain that the main kernel of the laws has come down from Hywel's time.

The codes deal with the court, the king's position, his rights, officers, court procedure and custom, and the extent of homage due.   Then follow details relating to tribal society in general, e.g. murder, theft, fire, land, animals, buildings, etc. It is with the references to houses that we are concerned here. Unfortunately these are not so comprehensive as to leave— without additional evidence—a clear picture of the tribal houses in the reader's mind.

All three codes stipulate that the villeins have to erect nine buildings for the king : the Demetian and 'Gwentian' versions list a hall, chamber, kitchen, chapel, barn, kiln-house, privy, stable and dog-kennel while the Venedotian has 'dormitory' for chapel! All the evidence points to the fact that the traditional Welsh house consisted of a number of separate buildings—'tei y Ilys', to quote *Manawydan*. This may account for the frequent use in the medieval poems of the plural form *tai* [houses] where 'house' is meant. For example, Dafydd Nanmor in his poem to Rhys ap Maredudd of Tywyn in Cardiganshire[1]:

> *I'r tai ynghwr y Tywyn . ..*

[To the *house* (lit. *houses*) on the edge of the Tywyn].
or Guto'r Glyn in his poem to Sir Siôn Mechain[2]:

> *Y mae curad a'm carai*
> *I'm dwyn oddyma i'w dai*

[There is a priest who so loves me that he would take me hence to his *house* (lit. *houses*).]

We shall see below that one of the characteristics of the later architecture was that it brought these separate 'houses' under one roof. This

---

[1] Roberts, T. and Williams, I.: *The Poetical Works of Dafydd Nanmor* (1923), P.I.

[2] Williams, I. and Williams, J. Ll.: *Gwaith Guto'r Glyn* (1939), p. 275.

had doubtless happened when many of the poets sang but the use of the plural form *tai* often persisted in their poems.

But the most important references for our present purpose occur in those sections of the laws which are concerned with the value of buildings. The houses of the period were naturally made almost entirely of wood: their liability to fire made necessary a detailed valuation which lists the various elements used in the structure of buildings. Ellis points out[1] that 'the Venedotian Code is clearest in its account . . the Demetian and Gwentian Codes are confused'.

The Venedotian version[2] divides halls into three grades, the king's, the freeman's (*uchelwr*) and the non-freeman's (*aillt'*). In the king's house, each '*gafael*' supporting the roof ('that is six columns' [*chwe cholofn*]) was valued at 40*d.*, the roof at 80*d.* and each penthouse (*godŷ*) 120*d.* In the freeman's house the valuations were 20*d.*, 40*d.*, and 50*d.*, respectively; in the non-freeman's, 10*d.*, 20*d.*, and 30*d.* The unfree's 'penthouses' are listed as his chamber, cow-house, barn, kiln, sheep-cote, pigsty, summer-house and autumn-house. The summer- and autumn-houses are also valued separately. The valuation then proceeds to specify individual elements of the house : large timbers (*pren bras*), doors (*dorau*), door-posts (*amhiniog*), beams (*trostau*), threshold (*trothwy*), fireback (*pentan*), poles (*pawl*], rods (gwïalen), staves (*cledren*), etc.

In the Demetian version each timber (*pren*) that supports the roof of the king's hall is valued at 20*d.*, the roof itself at 80*d.* For the winter house, the following valuations are given : every fork (*fforch'*) that supports the ridge-piece, 20*d.*; the ridge-piece, 40*d.* The 'Gwentian' version values both the ridge-piece and each fork supporting it at 30*d.* each. The Demetian Code also stipulates that 'if timber be cut in a person's wood without his permission other than the three timbers which are free for a builder on field-land', certain fees are to be paid. This is corroborated by a triad which runs 'three timbers which each builder upon field-land should have from the owner of the wood, whether the woodman will it or not, a ridge-piece and two roof-forks (*nenbren a dwy nenfforch*)'.

It will be noticed that in the Venedotian version, a *gafael* is valued at 40*d.* It is further explained that in the king's house, the *gafaelion* formed six columns. In the Demetian version, timbers supporting the roof of the king's hall are valued at 20*d.* each; forks supporting the winter-house roof are also valued at 20*d.* each.[3] What then were the *gafael* and *fforch*?

---

[1] *Op. cit.,* I, p. 378.

[2] For the references to the Laws in the two following paragraphs see Owen, A.: *op. cit.,* I, pp. 78, 292-4, 450, 486, 578, 586, 720, 772.

[3] In the 'Gwentian' Code, the valuations are not on the same scale.

The word *fforch* (cf. Latin *furca*) is cognate with the English 'fork'. Innocent[1] has discussed its significance in architecture. He points out that in certain parts of England, e.g. Durham and Yorkshire, 'a pair of the ordinary bent tree principals is known as a "pair of forks", so that each timber is considered to be a fork'. We are, I think, justified in assuming that the *fforch* (or *nenfforch*) was a cruck—i.e. a bent-tree principal— especially since in the Triad above, two forks are specified and since the *gafael* was double the value of a fork and probably represented a pair. Addy indeed (p. 27) assumes that the *nenffyrch* of the Triad 'are identical with the "crucks".'

The word *gafael* is difficult to explain. The Latin phrase is *de unoquoque retentaculo quod tectum sustinet*. I have failed to find *retentaculum* in any dictionary but its meaning is obvious—something to hold or support (retento = to hold fast).[2] The native word *furca* was *gafl* and one is tempted to see in the *gauael* of the corrupt manuscript of the Black Book of Chirk, the form *gauel* (= *gafl*). This *gafl* would be formed by the two crucks (cf. English 'a pair of forks'), the borrowed word *'fforch'* (from Latin *furca*, cf. as an analogy the English usage) being introduced to specify each of the single elements of the fork—the *retentaculum*—holding the ridge-piece. The fact however that the Latin text of the Laws gives *retentaculo* for *gafael* disposes of this possibility.[3]

---

[1] *Op. cit.*, pp. 36-8, 43, 65.

[2] Mr. Evan D. Jones, Keeper of Manuscripts in the National Library of Wales, draws my attention to the fact that *retentaculum* is also used (Owen, A.: *op. cit.*, II, p. 793) to indicate the *pentan haearn* (iron dog) which again 'held in' the fire. See C. Plummer : 'Glossary of Du Cange. Addenda et Corrigenda', in *Bulletin De Cange Archivum Latinatis Medii Aevi*, II (1925), pp. 25-6. Mr. Jones informs me that in the Latin-Welsh dictionary of Thomas ap William o Drefriw (Peniarth MS. 228) *retentaculum* does not occur but he explains *retinaculum* as 'daliat, pa vn bynac vo yn dala peth' [holder, whatever holds something], Thomas Thomas's Latin-English dictionary (1644 edition) gives the same *retinaculum* as 'any manner of thing wherewith another is stated or holden backe, a stay, the gable of an anker or anker rope : also the reine of a bridle'. Mr. Jones points out that Thomas ap William translated his definitions directly from such English sources, which explains why he overlooked the Welsh *gafael* and its Latin equivalent *retentaculum*.

[3] It is amusing to see Innocent, C. F. (*op. cit.*, p. 60) assert categorically that 'the Welsh in their turn borrowed the word "gavel" from the English'. Two other words in English use may here be mentioned. The first is 'gavel' used' to mean 'gable, gable-end' in parts of Ireland, Scotland, Northumberland, Durham, Cumberland and Yorkshire. This, with 'gable', is generally looked upon as derived from Old Norse *gafl*. The term 'gavel' may be cognate with the Welsh gaf(e)l. The second is 'gavelfork', 'the meaning of [which]' to quote Innocent 'is ... doubtful'. It is tempting to see in it the use of the Welsh *gaf(e)l*, the first element being explained by the second (*cf.* 'Masefield' = *maes* + field and 'Mainstone' = *maen* + stone). But the use and form as well as the meaning of 'gavel-fork' are doubtful, and, since we are not concerned with it, the matter can be left undecided.

On the other hand, *gafael* (= *gafl*) might possibly mean a fork in the sense of a pair of crucks which form a fork-like support, the *gafael* of the one Code being equivalent to the *fforch* of the other. If this be the case, the differences in valuations have not the significance suggested above but are merely due to regional variations. Here again the translation of *gafael* as *retentaculum*, in my view, disposes of this possibility too. In view of all the evidence, I incline to the belief that (*a*) two *ffyrch* formed one *gafael*; (*b*) *gafael* here has its normal meaning of 'hold, grasp', the one 'hold'— '*retentaculum*'—being formed of two forks (= crucks).[1]

If this interpretation holds, then the king's hall consisted of a building made of three pairs of crucks (*chwe cholofn*, six columns). Ellis describes it as consisting 'of three parallel rows of wooden pillars, two in each row. At a little distance from these pillars were rows of smaller pillars, the space between the larger and the smaller pillars being roofed over with beams and thatch or shingle, while larger, beams, similarly covered, stretched across the main pillars, roofing in the centre aisle. The side aisles were occupied by beds and were partitioned off from the main aisle by screens during the day. The main aisle was divided into two portions, the upper and the lower, separated from each other by a fire-place'.[2] Seebohm has given a similar description: 'Six well-grown trees with suitable branches apparently reaching over to meet one another . . are stuck upright in the ground at even distances in two parallel rows—three in each row. Their extremities bending over make a Gothic arch and crossing one another at the top each pair makes a fork, upon which the roof-tree is fixed. These trees supporting the roof-tree are called *gavaels*, *forks*, or *columns* and they form the nave of the tribal house. Then at some distance back from these rows of *columns* or *forks*, low walls of stakes and wattle shut in the aisles of the house and overall is the roof of branches and rough thatch. All along the aisles behind the pillars are placed beds of rushes called *gwelyau* (*lecti*) on which the inmates sleep. The foot-boards of the beds between the columns form their seats in the daytime. The fire is lighted on an open hearth in the centre of the nave between the two middle columns.'[3]

Sir John Edward Lloyd describes the king's hall as 'an oblong structure resting on six wooden uprights, of which two were placed at the one end with the door between them and two at the other; the central couple, having between them the open hearth, divided the hall into an upper

---

[1] I am indebted to Professor Henry Lewis, D.Litt., for drawing my attention to the form *retentaculo* and to various other points, and to Dr. Ifor Williams, F.B.A., for many suggestions and for confirming my belief that an equation of *gafael* with *gafl* here is unlikely.

[2] Ellis, T. P.: *op. cit.*, I, p. 35.

[3] Seebohm, F.: *The English Village Community* (1915), pp. 239-40.

section or "cyntedd" where the king and the greater officials sat at then-meat, and a lower section or "is-gyntedd" assigned to the less distinguished members of the royal train'.[1] The *cyntedd* and *is-gyntedd* have already been referred to (p. 67), the division between them being the *corf*,[2] the central pair of crucks.

While the Laws are explicit concerning the division of the hall and the positions to be taken up by the various officers of the king, there is no description of the 'aisles behind the pillars'[3] and the beds with their footboards as mentioned by Seebohm. The fact that the chambers of some of the officers of the court were in the hall is however inferred from the texts. The king's chamber is referred to without any details of its position. But it is stated that the page of the chamber makes the king's bed of straw and 'carries his messages between the hall and the chamber'. This suggests that the king's chamber is separate from the hall. But on the other hand, the Edling, however, 'is not to depart one night from the king' and *'his chamber is in the hall* together with the youths of the body-guard, the fire-kindler tending the fire and closing the doors'.

It is mentioned specifically that some members of the entourage did not sleep in the hall, e.g. the *penteulu* had the largest abode in the town, while the priest's lodging was in the chaplain's house and the chief falconer in the barn. The steward was to apportion the lodgings, his own being nearest the hall. It is therefore impossible, on the evidence, to determine who slept in the hall but it is certain that a number of persons did so, including the Edling or heir-apparent. Since the fire occupied the centre of the main floor which in turn was set out for the formal occasions of the court, it is probable that the sleeping accommodation was in side aisles and that the description given by Seebohm, Ellis, Rhŷs and Brynmor-Jones[4] and others is substantially correct. But the possibility that the hall may have been a nave without aisles (that is, a simple cruck house) cannot be entirely

---

[1] Lloyd, Sir J. E.: *op. cit.,* p. 314.

[2] Williams, Ifor : *op. cit.,* p. 131.

[3] The authority for this statement appears to be a reading of Giraldus Cambrensis's description (*Descriptio*, cap. x) of the sleeping arrangements of the Welsh : 'they sleep together, on a bed common to all laid along the sides of the house'. But the important fact is added that the fire was at the feet of all of them, from which may be inferred that the structure here described was a circular house. Rhys and Brynmor-Jones (*The Welsh People*, p. 200) indeed state: 'Giraldus describes the ordinary house as circular with the fireplace in the centre and beds of rushes all round it, on which the inmates sleep with their feet towards the fire'. But they quote Seebohm's description of the aisle beds which seems to have been based on the same passage !

[4] Rhŷs, [Sir] John and Brynmor-Jones, [Sir] David : *The Welsh, People* (6th edit., 1913), pp. 199-200.

dismissed, if we rely only on the evidence of the Laws.[1]

That the Welsh tribal house was of basilical character, with side aisles and a 'nave' is probable for two reasons other than the evidence of the Laws. The first is that this type was characteristic of Britain in Roman times: it was, indeed, as Collingwood has stressed[2] 'an early type in the Celtic world, perhaps established there before the Romans came . . . and superseded as the Romanization of the Celtic provinces advanced, by the corridor type. Its frequency in Roman Britain therefore is one of the many facts which show that Britain was a relatively backward area in civilization'. Such Romano-British houses—like the houses of the Welsh Laws—'possessed buildings other than the dwelling-house proper. These generally consist of cottages, barns, stables and so forth.' Collingwood and Ward[3] list a number of such houses in Britain. An example at Stroud near Petersfield, Hants, had its main block divided at first merely by two rows of wooden columns.

In the second place, such houses were universal in Ireland where the type dates from pre-Christian times[4]. Richmond suggests as we have seen

---

[1] The cruck construction of the tribal house has recently been questioned by Lady Fox in *Arch. Camb.*, 1939, pp. 177-8, where she seeks to explain *fforch* as a pronged upright post and holds that such a house would 'necessarily be rectangular and *central posted'*. The evidence on which her argument is based is the Triad referred to above which specifies 'a roof tree and two roof forks'. This, she states, 'makes clear that a "fork" is a single strut, not two tied together'. But it does not make clear that the fork is a pronged post: there is every reason to suppose, as has been shown above, that two forks made a *gafael*, a pair of crucks,. while the reference in the Laws to '*pob* gafael' and to the *gafaelion* forming six columns make it clear that the structure consisted of more than two forks, or two *gafaelion*. That the house was built of more timber than the three pieces mentioned in the Triad is evident from a clause in the Demetian Code (Owen, A.: op. cit., I, p. 586) fixing the prices of timber 'other than the three timbers which are free'. But it may be mentioned that houses whose main timbering consisted of a pair of crucks (*not* two pronged forks) and a ridge-piece (the three free timbers) were at one time common (see below, p. 162). I am unable therefore to accept Lady Fox's description of the tribal house, which I feel is based on insufficient evidence and on an incorrect interpretation of that evidence.

Lady Fox further suggests that the aisled structure posited by Seebohm and Ellis, i.e. the generally accepted interpretation of the tribal house, which I hold (above) to be substantially correct, is 'on the English pattern' and 'based on a late, possibly Normanized version of the royal hall at Abenfraw'. It will be seen below that this statement is untenable: the type is pre-Norman and owes nothing to either Norman or English influence.

[2] Collingwood, R. G. : *The Archaeology of Roman Britain* (1930), pp. 131-4.

[3] Ward, J.: *Romano-British Buildings and Earthworks* (1911), pp. 174-82.

[4] Richmond, I. A.: 'Irish Analogies for the Romano-British Barn Dwelling', in *The Journal of Roman Studies*, XXII (1932), pp. 96-106. According to *The Times* (2nd January, 1940) Dr. Seán P. O Riordáin, then Professor of Archaeology at University College, Cork, discovered during the summer of 1939 a house of Neolithic date with four rows of post-holes. The posts divided it into a long central space in which the fire was placed and side aisles 'which were

Collingwood do, 'that such buildings were not necessarily Roman but also part of the Celtic heritage'. The affinities in house construction and lay-out between Wales and Ireland which the present work shows, at almost all points, give strong support to the belief that a house-type universal in Ireland from prehistoric times and well-known in Roman Britain must also have been known in Wales. The partial reconstruction made possible by the references in the Laws—in particular the presence of parallel rows of columns—leads us to conclude that the tribal house in Wales was the Welsh counterpart of the well-established Irish structure and — bearing in mind the Romano-British evidence — that the Laws codified in the 10th century are here concerned with a culture which of course was not confined to the present borders of Wales : it had European associations and was of great antiquity.

The form of the Irish house repays study. The plan was 'undoubtedly oblong. If from nothing else, this would follow from the fact that there was a ridge-pole (*cleithe*). .. The main frame of the house was of timber beams. The walls between the framing-timbers were of woven wattles, coated with limed plaster [cf. the references in the Welsh Laws to 'hurdles' and 'wattle']. . . At each end of the building, the two roof-trees were crossed at their apex and the ridge-pole was fastened in the Y-rest thus formed [the normal cruck method]. . . The internal arrangements are equally clear. The chief space was taken by a great hall, very like the nave of a Norse stue and on each side there were partitioned bedrooms (*immdai*) containing one or more beds'.[1]

Richmond points out[2] that in the 9th century, 'a legal classification of society, conceived in much the same spirit as the Welsh Laws of Howell the Good' was prepared: this was the *Crith Gabhlach* which describes eight sizes of the Irish house, corresponding to eight types of chiefs. Probably a theorist's work, it may be compared with the theoretical classification of the Welsh house into three, the valuation and size descending with the social status. From an examination of this evidence, Richmond concludes that 'the aisled house ... emerges as the regular type of superior house in ninth-century Ireland and, as has been seen, there is evidence that it goes back

---

evidently the sleeping compartments'. Since this chapter was written. Dr. Ó Riordáin has kindly allowed me to examine his plan of the house. The reader should also study A. E. Van Giffen : 'Der Warf in Ezinge, Provinz Groningen, Holland, und seine westgermanischen Häuser', in *Germania*, 1936, pp. 40-7, where excellent prehistoric examples of this type are described, some of them corresponding very closely in size and lay-out to the house of the Welsh Laws. The outside rows of posts here and in the Irish example seem to conform to the construction mentioned on pp.48-9.

[1] Richmond : *op. cit.,* p. 98.

[2] *Ibid.,* pp. 100-1.

much further than that'. Richmond concludes that the -Romano-British 'basilical' house and the Irish house 'represent the highest level to which Celtic housing, unaided by Roman skill in stone, attained' and draws attention to the similarity of the lay-out of the Scandinavian *stue*. He hints tentatively that the prototype of all these houses may be found in central Europe, whence the type spread into Scandinavia, Britain and Ireland, with the Keltic wave.[1]

The problem of such origins however takes us beyond the scope of the present study but it is perhaps permissible to point out that here again we are dealing with a type whose varieties appear to be well-established over a long period in north-western Europe.

The houses of the *uchelwr* (freeman) and *aillt* (bondman) were built on the same principle as that of the king, but the valuations were lower. The references to hurdles, wattling, poles, rods, side-posts, etc. found in the Laws are also of interest. These can best be illustrated by a remarkable series of drawings of an old farmhouse in the Strata Florida district of Cardiganshire which were published in 1899.[2] These drawings (figs. 32-6) were prepared in 1888. They represent a long-house, the upper and lower end being separated only by a wattle-screen. 'The family lived with, and in close proximity to, their domestic animals: the cow and the pig occupied one portion of the house, screened only by the lattice-work partition probably plastered with mud, the poultry occupied the lattice-shelf to the right of the fireplace'. The writer, S. W. Williams, points out that 'the roof-principals spring direct from the ground instead of from the tops of the walls. Consequently, the walls are merely of use as screens to keep out the weather and perform no constructive function in supporting the roof. In the illustration, the ends of the principals have been cut off, probably due to rotting, for the house in 1888 was in a ruinous condition. It will be noticed too that the roof is strengthened by the use of upright supporting posts. The door-hurdle, poles and rods (*dorglwyd, polion a gwiail*) of the Laws are in much evidence. The fireplace has a wattle-and-daub canopy and is screened from the door with wattling. It is the dominant feature of the whole interior. The roof is of rough unhewn purlins covered with an underthatch of plaited rods under a layer of turf. The house was obviously medieval and may well

---

[1] C. A. Ralegh Radford (*Interim Report of Excavations at Castle Dore, Cornwall*, 1936, p. 5) refers to a Cornish Dark-Ages site 'closely related both to the basilican type of Roman Villa and to the neuadd or hall of the prince as described in the early Welsh tales'.

[2] *Arch. Camb.*, 1899, pp. 320-5.

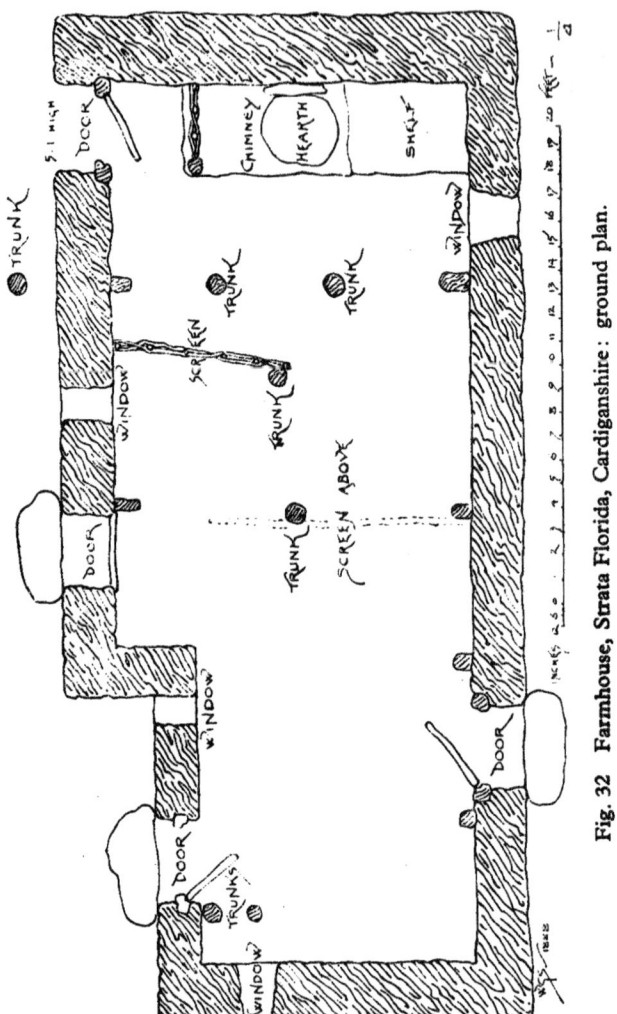

Fig. 32 Farmhouse, Strata Florida, Cardiganshire: ground plan.

represent the house of the Laws at the lowest end of the social scale: all the elements are here, the crucks, ridge-piece, door-posts, door-hurdle, fireback-stone, etc.

It is necessary here to notice briefly the importance of the fire and the hearth in the Laws. Ellis has pointed out[1] that 'the centre of social life was the hearth'. The central couple of crucks having between them the open

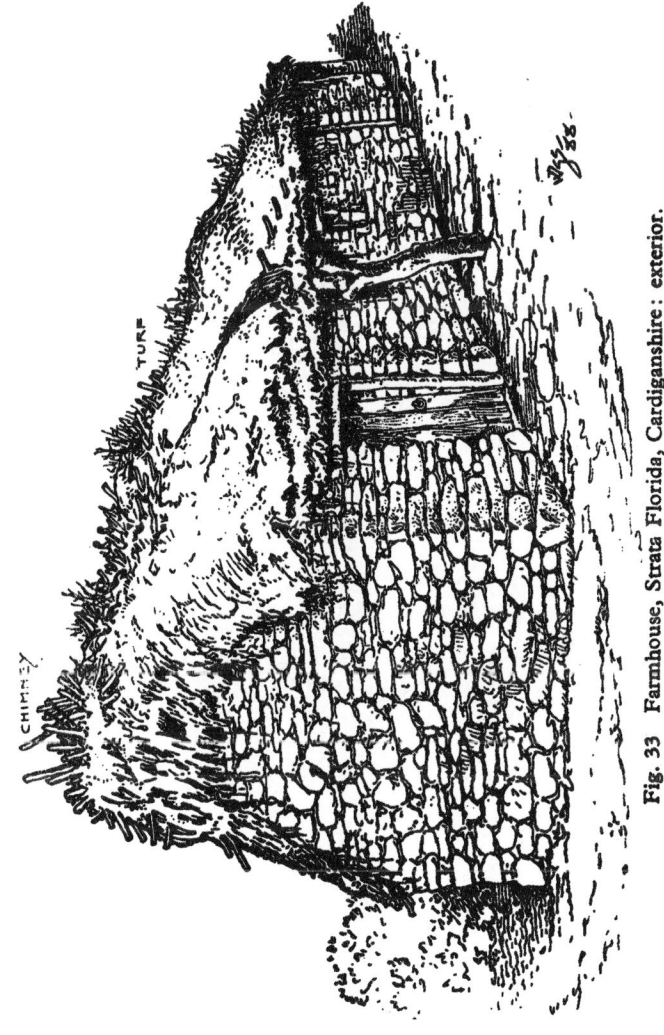

Fig. 33 Farmhouse, Strata Florida, Cardiganshire: exterior.

---

[1] Ellis, T. P. : *op. cit.,* II, p. 164.

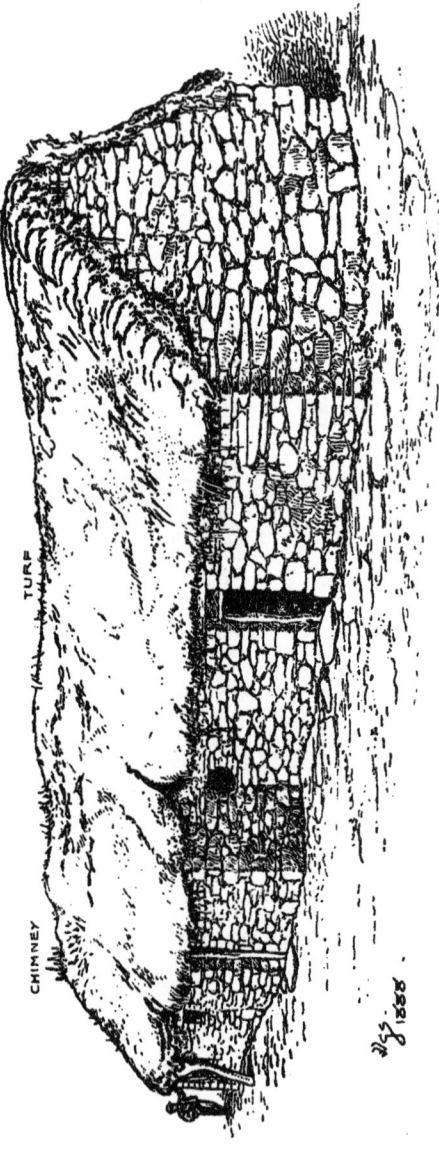

Fig. 34. Farmhouse, Strata Florida, Cardiganshire : exterior.

Fig. 35. Farmhouse, Strata Florida, Cardiganshire : interior.

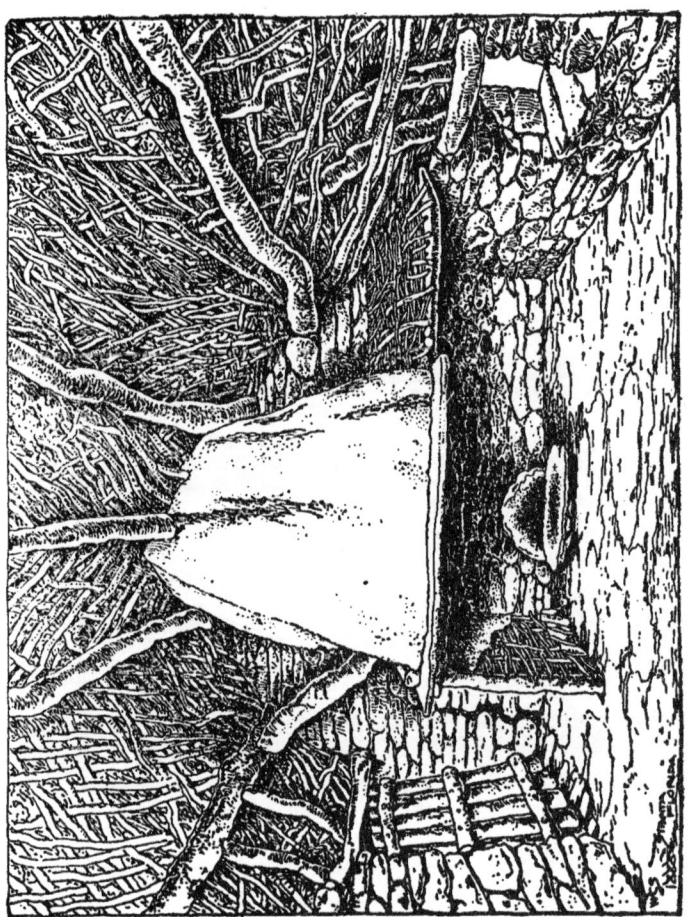

Fig. 36. Farmhouse, Strata Florida, Cardiganshire : interior showing fireplace.

hearth, divided the hall'.[1] Here was placed the *pentanfaen* (fireback-stone)[2], and once it was placed in position it was an offence to remove it. 'The house

---

[1] Lloyd, Sir J. E.: *op. cit.,* p. 314.

[2] A. W. Wade-Evans's translation of *pentanfaen* as 'hearthstone' (Welsh Medieval Law, p. 278) is misleading. The stone was placed vertically behind the fire, not, as 'hearthstone' suggests, horizontally beneath or in front of it. Richards (Cymru r Oesau Canol, p. 129) has fallen into the same error. 'Canolfan y cartref, he writes, 'oedd y pentanfaen, y garreg aelwyd, ys dywedwn ni heddiw'. [The centre of the home was the *pentanfaen,* the hearthstone as we call it

itself might be destroyed, the owners might desert the site . .. but the *pentanfaen* was never removed. It stood as a perpetual sign that the site where it stood was the site of an occupied homestead'.[1]

Campbell[2] has referred to a similar emphasis on the importance of the hearth in Ireland. He describes the fireback-stone, the *pentanfaen*, in Ireland : 'Standing at the back of the hearth is one large, thickish flag or often three or more stones forming the hob, *iarta*. . . The hob constitutes a protection for the wall behind. In Eastern and Southern Ireland even elsewhere the hob is built up carefully from stone and mortar'. He points out that this 'protection wall behind the fire' can develop in such a way as to constitute also two stone hobs (our modem *pentan*) on each side of the fire. In Ireland, as in Wales, the hearth has always formed 'the centre of family activity . . . the rallying point of the people. . . The place of honour is the corner seat near the fire, where the guests are invited to sit down'. This compares in detail with Welsh custom down to our own times.

The Welsh have always been primarily shepherds and herdsmen and, as Rees has stressed,[3] their homes, 'situated on the hill slopes at the edge of the woodlands, as described by Giraldus, were eminently suitable for a pastoral life'. But in the summer months the herds and flocks were frequently taken to the pastures on the higher ground. For this purpose the summer-house was necessary, this is the *hafdy* of the Laws, the *hafod* or *hafoty* as contrasted with the *hendref* or *gaeafdy* (winter house). Indeed, the Laws refer too to an autumn house, the *cynhaeafdy*. The *hafod* season in the Venedotian Code was from the beginning of May to August; in the Demetian, from the beginning of May to September; and in the 'Gwentian', from the beginning of May to the end of September.

The Laws have no details which make possible a reconstruction of the *hafdy*, but from the valuation, it is clear that the house was of a slight and even temporary character. This practice of transhumance however persisted throughout the ages and the many place-names testify to its former universality. Even today, in the sheep-farming districts of central Wales in particular, almost the whole household of some of the valley farms moves into a distant *lluest*, a moorland house often several miles away, for the sheep-washing and -shearing duties which extend over several weeks. As an

---

to-day]. The correct terminology is still maintained in west Wales, *y garreg bentan* is the fireback-stone, *y garreg aelwyd or carreg yr aelwyd*, the hearthstone immediately in front of the fire For a full discussion of the *pentanfaen* and *the pentan haeam*, see Peate, Iorwerth C.: 'The Double-ended Firedog' in Antiquity, XVI (1942), pp. 64-70.

[1] Ellis, T. P.: *op. cit.*, p. 164.

[2] Campbell, A.: *op. cit.* (II), p. 230; (I), p. 71.

[3] Rees, W. : *South Wales and the March 1284-1415* (1924), p. 217.

example, this is the practice of several valley-farmers in the Llanbrynmair (Montgomeryshire) district who with members of their families and their servants migrate annually for a short period to the high sheep-walks of the Pumlumon uplands. Another modern development of the same tradition of transhumance is the widespread Welsh practice of 'wintering' flocks, which have spent the summer months on the moorland, on the rich lowland of some of the valley farms often many miles from the holding of the farmer concerned.

That the *hafod* persisted without much development until the 19th century is obvious from the references to it in the literature. Thomas Pennant, writing in the last quarter of the 18th century,[1] refers to the Llanberis district of Caernarvonshire: 'They reside in that season in Havodtys or summer-dairy-houses. These consist of a long low room, with a hole at one end [of the roof] to let out the smoke from the fire which is made beneath. Their furniture is very simple : stones are the substitute of stools : and the beds are of hay ranged along the sides'. He adds : 'During the summer, the men pass their time either in harvest work or in tending their herds : the women in milking or making butter and cheese. . . . Towards winter, they descend to their *Hen Dref* or *old dwelling* where they lead, during that season, a vacant life'. It will be noticed that both men and women occupied the *hafotai*.

John Evans[2] at the beginning of the 19th century has a similar description of the Caernarvonshire practice : '[They] leave their winter habitations and take up their residence amidst the hills; where they erect what are termed *havodtai*, or summer dairy houses, which are merely huts. A few stones supply the place of chairs and bundles of rushes along the sides are in lieu of beds'. E. Owen, in 1867, refers[3] to eight *hafotai* in ruins 'in various parts of the Llanllechid [Caernarvonshire] mountains'. They were known at that time by such names as Hafoty Coed-yr-Ynys, Hafoty Lowri galed, Hafoty Alis, Hafoty Famaeth, Hafoty un-nos, etc. 'Persons lived in these houses, if they may be called houses, for several months in the year to attend to their flocks of sheep and cattle, and in them they made their butter and cheese. They are excessively small, being composed of two or three small rooms and it is strange how even for the summer months any one could have lived in them. To 'the beginning of the last century [the 18th] these huts were in annual requisition; in the time of Lhuyd they were in general use "about Snowdon and Cader Idris and elsewhere in Wales".'

---

[1] Pennant, T. : *The Journey to Snowdon* (1781), p. 161. See also the same description in the same author's *Tours in Wales* (1810), II, pp. 334-5.

[2] Evans, J. : *The Beauties of England and Wales* (1812), XVII, p. 321.

[3] In *Arch. Camb.*, 1867, pp. 106-7.

John Evans[1] had described at the end of the 18th century the habits of the mid-Wales farmers whose 'flocks like those of Estramadura and other mountainous parts of Spain are driven from distant places to those exposed pastures to feed the summer herbage'. He refers to farms and cottages in the Llanidloes district of Montgomeryshire 'which were only winter habitations'. Another reference to *hafotai* in Montgomeryshire (in 1873) relates to the parish of Garthbeibio: 'In the higher districts. of this parish there are several [*hafotai*]. The farmers in former times used to migrate from the lowlands into these dwellings and reside there during the greater part of the summer having their cattle with them and the things necessary for the dairies. It was then they generally harvested the . . *gwair rhosydd* [moorland hay]'.[2]

A systematic survey of the Welsh uplands would reveal many traces of human habitations and in view of the persistence of transhumance until a late date, many of them would probably show evidence of a long tradition of cattle-pens and sheep-folds all related to summer pasturage. Unfortunately for the student, the furniture and utensils used in such migrations to the uplands were of the most temporary character—probably wooden bowls, spoons, etc.—while most of the materials would be transported to and from the winter dwellings. It is likely therefore that even if the excavation of such sites were carried out on an extensive scale, little evidence could be obtained to estimate the chronology and history of transhumance in Wales. The practice, however, universal in the Age of the Princes, persisted in some localities in its original form—the winter *hendref* and the summer *hafod*—until the beginning of the 19th century. And in the 20th century a modified form of the migration still continues.[3]

---

[1] Evans, J. : *A Tour through North Wales in . . . 1798*, p. 65.

[2] *Montgomeryshire Collections*, 1873, p. 27.

[3] Sir Cyril and Lady Fox have described several upland structures found by them in south Wales. See *Antiquity*, 1934, pp. 345-413, *Arch. Comb.*, 1937, pp. 247-68, and 1939, pp. 163-99. The nature and purpose of these structures seem to me, on the evidence, to be still doubtful. But they may all have been *hafotai*. The position on the open moorland and the high altitude of all the sites —the Gelligaer examples are at an elevation of 1300-1350 feet—are the direct contrary to the siting of any *hendre* known to me. In her 1939 paper, Lady Fox holds that one of the homesteads 'was not a *hafod* ... on the evidence of the finds indicating metal working'. This in itself is not conclusive since the duties associated with pasturage were not onerous and provided long hours of leisure which could be spent in, e.g., metal-working. Nor is there reason to suppose that the occupants of the *hafotai* did not include both men and women for in the 18th century (see p. 127 above) persons of both sexes occupied them. The datable evidence on these sites is scarce. The terminal date for the occupation of one of the Gelligaer homesteads 'seems likely on the evidence' to have been in the first half of the 14th century. It is shown in the 1934 and 1937 papers that at the Margam Mountain and 'Dinas Noddfa' sites there was no datable material found; this absence of datable objects would be natural in a *hafod*. The excavation of a number of such sites is therefore desirable before their nature and purpose can be ascertained

APPENDIX TO CHAPTER VI

Certain houses mentioned in medieval literature may be referred to here.

(*a*) The late Dr. Kuno Meyer drew attention in 1902[1] to a house in the Irish statutes, with four doors, through the middle of which water flowed. He refers also to other Irish examples. Meyer then draws attention to Pen-y-bryn, Llanarmon-dyffryn-Ceiriog, Denbighshire, the birthplace of John Ceiriog Hughes, the poet. This house, situated on the gentle slope of a hill, had, when Meyer visited it, a small stream, confined within a stony ditch, flowing through its cellar. He quotes Isaac Foulkes, the poet's biographer: 'The dairy is in the cellar under the house : and it is hard to imagine a better place for keeping the milk cool and fresh. A clear stream, that springs from the heart of the rock, flows through the room summer and winter'. Meyer reminds us of a passage in *Tristan and Isolde*, where Tristan threw wood-shavings into the stream that passed through the room of his beloved and considers this type of house with water flowing in it to be Keltic.

This feature—a spring or overflowing well in a house—is still to be found in some parts of Wales. I have been informed of such a feature in several houses in more than one district in west Wales, for instance. At Pennantwrch, Garthbeibio, Montgomeryshire, Mr. Sam Ellis informs me that the pistyll (waterspout) was in the back-kitchen and the water flowed through a conduit under the floor. Dr. W. F. W. Betenson, Medical Officer of Health for Brecknockshire, informs me[2] that in the district of Cwm-nant-gam, Llanelly Hill near Bryn-mawr, in that county 'is quite a solidly-built terrace of houses on the hillside and two of these, to my certain knowledge, have wells inside and I rather think that the whole terrace is similarly built. . When the well gets particularly full in the rainy season it overflows and the water is liable to run out of the front door'. Dr. Betenson described such houses before the Committee of Inquiry into the Anti-Tuberculosis Service in Wales and Monmouthshire[3] : 'There were wells in the middle of the houses between the front and back rooms. In one house, the well was big enough for a baby to fall into, and, in another, an adult could have bathed in it. He said that the opening to the well resembled the entrance into a dog kennel'.

---

with any certainty. The problematical character of the structures precludes any further discussion of them in this book.

[1] In *Zeitschrift fûr Romanische Philologie*, XXVI (1902), pp. 716-7.

[2] In a letter dated 5th February, 1938.

[3] *Report*, p. 149.

In the parish of Llanfigan, Brecknockshire, about four miles south-east of Brecon is the farm-house of Pantllefrith. This (Mr. T. M. Thomas, Llandrindod, informs me) has a well in the cellar from which the household is supplied. No 91, High Street, Pwllheli (information from Mr. R. E. Thomas, Bodorwel, Pwllheli), Caernarvonshire, a three-storied cellared house had in the 19th century a stone-lined well in one of its cellars. Mr. S. M. Powell, M.A., Tregaron, Cardiganshire, writes that a house in that district, called Dewi Well, has a well in the kitchen. 'In *Llyfr Ancr Llanddewi-brefi'* he writes, 'there is a tale of Dewi Sant [S. David] passing this spot on his way . . . when the woman who lived there prayed him to do something for her child who was dead. Forthwith Dewi went into the house and brought the child to life. The story goes that a well gushed forth on the spot. In fact the whole area of the lower ground is full of springs'. A similar internal well is reported (*Western Mail*, 5.12.1940) at Maes-y-cwarre, Betws Mountain, Ammanford, Carmarthenshire.

Whether these house represent the survival of the old tradition discussed by Kuno Meyer is a matter for conjecture. They are noted here in the hope that their characteristics and the distribution of the type—if, indeed, it be a type—may be studied more closely by future workers.

(*b*) Iolo Goch, a 14th-century poet,[1] has a poem describing[2] the hall of the Welsh leader, Owain Glyn Dwr, at Sycharth, which was burnt down at the beginning of the 15th century[3]. The poem awaits translation by a competent literary and architectural scholar. Sycharth was a motte-and-bailey site, the house being of timber. The reference to *cyplau* (couples) :

> Cyplau sydd, gwallh cwplws ŷnt,
> Cwpledig bob cwpl ydynt.

[It has couples, they are tied, each couple tied together.]
indicate the nature of the roof, while

> Tŷ pren glân mewn top bryn glas
> Ar bedwar piler eres

[A fair wooden house on the crest of a green hill, upon four wondrous pillars.]

---

[1] For a study of his dates, etc., see Lewis, H., Roberts, T., and Williams, I. : *Cywyddau Iolo Goch ac Eraill, 1350-1450* (1925).

[2] *Ibid.,* pp. 41-4

[3] Richards, R. : *op. cit.,* p. 318.

suggests that here we have an example of a framed building of post-and-truss type, not a cruck building. The poem mentions also eight upper rooms, a tiled roof, a chimney, and nine 'wardrobes'. The house must therefore have reflected to a high degree the Norman and English developments in architecture.

(*c*) Two poems describing houses, written by Howel Davi, a native of Brecknockshire, of 15th-century date, were published in 1918[1]. One house has a

> *Simnai sgwar val tai m haris . . .*
> *Maint Llong yn y mantell hi*
> *Main nadd or tu mewn iddi*

[square chimney like houses in Paris. ... the size of a ship in its mantel, hewn stone inside it].
He speaks also of

> *bwrw swnd a beris yndi*
> *briwio kalch hyt y bric hi*

[its interior is sanded, lime has been ground over its roof].
The other house described has

> *Ar y vric keric kwarel*

[on its roof quarry stone].

> *gwalau megis mvryav mon*
> *gwewyt trwyddynt goet rvddyon*

[walls like the walls of Anglesey (i.e. white): timber was woven through them]—probably a description of the 'black-and-white' technique.

There are several references to and descriptions of houses incidental in the literature of the 15th-17th centuries, of which the above may be taken merely as examples. But unfortunately most of the material has not been published.

(*d*) Guto'r Glyn, a mid-15th century poet, has a description of the house of Sir Siôn Mechain, who was vicar of Llandrinio, Montgomeryshire. He describes it as

---

[1] Roberts, E. Stanton : *Peniarth MS. 67* (1918), pp. 70-1, 99-101.

Neuadd hir newydd yw hon
Nawty'n un a'r tai'n wynion:
Cerrig, ar frig awyr fry,
Cornatun yn cau'r nawty
Lwfer ni ad lif o'r nen
A chroeslofft deg a chryslen ...
Plas teilys . . .[1]

[A new long hall is this, nine houses in one and all white. Corndon stone on the roof closing the nine houses. A louvre prevents a downpour from the heavens and a fair crossloft with a screen. . . A tiled palace . .] The reference to *nine* houses should be noticed, and compared with the nine houses of the Laws (p. 113). Here in the normanized architectural style of the middle ages the nine separate 'houses' of the old Welsh tradition have been brought together under one roof.

In another poem he describes a mansion, Coldbrook, Monmouthshire. Here again

Mae obry naw tŷ'n y tŵr

[There are below nine houses in the tower]
but

Mae fry ganty ac untwr.
Tref fawr mewn pentwr o fain
Tŷ beichiog o'r tai bychain.
Ei gaerau yw'r graig eurin,
Ei grib sy goch fel grâps gwin.

[Above there are a hundred houses and one tower. A large town in a heap of stone, a house laden with small houses. The golden rock is its walls, its ridge is red like wine-grapes].

In a third poem, another Montgomeryshire house is described: here again are the inevitable nine houses :

---

[1] For Gutor'r Glyn's poems, see Williams, I., and Williams, J. Ll.: *Gwaith Guto'r Glyn* (1939), pp. 109-11, 132-4, 275-6. See also *Mont. Coll.*, 1904, pp. 151-2. Corndon (Welsh, Cornatun) Hill is just within Montgomeryshire on the Shropshire border. Its quarried stone is well-known and this 15th-century reference to its use for tiling purposes proves that the quarries have been worked over a long period. I am indebted—indirectly—to Sir John Edward Lloyd for this reference.

Yntŵy a wnaeth naw tŷ'n un,
I'r nawty yr awn atun.

[They made nine houses into one, we shall go to them to the nine houses.]

(*e*) A description of Cae Du, Llansannan, Denbighshire, was published in 1910[1]. The description, here translated from the Welsh, runs as follows : 'The old house stands with its gable to the lane, and its wall on that side deep in the earth, while the lower gable, because of the slope, well above the ground-level, and its floor high enough to form a cellar at that end. The old house had three rooms on the ground floor and two up, as well as the cellar already mentioned, and the famous little room in the chimney, where Salesbury is said to have translated the New Testament.

The overall length of the building was about 72 (? 52) ft., and its breadth from wall to wall about 14 ft. The first room was about 9 ft. long, but it had no fireplace and stood deep in the earth. The next, the central room, was the principal room, and measured 16 ft.: in it was the hearth and chimney. The two rooms were separated by a stone partition reaching to the roof and a wide mantel thrown out over the hearth also reached to the roof. There was no loft above the first room, but there was one above the other two, and a small room formed in the chimney between the mantel (or the partition-wall above the mantel) to the end wall of the room, and above the hearth. The loft above the kitchen was therefore smaller than the kitchen by the width of the chimney. There was no door from the principal bedroom into this small room, and no one could imagine that the room existed : the only entrance into it was by climbing up through the chimney. And this is the kind of place—the secret or sacred chamber as it can well be called—where was performed the holy work which gave the house such fame'.

(*f*) *The Black Book of St. David's*, 'an Extent of all the lands and rents' of the Lord Bishop of St. David's made in 1326[2] has references to medieval custom which show the persistence in modified form in the 14th century of some of the arrangements described in the Laws. For instance, 'they ought to carry the heavy materials which cannot be drawn by one horse from the forest of Atp[ar] to the Manor of Landogy for building five houses there, namely the Hall, the chamber of the Lord, his kitchen, stable and grange, at their own cost':[3] which again should be compared with the nine buildings of the Laws which the villeins had to erect for the king. There are also several references to the use of wattle and wood, and to

---

[1] Jones, R. W. : *Hanes hen furddynod plwyf Llansannan* (1910), pp. 24-5.

[2] Willis-Bund, J. W. : *The Black Book of St. David's* (1902).

[3] *Ibid.,* p. 201.

numerous buildings both of wood and of stone. Unfortunately none is described.

CHAPTER VII

Some Stone and Half-Timbered Houses

REFERENCE has been made to the use of stone in various parts of Wales for building purposes. It is beyond the scope of the present work, however, to deal with all stone-built houses throughout Wales. Such a study would involve a parish-by-parish survey of great length and detail which can only be accomplished in future years and would involve issues wider than those with which we are at present concerned, e.g. a treatment of manor houses, castles, etc.—in short, a sophisticated tradition other than the 'unconscious artistry' of the traditional building. On the other hand, the Welsh builder has used stone as his medium, when there is a plentiful supply, to produce long-houses and cottages whose lay-outs do not differ in any fundamental way from those built of mud or other materials. This aspect of the subject is dealt with in Chapter VIII.

In Pembrokeshire, however, a type of stone house has been evolved which is so individual and so different from houses in other parts of Wales that it deserves separate treatment here. Pembrokeshire has a large number of houses of a well-built and sturdy character. 'No district of the Principality', writes Barnwell[1] of south Pembrokeshire, 'is richer in castles, churches or houses'. He lists the castles of Haverfordwest, Picton, Wiston and Narberth, the 'episcopal castle' of Llawhaden and the commandery of Slebech, and proceeds to enumerate Wolf's Castle, Roche Castle, and the castles of Amroth, Tenby, Manorbier, Castle Martin, Walwyn's Castle, Benton, Upton and Carew with the great fortress of Pembroke over all. 'So completely fortified was the whole district that even the churches with their vaulted roofs and lofty towers' seem to have been adapted for defence. The large country houses— Eastington, Bonville Court, etc.—showed the same strength of structure and many of the structural characteristics of the castle-buildings.

One such characteristic is the massive round chimney which has been popularly considered for many years to be of Flemish origin, the work of the Flemish colony settled in part of Pembrokeshire in the time of Henry I. Barnwell and others have completely disposed of this theory.. The round chimney is found in some of the Pembrokeshire castles (e.g. Manorbier): it occurs in houses at Tenby and its district, e.g. Drusselton and Bubbington), Manorbier, Pembroke (Monkton), Templeton, Lamphey, St. Florence and in (formerly) a large number of farmhouses in the St. David's district. The dis-

---

[1] Barnwell, E. L. : 'Domestic Architecture of South Pembrokeshire', in *Arch. Camb.*, 1867, p. 193.

tribution of this feature does not therefore coincide with the boundaries of the Flemish colony. Barnwell's conclusion is reasonable: 'If not actually

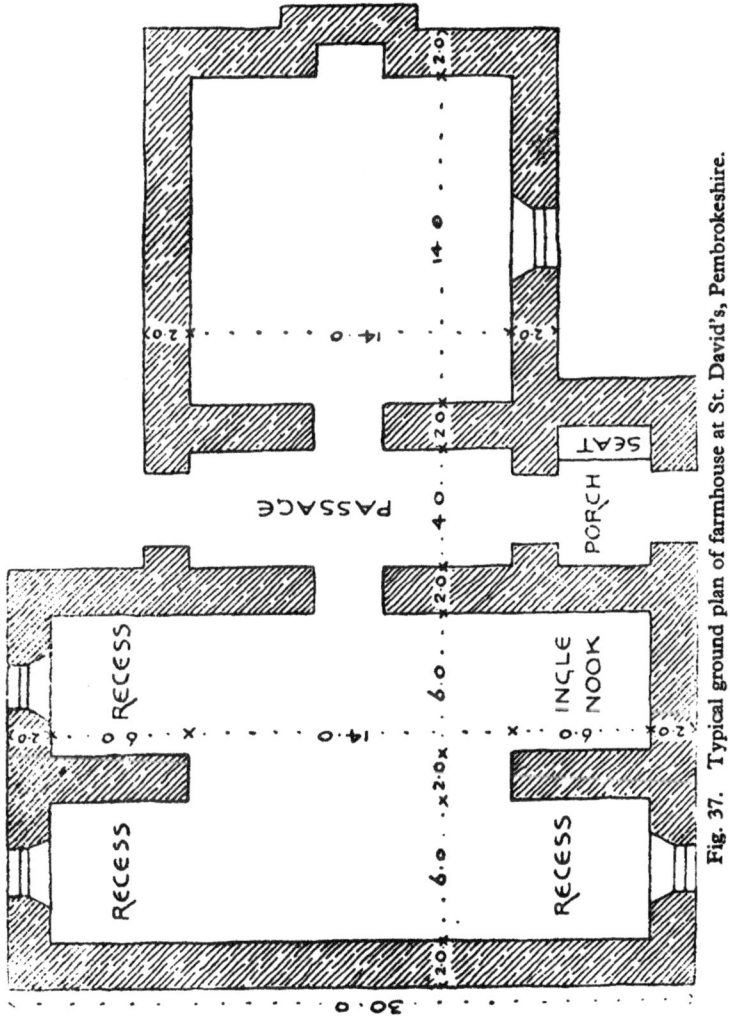

Fig. 37. Typical ground plan of farmhouse at St. David's, Pembrokeshire.

Norman, they are imitations of Norman; the form was well-suited to the kind of stone at hand and having once got into the fashion, continued so to a late period.

This Pembrokeshire type, as it may well be called, is best illustrated in 'the farmhouses of the St. David's district. These have been admirably described by the late J. Romilly Allen in an extensive paper published in 1902.[1] His records were made in 1883 : when his paper was published several of the houses had been 'swept away to make room for modem Impr-

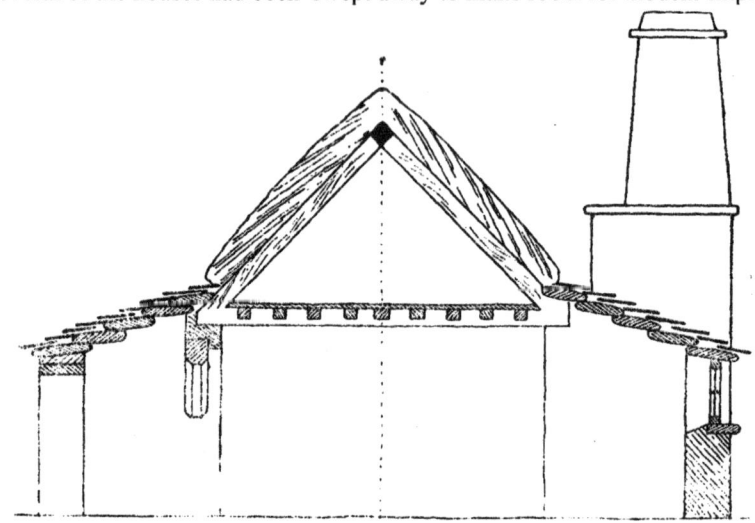

Fig. 38. Llaethdy, St. David's, Pembrokeshire : cross-section.

ovements'. He adds: 'I did not anticipate that the process of demolition, once begun, would go on so quickly as to prevent my ever 'being able to correct the observations I made twenty years ago.' The present writer was enabled to spend several days in the area during the -course of the present survey. It was then found that a still greater number had disappeared since Romilly Alien's paper was published and of the -few remaining examples, some had been much renovated and altered. Clegyr Foea, Hendre Einon, Rhoson and Pwllcaerog still remain, some in altered form, while to the list should be added TrefElydr and Croftufty (planned and photographed by the writer in 1942).[2] The present description is therefore based to a great extent upon Romilly Allen's detailed account, the illustrations being those which accompanied his paper.

---

[1] Allen, J. Romilly : 'Old Farm-Houses with round chimneys near St. David's' in *Arch. Camb.*, 1902, pp. 1-24.

[2] I am indebted to Mr. J. J. Evans, M.A., St. David's, for much information and for drawing my attention to references in *The Black Book of St Davids* (1326) to 'the mill at Poulthcauok' (p. 13), 'Pwllcauerok' (p. 107) and 'Trefelydyr (p. 51). He informs me (8th January, 1940) that Tref Elydr (Treleidyr) caught fire a fort-night ago and the thatched roof was completely burnt out.

These farmhouses have certain peculiarities of ground plan and construction. In nearly all cases they have a central passage (figs. 37,41) about 4 ft. wide with the front door at one end and the back door at the other. This

Fig. 39. Porch and doorway, Llaethdy, St. David's, Pembrokeshire.

feature may originally have been related to the similar passage-way-in the long-houses. On each side is a door leading to the two principal rooms on the ground floor, smaller rooms opening out of the larger ones. in certain cases. Allen points out that the most remarkable feature in the construction of the houses 'is the device adopted for increasing the area of the ground floor without the necessity for making a roof of unduly wide span. This is done by adding what may be termed side aisles. The central part of the house is covered by a thatched roof, of from 14 ft. to 15 ft. span inside and with the sides sloping perhaps at an angle of 45 degrees. Along one or both sides of the house are a series of recesses 6 ft. square inside, roofed over, pent-house fashion, with large slabs of slate, covered with ordinary roofing slates on the outside. The roof of the side aisles or recesses slopes at a much less steep angle than that of the main roof of the central part of the house' (fig. 38). These recesses are shown in fig. 41, where they form (*a*) a porch at the main entrance, (*b*) the hearth recess and (*c*) a recess lighted by a window, in which a table was placed. Other recesses, states Alien, were used for beds and for scullery purposes. In plan therefore the houses show a convergence of the tradition of a central passage with opposite doors and that of the old Keltic aisled house, translated completely into a stone technique.

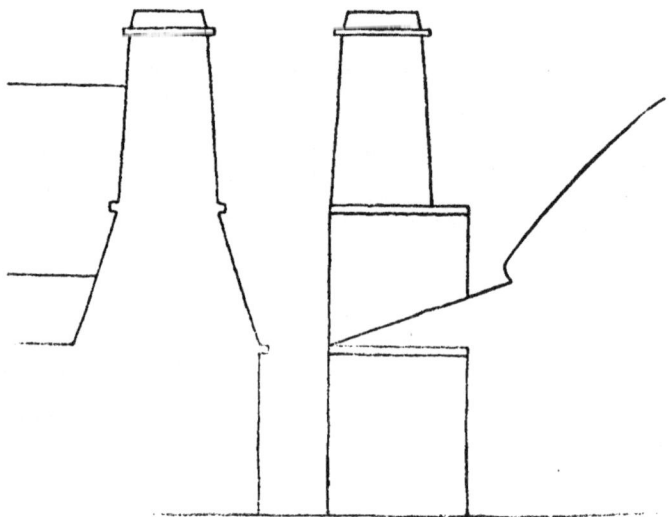

Fig. 40. Round chimney, Llaethdy, St. David's, Pembrokeshire.

In construction, the houses are greatly influenced by the castle-building technique as found in Pembrokeshire. The thick stone walls with deeply-recessed windows, the arched doorways (figs. 39, 50), the stone staircases and benches, especially when considered *in toto* are strongly reminiscent of the Norman builders' technique. And this is also true of the massive chimneys (fig. 40). These are from 18 ft. to 20 ft. high and are 3 ft. wide at the top. They are built in three stages : (*a*) the top, which is round, (*b*) the middle stage, with a batter to two of the side walls so as to increase the width to cover the hearth below, and (c) the bottom, which is rectangular. The roofs of the porch and the side-aisle recesses abut on each side against the lowest stage of the chimney (fig. 46).

Romilly Allen lists eight sites. These were visited during the course of the present survey. Only four of these now remain in a condition approximately similar to that described by Allen : one at least has been. re-roofed and its exterior cemented.

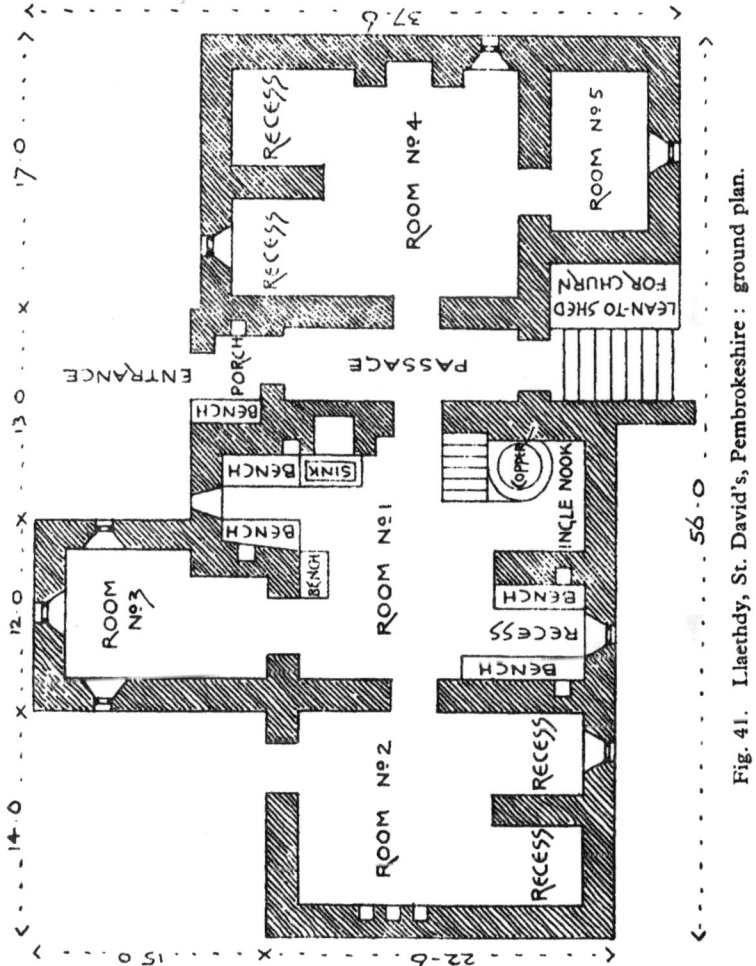

Fig. 41. Llaethdy, St. David's, Pembrokeshire : ground plan.

Llaethdy (figs. 38-42 and plates 51-2) conforms to the normal type,. It has a passage, 4 ft. 6 in. wide, crossing the house transversely, with doors at each end. On one side a door leads into the kitchen, from which two other rooms can be entered. In Room 1 the hearth and the space on its right constitute two recesses. There are two more in Room 2. On the other side of the kitchen is another recess together with Room 3. On the other side of the passage-way, a door leads to Room 4 which has two recesses on the left and Room 5 as a recess on the right. The house is therefore completely side-aisled throughout. Plate 51 illustrates a corner of the kitchen, the principal living-room, with its hearth, hearthside-recess. with benches, the boiler and stone steps leading to the attic. The opposite recess in the kitchen is shown in plate 52. Here the various dairy utensils were kept.

Fig. 42. Llaethdy, St. David's, Pembrokeshire : exterior view.

Room 2 had beds in each of its recesses and in the end wall 'a triple cupboard . . . covered with a single slab of stone'. Room 4 was the 'best: room' and Room 5, as far as Allen could recollect, the dairy.

Porth-mawr (figs. 43-4) again has a central through passage but appears to consist of two blocks joined together by this passage Again the hearth and its accompanying recess are in the same relationship, with another recess opposite. The roofs of the recesses are slated, but that of the central part thatched.

Clegyr Foea (fig. 45) is on the usual plan with a central passage. Here the roof of the 'nave' is higher than those of the 'aisles', providing an upper floor.

Rhoson Uchaf (figs. 46-7) has remained to the present day without any considerable alteration, except that the thatched roof has been replaced by slate. Here again there is an upper floor, the hearth and the recess. nearby together with the porch providing the principal 'aisle'.

Trefeiddan (figs. 48-50) as described by Allen provides a good example of the nave-and-aisle character of these houses, the central roof again being thatched and the side roofs slated.

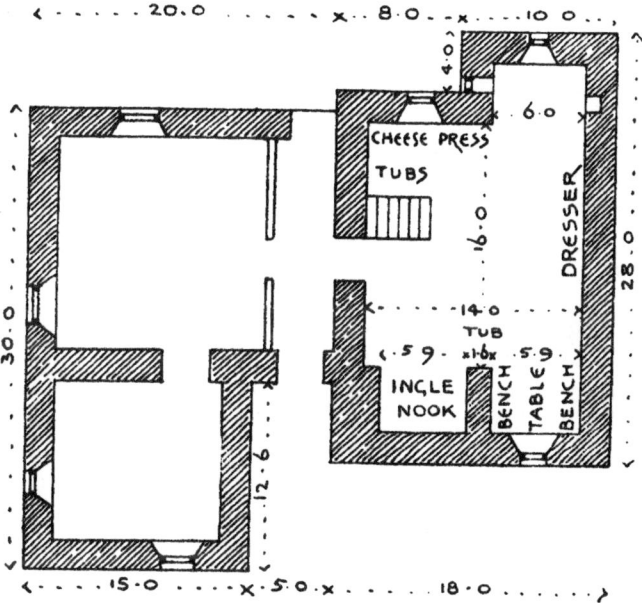

Fig. 43. Porth-mawr, St. David's, Pembrokeshire : ground plan;.

Gwrhyd Bach (plate 50) is described as a rectangle, 44 ft. by 30 ft., with a central passage with a room on each side of it. The room on the left of the passage has four recesses, two on each side of the room opposite each other, containing respectively a bed, a table, and shelving. The other room has a hearth-recess on one side and a dairy recess on the other. In this case all the recesses are barrel-vaulted.

Hendre Einon (fig. 51 and plate 53) conforms in general lay-out to the normal plan. In recent years it has been considerably altered and the whole of the exterior cemented.

The last example, Pwllcaerog, is illustrated in fig. 52 and conforms to the normal type of these houses.

One of the features of all these houses is the spacious fireplace in the lowest stage of the massive chimney, placed without exception at the side of the house adjacent to the entrance, the fireplace-recess forming a projection— a part of the 'aisle'. As far as I can judge this layout is unique in

Wales. But the chimney has parallels in Somersetshire and Devonshire and—in the far north—in the English Lakes district. Oliver[1] writes: 'Somerset cottages, and many in Devonshire also, originally had only one fireplace, with external projection, and that at the side of the house often adjacent to the entrance.' The well-known cottage at Selworthy, near Minehead, Somersetshire (plate 54) illustrates his point. The chimneys in these west-of-England examples have much in common with those of Pembrokeshire. They are all massive and many are in two stages (e.g. at Allerford near Porlock, Somersetshire)—a round top stage and a rectangular bottom stage with slight intermediate battering. But it is only in the chimney and its position that we find a parallel. The central 'nave' and side 'aisles' do not appear to be a feature of the west-of-England houses.

Why should these west-of-England chimneys and those of Pembrokeshire provide such close parallels ? The problem is an interesting one. We know that from prehistoric times onwards the cultural connexion between the country south of the Bristol Channel and south Wales has been a close one in several respects. But if the explanation were to be found in this direction we should expect similarities between Somerset and the Vale of Glamorgan, not Pembrokeshire. A clue may be obtained in the commerce of the Middle Ages. Lewis[2] points out that at the end of the 12th century, Welsh trade seemed to be confined to a dependence upon England for many commodities. 'The Welsh people themselves paid no attention to commerce, shipping or manufacture. The Flemings, settled by Henry I in Pembrokeshire, were the only commercially-minded people in Wales.' The contemporary Pipe Rolls yield a few instances of commerce between Pembrokeshire and the castles and towns on the south-west coast.

That commerce continued and George Owen points out[3] how at the opening of the 17th century 'the wools of south Pembrokeshire were drafted to Somersetshire and other West of England counties'. At the same time, the ports of Glamorgan 'being baronial foundations, were denied the prestige of the status of staple towns'.[4] Consequently the close relationship of Pembrokeshire, but not Glamorganshire, with the west of England at that period is explicable. The Welsh Port Books published by Lewis[5] give instances of trade between St. David's and Bamstaple and between Tenby

---

[1] Oliver, B.: *op. cit.,* p. 21.

[2] Lewis, E. A.: 'A contribution to the commercial history of medieval Wales', in *Y Cymmrodor*, XXIV (1913), pp. 88-9.

[3] *Ibid.,* p. 97.

[4] *Ibid.,* p. 100.

[5] Lewis, E. A. : The Welsh Port Books (1550-1603), No. XII in the Cymmro-dorion Record Series (1927).

Fig. 44. Porth-mawr, St. David's, Pembrokeshire : exterior view.

and Minehead, Ilfracombe and Barnstaple. We are justified, I think, in concluding that the commercial and cultural contacts between Pembrokeshire and the west of England over a long period may provide an adequate reason for the existence in those two regions only (in south Britain) of the chimney-type under discussion.

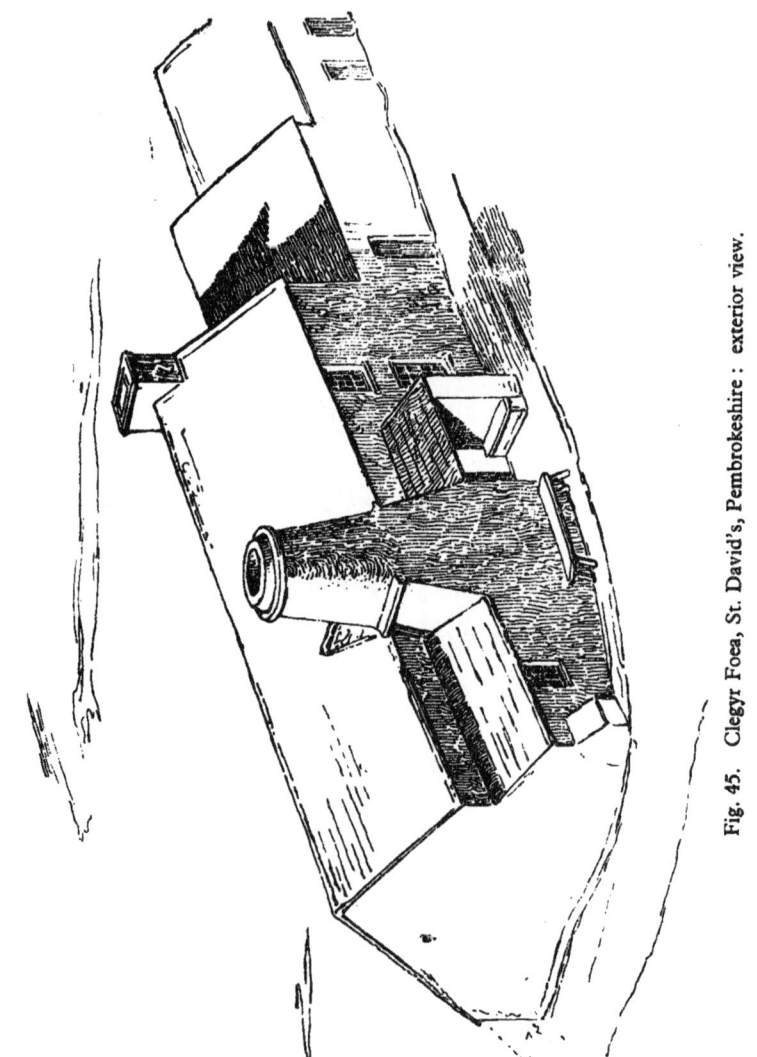

Fig. 45.   Clegyr Foea, St. David's, Pembrokeshire : exterior view.

To sum up, it appears probable that in the north Pembrokeshire farm-houses we have the convergence of two or more traditions. The central passage way and the opposite doors which occur regularly are a feature of folk buildings found throughout the whole of north-western Europe as we have seen. The nave-and-aisle lay-out of the houses which was 'the most remarkable feature' noted by Romilly Allen is strongly reminiscent of the houses of the Welsh Laws which were codified at the neighbouring town of Whitland. The fact that many of the recesses are still used for the housing of beds is not without interest: it may point to the persistence of a long tradition. In which case, the recesses correspond to the *immdai* of the Irish house. Finally, the whole of Pembrokeshire is so permeated with' the technique of the Norman builder in stone that the traditional wooden form has been completely metamorphosed by a stone technique well illustrated in the many castles and large houses of the area. Even the bed- and other rece-

Fig. 46. Rhoson Uchaf, St. David's, Pembrokeshire : exterior view.

sses of one house, as we have seen, were barrel-vaulted. In the same way, some of the stone fixtures of the farmhouses found their way in time into the one-roomed cottage of the native tradition where there appears in the *croglofft* cottage, for instance, the *mainc* near the hearth. When we consider, therefore, all the evidence and the probabilities, it is reasonable to conclude that the north Pembrokeshire farmhouses are not an exotic type but represent the survival and modification of a well-established Welsh lay-out adapted to a new stone technique introduced by the castle-builders of Norman and English times. They have preserved, in a greatly modified form, through the durable nature of their stonework, a lay-out, which, because its natural medium was wood, would otherwise have disappeared completely from Wales. The position and character of the massive chimney would appear to be a feature introduced with the new constructional technique.

Fig. 47. Rhoson Uchaf, St. David's, Pembrokeshire : front.

Against these conclusions, it may be argued that the side-aisles of these houses represent merely a solution of the problem of increased space, as Allen has suggested, and that such space was made possible by the front. addition of a number of 'outshuts', for the aisles on both sides do not run the whole length of the 'nave'; furthermore, that one might expect in a stone interpretation of the technique of the wooden basilical house of early Wales the presence of stone pillars where formerly the wooden posts were to be found. I am inclined to doubt such an argument. The side-aisles appear as integral parts of the construction and occur consistently in all the houses. If they were built merely 'to increase the area of the ground floor' the method seems unduly laborious and unpractical when the 'nave' was already roomy enough and extra ground space could be obtained much more easily by an addition to the length of the house which would not involve the roofing problems present in the aisled house. But if it is believed that the builders were working in a long-established tradition— that of the basilical wooden house—then the method adopted in the lay-out of these houses is easily understood. Indeed the peculiar roofing arrangements and the frequent recesses can be adequately explained only if some such tradition is postulated.

Fig. 48. Trefeiddan, St. David's, Pembrokeshire : exterior view.

In such a transition from a wood technique to stone, it is natural to expect a modification—indeed almost an atrophy—of the side-aisles which were only of secondary importance compared with the great 'nave' of the Fig. 49. Trefeiddan, St. David's, Pembrokeshire : detail of front. wooden house, and whose regularity along the length of the wooden house was an integral part of the construction. In a stone technique such regularity was unnecessary and the gradual disappearance of the side aisles would be normal in the development of the traditional house in a new medium.

Fig. 49. Trefeiddan, St. David's, Pembrokeshire : detail of front.

Finally, the posts of the wooden house performed a fundamental function. They held the complete roof (see p. 158). The wattled walls had no constructional significance : they merely enclosed the house. But in the new construction introduced by the castle-builders, the solid stone walls usurped the function of the crucks and bore the weight and thrust of the roof. Consequently stone pillars were not necessary in the new technique which provided recesses walled on three sides.

The conclusion, therefore, that the builders of the first stone houses of this type were working in the well-established native tradition of the wooden basilical house is likely although it cannot be proved.

Fig. 50. Trefeiddan, St. David's, Pembrokeshire : doorway.

§

Half-timbered houses or houses with timber framing have a wide distribution throughout Europe.[1] If the half-timbering technique of the English lowland can be considered one of the glories of English building

---

[1] See for instance the works of J. Strzygowski, e.g. *Der Norden in der bildenden Kunst Westeuropas* (2nd edit., 1928); Brunhes, J. : *Géographze humaine de la France* (1920-6); Trefois, Cl. V. : 'La Technique de la Construction rurale en bois' in *Folk*, 1937, pp. 55-73.

tradition, as indeed it is, 'it is', as Batsford and Fry have emphasized,[1] 'but a little insular flowering of a plant which has other stems and blossoms. The *chalets* and farm buildings of the Swiss and other Alpine peoples are tremendous structures entirely in timber, like that other very individual manifestation, the mast churches of Norway. More nearly akin to our own buildings are the many-storied half-timber houses of western Germany and Alsace—the towering structures of Nuremberg, Rothenburg, and their fellows.' The houses of the Welsh borderland belong to this larger unity but at the same time they show many traces of environmental influence and possibly of native tradition.

Fig. 51. Hendre Einon, St. David's, Pembrokeshire ; fireplace.

The origin of the half-timbering technique in Britain is a problem which has given rise to much conjecture. Associated since the late Middle Ages with a pure English building-tradition it has been assumed that here we have a non-Welsh technique. But we have already seen how the Keltic house in Britain and in Ireland from prehistoric times down to the 9th - 10th

---

[1] Batsford, H., and Fry, C.: *op. cit.*, p. 40.

Fig. 52. Pwllcaerog, St. David's, Pembrokeshire : exterior.

centuries was of timber with the walls between the timbers of woven wattles plastered with lime or clay. In the *Mirabilis Historia Ecclesiastic* III, xxv of the Venerable Bede, the writer speaks of Lindisfarne as *'ecclesiam more Scottorum non de lapide, sed de rohore secto totam composuit'*—this in the year 582. Strzygowski[1] points out that Bede speaks not only of wood-building in general, but also of hewn oak used in this kind of wooden architecture. The phrase is *'tabulis dedolatis iuxta more Scoticorum gentium'*. The *mos Scottorum*, 'the Scotic manner', was to build 'from pieces of oak, with boards hewn off'. This was in contrast to the *mos Romanorum* which was to build in stone, in particular quarried stone. Professor Baldwin Brown[2] concludes that the mos Scottorum was a type of wood-building characteristic of Keltic tradition, and Strzygowski is dogmatic that the 'Scotic manner' 'must clearly have been framework'.[3]

We have to span several centuries to come from the Venerable Bede to John Leiand who travelled in Wales in the 16th century, but in reading his Itinerary we are struck by his insistent description of the building of the Welsh-border towns as *'after the Walche fascio'*[4] *'Mos Scottorum'*, *'Walche fascion'*,—we may be dealing with the same tradition. Newtown (Montgomeryshire) was 'meately welle buildyd after the Walche fascion'; Knighton (Radnorshire), 'a praty towne after the Walsche buildinge'; 'Walsch Pole . . . wel buildid after the Walsch fascion'. It is well to recall here that several Welsh churches are known to have been built of wood, Llanfair Waterdine in the Teme Valley, Trelystan (Montgomeryshire)[5] and 'St. Asaph church was first built of wood'.[6] We know also from old prints that half-timbered work was formerly found well inland in Wales, e.g. at Conwy—a half-timbered street is illustrated by R. Richards (*op. cit.*,p. 204). Early examples still remain at Machynlleth (Montgomeryshire) and were known at Llantrisant (Glamorganshire).

We know therefore that timber framing was a characteristic of building in Wales as in other countries. But whether there was a native Keltic timber-framing tradition is an open question. One view may be

---

[1] Strzygowski, J. : *Early Church Art in Northern Europe* (1928), p. 87.

[2] Brown, G. Baldwin : *The Arts in Early England* (1925), II, p. 42.

[3] *Op. cit.,* p. 88.

[4] Leland, J.: *Itinerary in Wales 1536-9* (1906 edit.), pp. 11, 12, 125. It will be seen below (p. 156) that even two centuries after Leiand's time, Newtown for instance had a preponderance of timber-framed houses. The same was the case in the other towns mentioned and it is reasonable to suppose that this was the feature to which Leiand referred when he wrote of 'buildinge'. In later times the universal practice of plastering and rough-casting these houses concealed their character.

[5] Willans, J. B. : *The Byways of Montgomeryshire* (1905), plate on p. 89.

[6] Pennant, T. : *The Journey to Snowdon* (1781), p. 18.

quoted. 'Fortunatus, if we have read him aright', writes Strzygowski,[1] 'an Italian appointed to a Keltic bishopric admired half-timber work on the Moselle and Rhine; that is to say, that it was not usual in Roman and Keltic territory for houses but was an essential feature of Teutonic houses'. Strzygowski is prepared to believe that half-timbering 'was already the normal pre-Christian type among Teutonic peoples' on the Continent and that in these isles the Keltic peoples were forerunners in the same technique. Whether the timber-framed houses of the border counties of Cheshire, Shropshire and Herefordshire are a development of a Teutonic tradition or whether they represent the persistence of a 'Walsche fascion' of early times is not a matter which can or need be determined by the present writer. It is at any rate clear that the timber-framed houses of Wales belong in character to the tradition represented in those counties. The characteristics of the building-tradition in those three counties have been discussed at such length by several writers that it is unnecessary here to discuss them in detail.[2]

Jones[3] has pointed out how in Cheshire great elaboration is shown due to the introduction of oblique struts, curved braces, pierced quatrefoils and fleurs-de-lys, geometrical patternings and gables and dormers over-sailing. In Shropshire and Herefordshire on the other hand the elaboration is less marked. The timbering is simpler and shows less striving for effect, depending mostly on vertical and horizontal lines. In those two counties 'stout oak sills are laid horizontally upon a low wall of stone or brick and into these are tenoned upright posts, the larger ones being placed at the external angles. Upon these upright posts, horizontal heads are placed just below the level of the chamber floor, and the intervening spaces formed into panels with thinner pieces, the whole being framed and tenoned together and pinned with oak pins. The joists of the floor are then laid, resting upon the horizontal heads, and frequently being partly supported by internal beams, which appear in the ceilings of the house. Upon the ends of the joists the sill of the upper storey is laid, and the framing is, more or less, a repetition of that below, the head forming a support for the spars of the roof, and being frequently carried over at the ends as a wall plate to carry the overhanging gables.'[4]

It is these styles that we find in eastern Wales, most of the houses being in the Shropshire-Herefordshire style although the influence of

---

[1] *Op. cit.*, p. 110.

[2] See for instance Hoime, C.: *Old English Country Cottages* (1906); Jones, S. R. : *English Village Homes* (1936); Moss, Fletcher : *Pilgrimages to Old Homes mostly on the Welsh Border* (1903), Oliver, B. : op. cit. ; Parkinson, J., and Ould,, E. A. : *op. cit.*

[3] Jones, S. R. : *op. cit.,* p. 112.

[4] Parkinson, J., and Ould, E. A, : *op. cit.,* p. 70.

Cheshire is to be seen in the Vale of Clwyd and the north-eastern area.
Rhydonnen, Gellifor (plate 55) and Galch Hill, near Denbigh (plate 56)—

Fig. 53.   Bachelldre, Churchstoke, Montgomeryshire.

the home of Sir Richard Myddelton (died 1575-6)—are examples of the simplest form of this technique. Plas Uchaf, Eglwysegl (well illustrated by Moss: op. cit., pp. 74-81) is an excellent instance of the simple Denbighshire fashion (plate 57). Any traveller in the Vale of Clwyd who has time to wander around the town of Ruthin will find a large number of such half-timbered houses.

But the technique in all its glory is to be found in east central Wales;, in the whole of the upper Severn valley from Welshpool to Llanidloes and to Caersws. South of Caersws it spreads into the Trefeglwys-Llawr-y-glyn area; westwards, examples are found in the Carno area, and far beyond the watershed in the Dyfi Valley. The westernmost example is Tyno Hir on the Montgomeryshire-Cardiganshire border overlooking the Dyfi estuary and Cardigan Bay. In north-east Montgomeryshire, good examples are found in the Llanfyllin area.

Llanidloes was described in 1798[1] as a town of 'houses . . . built with laths and mud filling up the intermediate spaces of a timber frame', 'a mean town, composed chiefly of lath and plaster houses'.[2] Newtown too was 'rather mean, from the number of lath and plaster buildings with which [it] abounds'.[3] John Evans[4] writes of Newtown: 'The houses being principally half-timbered, i.e. timber frames, with the intermediate spaces filled up with whattle and dab.' These descriptions are quoted here since they show how universal in these towns was the timber-framing technique. The 19th century however saw a widespread destruction of a large number of the buildings in these towns and in other areas of the timber zone, so that the examples left to the student are far less numerous than formerly. One such house recently demolished was Lymore (plate 58), 'in date probably one of the last half-timber houses constructed in the kingdom and in size and interest the most important in Montgomeryshire'.[5] Lymore was situated in the Montgomery district and was built as late as 1675 by Edward, third Lord Herbert of Chirbury. Its internal arrangements have been fully described.[6] The greater part of the house fabric was constructed of timber framing.

Another house which has now disappeared was Penrhos (plate 59) in the Meifod district. It has been well illustrated by Moss[7] and Willans.[1] It

---

[1] Bingley, W. : *op. cit.,* I, p. 484.

[2] *Pinnock's County Histories : North Wales* (1822), p. 83.

[3] *Ibid.,* p. 82.

[4] Evans, J. : *North Wales,* p. 31.

[5] *Mont. Coll.,* XVIII, 1885, p. 168.

[6] *Ibid.,* pp. 155-63.

[7] *Op. cit.,* pp. 277-9.

was built in the early 17th century and was a good example of the 'brick-nogging' method of filling the spaces of the timber-framework. Other examples (illustrated by Moss) in Montgomeryshire are Llwyn and Treder-

Fig. 54.   Lack, Churchstoke, Montgomeryshire.

---

[1] *Op. cit.*, p. 197.

wen. Trewem (plate 60) about a mile from Buttington, of early 17th century date, is a good example of the type in which the hall is the dominant feature.[1] The village of Berriew has a large number of timber-framed houses. Bachelldre (fig. 53) and Lack (fig. 54) in the Churchstoke district should also be noted.

In the district centring upon Caersws there are several excellent examples of half-timbered work. At Caersws itself is Maes-mawr,[2] a house of interesting plan (plate 61). Here the rooms are not grouped around the hall but the hall itself, the parlour and the staircases are all grouped around, a great central chimney. Penarth (plate 62), in the Newtown district is on the normal H-shaped hall plan,[3] in plain, heavy timbering. Parc-pen-Prys,[4] Llandinam Hall,[5] Pertheirin,[6] Plasau Duon[7] and Ysgafell—, well-known in Welsh Nonconformist history—are all in the Newtown-Caersws-Carno district.

The Trefeglwys area, south of Caersws, has a number of fine examples of,timber-framed work. Of these Talgarth[8]—once the seat of the Lords of Arwystli—and Rhyd-y-carw[9] are amongst the finest. Talgarth (plate 63) has timber-framed walls worked with upright quarterings with heavy sills, angle-posts and braces and the gable is enriched by quarterings framed diagonally. The house has been considerably mutilated. Rhyd-y-carw (plate 64) has undergone less restoration. Its lower storey is framed of uprights on a sill laid on stone foundations. The upper storey is divided into squares filled with diagonal quartering. Each gable-end is of stone with projecting chimneys.

The third area of half-timbered houses is the east-Radnorshire-Brcck-nockshire district. Here we come to the John Abel country and it has already been indicated how the technique spreads along the valleys of the Usk, Wye and Teme as indeed it does along the Upper Severn valley.

Brecon town today shows little evidence of half-timbered work but it is of interest to note that John Abel is said to have been the builder of the old town hall there. John Abel's dates are generally given as 1577-1674 but

---

[1] *Mont. Coll.* XVII, 1884, pp. 157-61 ; Moss, F. : *op. cit.,* pp. 283-6.

[2] *Ibid.* pp. 152-7 ; Moss, F.: *op. cit.,* pp. 269-71.

[3] *Ibid.* pp. 359-60 ; Moss, F. : *op, cit.,* pp. 272-3.

[4] *Ibid.* pp. 361-8 ; Moss, F. : *op. cit.,* pp. 264-8.

[5] *Ibid.* XIX, 1886, pp. 351-4.

[6] *Ibid.* pp. 125-8.

[7] *Ibid.* XXXIII, 1904, p. 169.

[8] *Ibid.* XXI, 1887, pp. 303-6.

[9] *Ibid.* pp. 306-10.

Wickham[1] points out that the date of his death as recorded on his tombstone at Sarnesfield is 1694. If this is correct his birth-year must have been later than 1577. It has been stressed[2] that the Herefordshire—Shropshire technique is superior to that of East Anglia, due not only to the abundance of timber material but also to the influence of Abel himself. He is said to have been a native of Hereford and his influence on the building-technique of this part of the Welsh border was very considerable. According to Theophilus Jones[3] Brecon Town Hall was built by Abel in 1624 and the facade is illustrated in his plate V.

This southernmost area of the timber-framing technique extends throughout east Radnorshire and east Brecknockshire—indeed from Tretower on the Monmouthshire border northwards—while isolated instances have been known as far south as the edges of the Vale of Glamorgan, e.g. at Llantrisant. The towns of Presteigne and Knighton present excellent examples of the technique. Most students of Welsh architecture know of the wealth of timber work of a fine quality in the churches (e.g. Partrishow and Llananno) of this area. A detailed survey parish by parish is necessary to discover the present distribution of such houses and it is to be regretted that in the past the Royal Commission on Ancient Monuments in Wales neglected this aspect of their work. The Inventories relating to Denbighshire, Montgomeryshire and Radnorshire do not illustrate any such houses. Finally it should be stated that while most of the examples referred to are small mansions, the same technique is found throughout the area in the construction of cottages. There is the same low wall and the same timber framing.

In those districts where the timber-framing zone merges into the moor-land, the timber-growth is smaller in quality and quantity and here a modification in type is noticeable. Many of the houses have their exteriors boarded horizontally and the characteristic black-and-white pattern is less in evidence. This is well illustrated in the Trefeglwys-Llawr-y-glyn district. The valley floor here as we have seen has magnificent examples of timber-framing at its best, as at Talgarth and Rhyd-y-carw but in the moorland between Llawr-y-glyn and Staylittle the boarded type is evident. A small farmhouse from this district is illustrated (plate 65). Such boarding is frequently to be met with throughout eastern Montgomeryshire. This is also true of the other districts, e.g. Radnorshire.[4] At the same time, simple

---

[1] Wickham, A. K. : *The Villages of England* (1932), p.44.

[2] Parkinson, J., and Ould, E. A. : *op. cit.,* p. 75.

[3] Jones, Theophilus : *A History of the County of Brecknock* (1809), II, p. 109.

[4] See for example, Llanbedr Hall in the parish of Llanbedr Painscastle, figured in the *Inventory of Ancient Monuments in Radnorshire*, fig. 33.

timber-framing of an unpretentious character also occurs on the moorland, as may be seen at Abernodwydd, Llangadfan (plate 9), and in several other instances.

CHAPTER VIII

Building Construction

THE many details of the construction of Welsh houses deserve the close attention of the serious student of folk culture and in particular of Welsh architecture. It is impossible in a volume of this nature to do more than draw the reader's attention to general considerations and to some outstanding features. For information of a technical character, a comprehensive series of scale drawings of the various constructional details is required, and it is to be hoped that much material of this character will be prepared for the remaining volumes of the Inventories of the Royal Commission on Ancient Monuments in Wales and Monmouthshire. Any treatment of the practical aspects of construction must be perfunctory until the Royal Commission and our trained architects collect a mass of measured drawings of buildings from every part of Wales. The interested reader should also consult the various volumes of *Archaeologia Cambrensis*, in particular some of the papers of the late H. Harold Hughes.

Cruck Construction

We have already referred in more than one chapter to houses of cruck-construction and this method must now be considered in greater detail. The only extensive study of the method in England is to be found in Innocent's book[1] but the information there given concerning cruck-buildings in Wales is both inadequate and at times incorrect. His frequent uncorroborated references to 'the Welsh tradition', in particular,[2] may well lead the unwary astray.

Cruck-constructed buildings consist of pairs of curved timbers set up in inverted V form, the timbers crossing at the apex of the triangle thus formed, so forming a fork in which the ridge-piece is fitted (figs. 55-6 and plates 67-8). The rafters and purlins are placed on the crucks which therefore bear the whole weight of the roof. The walls of such buildings were therefore of secondary importance and served principally to enclose them: they bore no constructional relationship to the roof.

The fact is often overlooked that in past ages Britain was extensively covered with forests. Oak trees were easily found of such a variety of

---

[1] Innocent, C. F.: *op. cit.*, pp. 23-72.

[2] *Ibid.*, e.g. pp. 28-9.

growth that building timbers of every kind were obtainable from them. And so, as Innocent points out,[1] 'it was possible to find an oak-tree naturally bent in such a form that, when set up in the building, part would be up-right and parallel to the wall and part sloping in line with the roof, or to find one with a great branch bent at such an angle to the bole that when the tree was set up in the building the branch would be in line with the roof. If such a tree were split and the halves placed opposite to each other, with the ends of the bent trunk or branch crossing at their summits, they would form a fork in which the ridge-tree would securely rest.'

Evidence from Wales shows that this method of construction was at one time widespread through the country. Here again it must be stressed that only a parish-by-parish survey can determine accurately the former distribution of the technique in Wales and unfortunately many of these buildings have been destroyed. It is of interest however to note the extent of the technique in Wales as far as our present information reveals it. Hughes and North[2] have described a large number of houses so constructed in Caernarvonshire and several are illustrated by them. The technique occurs in Denbighshire (plates 67, 68); in Flintshire (plate 69); Merionethshire (plate 70 and fig. 55); Montgomeryshire (e.g. Bryn-mawr, Llanerfyl, plate 48 and Llansilin, fig. 56 and plate 71); Radnorshire (Ciloerwynt and Llannerch-y-cawr, figs. 19,20 and plates 31,34 were so built) ; Cardiganshire (plate 72. I found that several buildings recently destroyed in the county were of cruck-construction, e.g. one at Blaenpennal), Carmarthenshire (there were formerly good examples at Cwm Crymlyn, Llandeilo and Pant-mawr, New Inn. Glan'rafon-ddu ganol, Tal-y-llychau, is another instance. I am informed that in the old house, six pairs of crucks still stand).

Many examples have been recorded from Caernarvonshire. William Williams[3] writes of Ty'n-y-weirglodd, Llanberis : ' . . yr hen gwpwl coed sydd â'i ddeupen yn y ddaear. Chwilid am goeden yn meddu cangen yn taflu allan ar ongl osgoawl tebyg i gwpl tŷ : wedi ei chael torid y goeden yn y bôn, yna plenid hi ar ei phen yn y lle y bwriedid i'r tŷ fod, a'r gangen gam yn taflu i fyny at Ie y grib fel cwpl. Wedi cael digon o'r cyfryw goed, plenid hwy yn gyfochrog ac adeiladid mur cerrig amdanynt.' [the old timber couple with two ends in the earth. A tree was searched for having a branch thrown out at an oblique angle like a house-couple; when it was found, the tree was cut at its base and then set up where the house was to be, the branch throwing itself up to the ridge like a couple (i.e. a normal rafter).

---

[1] *Ibid.*, p. 27.

[2] *Op. cit.*

[3] Williams, W. : *Hynafiaethau. . . Plwyf Llanberis,* p. 66.

After securing a number of such trees, they were planted in parallel rows and a stone wall built around them]. It will be seen that this description tallies in detail with Innocent's statement, Hughes and North, in their study of a number of houses so built, several of which they illustrate, ascribe them to the 14th - 15th centuries. 'The characteristic of these cottages, they write,[1]

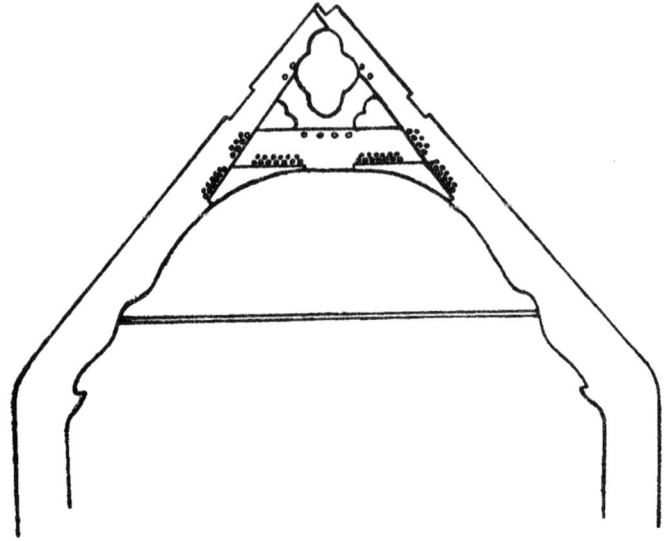

Fig. 55. Cruck at Hafod Ysbyty, Merionethshire.

seems to have been that the roof principals were composed each of two great curved pieces of oak, starting from the floor, against the side walls and meeting at the ridge.' They illustrate and describe examples where the main timbering consists only of one pair of such crucks, set near the centre of the building, and a ridge-piece whose centre rests in the cruck-fork and its ends on the stone gables. These, in fact, seem to be the three free timbers of the Welsh Laws (see p. 111) and as Campbell has pointed out[2] 'these houses consisting] of a pair of crucks and a ridge-tree . . . can be shown to be of great antiquity. . . This form . . . can be studied over a large area' and can well be pre-Christian in type. Other examples, consisting of these three timbers were examined during the present survey in at least three other counties.

---

[1] *Op. cit.*, pp. 5-6.
[2] *Folkliv*, 1937, p. 213.

Hughes and North stress the important point that this type of construction 'was doubtless a survival of wattle or wood-building where it was obviously necessary for the principals to carry the thrust to the ground'. They add that 'the nave of old Llanfair Fechan church was roofed in this manner and there is good ground for thinking that the old churches were roofed in this way previous to the introduction of the close-couple roofs by the Latin monks'. These authors' argument therefore is that the cruck method of construction was that of the native Welsh tradition, a view supported—as we have seen—by the evidence adduced in Chapter VI. Innocent, following the widespread English view that little or nothing in architectural tradition in Wales could have been pre-English, doubts the conclusions of Hughes and North in this instance and maintains that what probably occurred was 'an English superiority in building, which was followed by the Welsh'. This conclusion he bases on a 'tradition' which he discovered 'by personal enquiries among old men in North Wales' that cruck buildings 'were forced upon the Welsh by their English conquerors'! Later he asserts dogmatically that 'Welsh tradition tells that the bent-tree principals were introduced by the English'.[1]

A tradition of a somewhat different nature is referred to by a Welsh writer in 1901. Describing Cwm Berwyn, a farmhouse in the uplands above Tregaron (Cardiganshire) he writes :[2] 'Tŷ hir cadarn gyda'i furiau yn agos ddwy lath o drwch a'i ffenestri uchaf yn onglog, ac yn myned trwy y to, a grisiau cerrig llydain yn arwain i'r llofft, gyda holl goed ei do o ruddin derw, a'i gyplau yn cyrraedd i'r ddaear, fel yr oedd cyplau holl hen dai Cymru hyd tua'r 16eg ganrif... Yn agos i gychwyniad y gormes Normanaidd gwnaed dcddf na châi Cymro adeiladu tŷ yn uwch nag uchder y cyplau. . . Er mwyn osgoi cael eu pennau beunydd yn y to darfu iddynt osod traed i'r cyplau. Yr oedd y traed yn rhan o'r cyplau, ac yn cyrraedd i'r ddaear ac yn y modd hwnnw yr oeddynt yn llwyddo i gadw llythyren y gyfraith a chael yn fynych ddau lawr i'r tŷ. Byddid yn adeiladu muriau o dan y to uchder traed y cyplau ond ni fyddai y cyplau'n pwyso ar y muriau. Dyfais ychwanegol oedd adeiladu gwadn llydan gryn lawer yn lletach na'r muriau llydain uchder llawr isaf y tŷ ac ar hwnnw gosodid sail y muriau a byddai traed y cyplau'n gorffwys arno. Yr oedd y ddwy ddyfais hon i'w gweld yn Cwm Berwyn.' [A long solid house with its walls nearly two yards thick and its top windows angular and going through the roof (i.e. dormer windows), wide stone steps leading to the upper floor; all the roof timbers of heart-of-oak, the couples reaching to the earth, *as did the couples of all old Welsh houses until about the 16th century. . .* About the beginning of the Norman conquest, a law was

---

[1] Innocent, C. F.: *op. cit.,* pp. 28-9.

[2] Parry, W. T., in *Cymru,* 1901, II, pp. 282-3.

passed that no Welshman was to build a house higher than the height of the couples. . . To prevent their heads from continually striking against the roof, they gave the couples feet. These were part of the couples and reached to the floor and in this way they managed to succeed to keep the letter of the law and have also two floors in the house. They built walls under the roof the height of the lower stage of the couples but the couples did not rest on the walls. An additional device was to build a broad base much wider than the thick walls to the height of the ground floor of the house : on this was placed the foundation of the walls and the feet of the couples. Both devices were to be seen at Cwm Berwyn.]

While this passage describes the cruck method in detail and shows that it was a normal technique in Wales, its attempt at explaining the reason for the adoption of crucks is unfounded. No law of the kind referred to is known and I am grateful to Sir John Edward Lloyd, F.B.A., for confirming this.[1] The statement is obviously a popular attempt, probably originating in the 19th century, at explaining the 'strange' cruck construction and has no foundation in fact. But it should be noted that Parry does not maintain that 'bent-tree principals were introduced by the English' as Innocent's 'tradition' asserts.

Many of the examples of crucks in north Wales have angularly-bent timbers (see for instance plate 68) and Innocent believes these to be 'apparently older than the forms in which the timber is bowed or irregularly curved. This is to be inferred from their rare occurrence in England and their prevalence in Wales, and the difficulty which there must have been in obtaining timber of the required shape.'[2] It is difficult however to know whether such chronology is possible and whether the shape of the crucks did not depend at all times on the local material available.

Crucks in Denbighshire are here illustrated by an example from the Yale district (plate 68) and another from Llandyrnog (plate 67). On the Montgomeryshire-Denbighshire border at Llansilin, Monroe[3] has described and illustrated (fig. 56 and plate 71) a magnificent example which he believes to be late 16th or early 17th century in date. Fig. 55 illustrates an interesting cruck at Hafod Ysbyty in the parish of Ffestiniog.[4]

---

[1] In a letter dated 23rd July, 1939. Sir John adds that 4 Hen. IV, cap 31 (that no Welshman was to keep 'castle, fortress nor house defensive other than was permitted in Edward I's time) may have been the basis of the tradition .

[2] Innocent, C. F. : *op. cit.*, p. 33.

[3] Monroe, L. : 'A Crutch Roof truss at Lloran Ganol, Montgomeryshire' in *Arch. Camb.*, 1933, pp. 122-5.

[4] Williams, G. J. : *Hanes Plwyf Ffestiniog* (1882), p. 56.

Several examples of crucks were noted in Cardiganshire. Llwyn-rhys (above p. 68)—like Cwm Berwyn—was built in this way, with large curved pieces of oak resting on stones at the floor level. It is fortunate that these were photographed in 1901[1] (plate 72). Such stone-rests were a normal feature of many cruck-buildings.

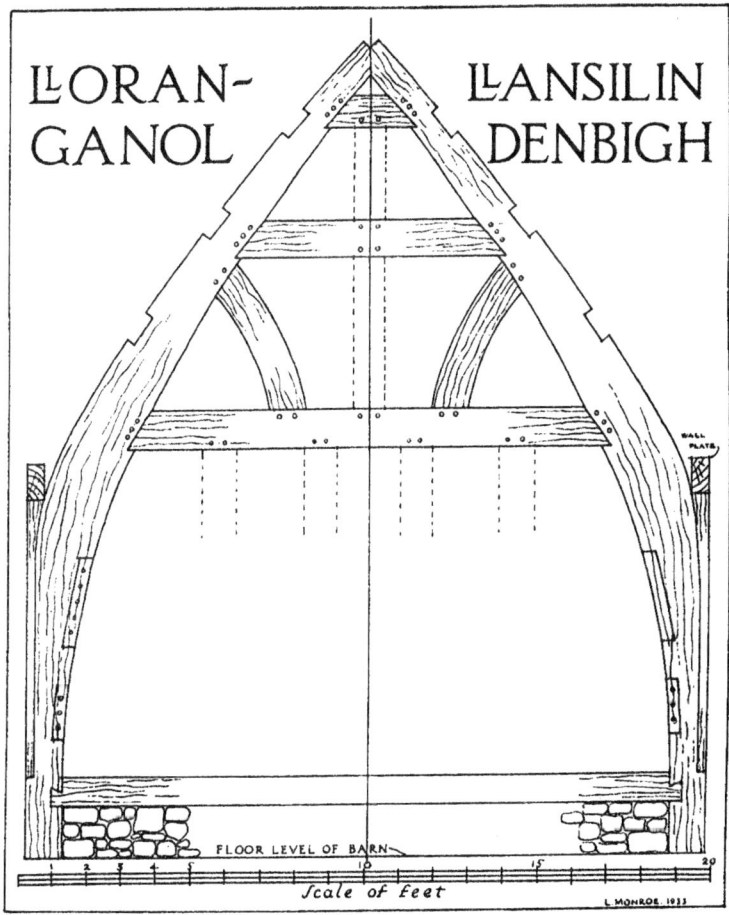

Fig. 56. Cruck at Lloran Ganol, Llansilin, Denbighshire.

The later development of cruck construction is fully discussed by Hughes and North. They show how in a house near Conway the side posts

---

[1] See also Cymru, 1901, II, p. 271.

and rafters are separate. In this case, the wall-piece or side-posts do not extend down to the floor but are carried half-way only down the wall. Innocent draws attention to an example (plate 73) at Cae Crwn, Glanmorfa, Portmadoc, where the curve of the crucks is reduced to a bend at the foot of the principal rafter and the crucks here 'approximate in arrangement to a collar beam-truss'.[1] These examples are obviously experiments in new manners. How the new methods developed in Wales is a long and complex

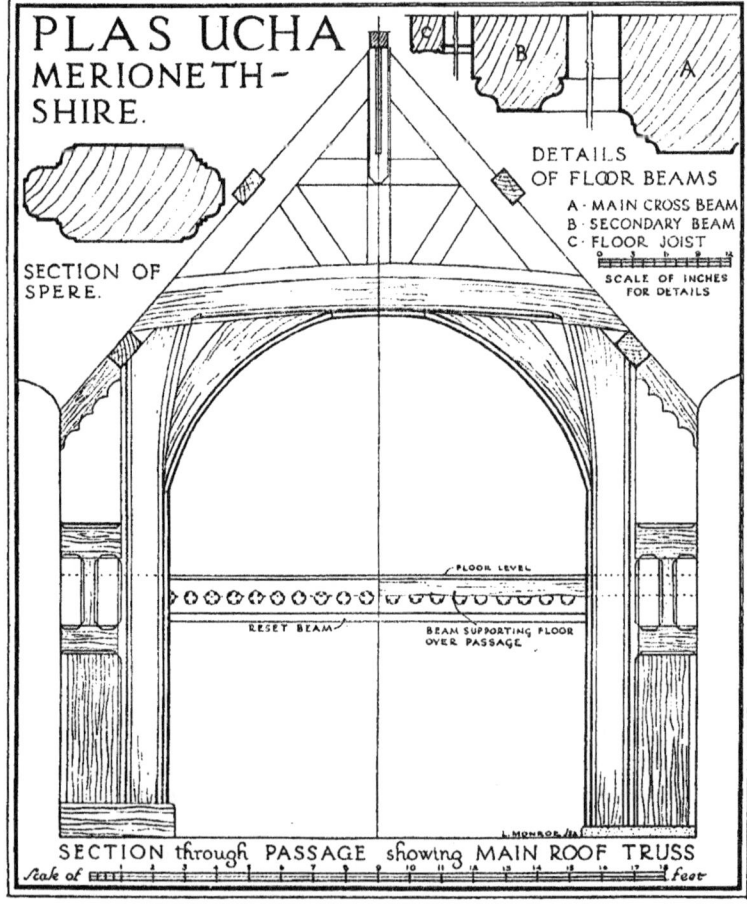

PLAS UCHA
MERIONETH-
SHIRE.

DETAILS
OF FLOOR BEAMS
A · MAIN CROSS BEAM
B · SECONDARY BEAM
C · FLOOR JOIST

SCALE OF INCHES
FOR DETAILS

SECTION OF
SPERE.

FLOOR LEVEL

RESET BEAM

BEAM SUPPORTING FLOOR
OVER PASSAGE

L. MONROE fu.

SECTION through PASSAGE showing MAIN ROOF TRUSS

Scale of   feet

Fig. 57. Truss at Plas Ucha, Llangar, Merionethshire.

---

[1] Innocent, C. F. : *op. cit.*, p. 64.

story with which we are not concerned but one aspect of it may be illustrated. Monroe has described[1] the elaborate timbering (fig. 57) of Plas Ucha, Llangar, Merionethshire, where there is found 'so far west as this part of Merionethshire an example of a type of roof described. . . as being typical of the west of England'.

What is the history of the cruck method of construction? 'The cruck buildings' writes Innocent, 'seem to be as peculiarly British as the bull-dog or the red grouse.' Is this view justified? We have already seen that the method seems to have been a feature of early Keltic building in these isles. But it would be wrong to allow the reader to suppose that the matter can be left there. The *stritsular* of the Jutland peasant buildings of Denmark should be regarded—though not identical—as parallel examples of this construction[2] but as Erixon has pointed out[3] they 'do not show the arch form'. Erixon makes a tentative statement that while evidence is wanting outside the British Isles of supports of exact cruck form, 'certain indications are to be found that it had at one time a considerable distribution in West Europe. Thus in Northern Spain . . . I have met with arched sloping struts to vertical roof supports and in France as in Belgium, Holland and north-west Germany are to be found half-timbered gable-ends with inclined, often arched struts and inclined supports which should be relics of cruck-like roof supports occurring there at one time in the far past.'[4] Similar evidence is forthcoming from prehistoric times in Denmark and Gotland and even from the Stone Age in Sweden and west Germany, according to Erixon, who concludes that cruck-construction 'in its wider, more primary significance' should be regarded as a local west European-Scandinavian form. That the method was normal in the highland zone of Britain is to be seen from the fact that it occurs throughout Wales and also in the Scottish Isles.[5] In the same way Vrcim[6] has shown that the *bael'lje* construction of the Lapps is the equivalent of the cruck method and holds that the stave-buildings of north and west Norway have also passed through the cruck stage. We are therefore justified in concluding that the cruck technique, in variations probably affected environmentally, (*a*) is a feature of building-construction throughout north-western Europe; (*b*) was well-established throughout the greater part of Wales.

---

[1] Monroe, L.; 'Plas Ucha, Llangar, Merioneth', in *Arch. Camb.*, 1933, pp. 80-7.

[2] Zangenberg, H. : *op. cit.,* p. 82.

[3] Erixon, S., in *Folkliv*, 1937, p. 141.

[4] *Ibid.,* pp. 141-2.

[5] Roussell, A. : *op. cit.,* p. 46.

[6] Vreim, Halvor: 'The Ancient Settlements in Finnmark', in *Folkltv,* 1937,, pp. 198-202

Walls

It is axiomatic that there are few areas where the use of stone as the principal building material for the walls of country buildings of modern type is of any great antiquity. Consequently it is logical to consider first the various methods adopted to build walls in materials other than stone.

The Laws, as we have seen, refer to wattled walls, i.e. walls of timber hurdles with twigs or wattles interwoven between the posts. The Black Book of St. David's speaks[1] of 'rods for making and covering houses', 'all the materials and rods for the mill and build and wattle at their own cost', and 'they should wattle all houses requiring it'. This wattling is the *bangor* of the Welsh Laws and its use reaches back to prehistoric times : there are examples of wattling from the Glastonbury Lake Village, and from Romano-British sites. The Romans used wattling for various purposes, such as at Caersws, Montgomeryshire, for the lining of wells. We have seen (p. 38) Giraldus's reference to its use in Wales in his time.

A natural development was the application of daub to the wattle : this might be clay or lime plaster, strengthened with straw or cowhair and cow-dung, the finished walling being known as wattle-and-daub. The foundation for the daub varied. I have noted in addition to the use of interwoven twigs or wattles the use of reeds (as at Rumney, Monmouthshire), brambles in Merionethshire (Innocent too quotes their use at St. Florence, Pembrokeshire[2]), straw at Tal-y-llyn (Merioneth—see p. 91—and Llŷn (Caernarvonshire) and riven oak laths at Welshpool (Montgomeryshire). Innocent has shown how the natural round rods of the wattle gave way to squared timbers[3] as at St. Issell's (Pembrokeshire), and Conway (Caernarvonshire) while at a cottage near Marros (Carmarthenshire) the square uprights were fixed horizontally in imitation of contemporary plaster on laths. A late 19th-century observer[4] describing the construction of cottages in west Montgomeryshire, writes : 'Gwnelid y bythynod . . . ar gyn lleied o draul ac a ellid. Gwnelid y talcen lle y byddai'r tân ac weithiau'r ddau o ga-ig wedi'u gosod mewn cymrwd clai, ac yn wir ar adegau gwneid muriau da yn y dull hwn. Yn yr wyneb a'r cefn gwnaethid ffrâm o goed a rhwng y coed hynny drachefn plethid gwiail ac yna byddid yn plastro y gwiail â chymrwd clai eto.' [The cottages . . . were made at as

---

[1] *Op. cit.,* pp. 81, 113, 317.

[2] Innocent, C. F.: *op. cit.,* p. 130.

[3] *Ibid.*

[4] Peate, D.: *op. cit.*

little expense as possible. The gable end where the fire was placed and sometimes both ends were made of stone fixed with clay-mortar, and indeed at times good walls were made in this way. In the front and back, a wooden frame was made and between the timbers rods were woven : these rods were then plastered with clay-mortar.] The demolition of several cottages in the area recently—all of them of 19th-century date—has revealed a widespread use of wattle-and- daub, particularly in interior partition walls. The use of wattle-and-daub in half-timbered work is too well-known to need discussion here.

Innocent has described a form of wattle-and-daub wall in which the wattle is of two thicknesses, with the daub and mud packed between them. W. K. Sullivan[1] has shown that some of the round houses of Ireland 'were made by making two basket-like cylinders, one within the other and separated by an annular space of about a foot, by inserting upright posts in the ground and weaving hazel wattles between, the annular space being filled with clay'. Innocent has seen[2] in some remains in Caernarvonshire 'round banks of earth which indicate former round houses' constructed in this way.

It is probable that this double-wattling method gave rise to the mud wall in its many forms. The inevitable decay of the wattlework would show the builders that the clay or mud filling itself provided a good durable wall. Reference has already been made (Chapter II) to the distribution of houses with mud walls, but certain types deserve notice here. J. Evans refers to the cottages of Caernarvonshire as of 'turf or clay with chopped rushes';[3] he refers in particular to cottages in Llŷn as having 'walls built of what in Devonshire is termed *cobb* ; that is an argillaceous earth having straw or rushes mixed with it while in a state of paste, and then laid layer upon layer, between boards'.[4] Culley in 1867 describes the cottages of south-west Wales as 'of mud (clay and straw mixed)'.[5] Many of the cottages of Dyffryn Aeron and mid-Cardiganshire are described by a contemporary observer as having 'welydd pridd a gwellt, weithiau'n 4 troedfedd o drwch.   Ceid rhes ohonynt ar eu traed felly tua 1913 yn ardal Llwyncelyn'[6] [walls of mud and straw, sometimes 4 feet thick. A row of such houses remained about 1913 at Llwyncelyn]. This writer adds : 'Nid oes dim arbennig yng ngwaith coed yr

---

[1] Quoted by Innocent, *op. cit.,* pp. 133-4.

[2] *Op. cit.,* p. 134.

[3] Evans, J. : *Letters . . . North Wales in the year 1798,* p. 160.

[4] Evans, J. : *The Beauties of England and Wales,* XVII (1812), p. 322.

[5] *Third Report of the Commission on the Employment of Children, Young Persons and Women in Agriculture* (1867), p. 48.

[6] Mr. W. Beynon Davies, M.A., in a written communication, August, 1939.

hen fythynnod rhagor na mai derw wedi'i naddu â bwyell ydoedd. Ni cheid hoelion ond *pinolion* pren i'w cadw yn eu lle.' [There is nothing to note specially in the woodwork of the old cottages except that it was adzed oak. Wooden pins, not nails, were used for securing the woodwork.] Hughes and North[1] refer to a cottage near Llanbedr-y-cennin, of 14th-century date, whose walls averaged 3½ ft. These were built of mud on inside and outside but the core was filled with bran, 'doubtless with the idea of keeping damp from the house'. Finally we have seen that clod houses were known in Radnorshire and in north Wales.

It may be concluded therefore that turf or clods on the one hand and mud, prepared in various ways, were the normal materials used in many parts of Wales until recent times and in houses constructed of these materials, the older technique of wattle-and-daub persisted in the interior partitioning. Evans in the quotation above referred to 'cob' walls; the term 'clom' is also known in Pembrokeshire. 'Clom' is possibly related to Welsh *clwm*, *clymu*, 'to tie up, to bind'. The term 'cob' is well known in Devonshire. The practice was to lay a stone foundation and subsequently to build the clom (when wet and soft as mortar) in layers, periods of a week or more being given each layer to dry and harden before the next was put on.

When stone walls superseded wattle in north Wales, the stones were at first daubed like the wattle with a mixture of clay and cow-dung,[2] a practice also found in England. In most of the stone cottages of Caernarvonshire, boulders of enormous size have been used for the foundations (plate 74) extending up to the ground floor level, the walling above being of smaller stones. One reason for this was that the large stones could be more easily handled at the base of the wall but such a use, it has been pointed out,[3] is a survival from the times when the walls were built of wood and wattling. The earliest use of stone in folk building appears to have been to form a foundation on which rested the sill of the wooden framework of the wall and such stones were used without having been dressed—and were often river stones or stones from boulder-clay. They often formed a projecting plinth rising to the floor level. Hughes and North have shown how in the early 19th-century when the walling stones of houses in Caernarvonshire were trimmed with hammers, the chippings from them were used for pegging the work, with the result that because of the neatness of the pegging, whitewash was abandoned.[4] Pegging of a similar character

---

[1] *Op. cit.*, pp. 12-13.

[2] North, H. L. : *Old Churches of Arllechwedd* (1906), p. 78.

[3] Innocent, C. F.: *op. cit.*, p. 118.

[4] *Op. cit.*, p. 32.

with small stones, the wall being then whitewashed, was a pre-19th century feature.

Most of the slate buildings of north Wales show a similar gradation of stones, large at the base of the walls and becoming smaller as the walls rise. The feature adds to the attractiveness of the building.

Dry walling is met with throughout Wales in old buildings. Plate 75 shows the dry-walled porch of a cottage at the foot of Snowdon. Wigstead (1797) described the houses of Dolgelley as 'composed for the most part of stones piled up with neither mortar or cement of any sort'.[1] Evans (1798) writes of the cottages of the Mawddwy district (Merionethshire) as 'built of fragments of quartz and limestone, piled one upon another in an irregular manner, with the interstices filled up with lumps of turf or peat'.[2] Aikin gives a similar description of the houses of Cwm Cyn-llwyd in the same neighbourhood.[3] The Education Commissioners (1847) describe the houses of the Tal-y-llyn district in the same county as 'formed of a few loose fragments of rock and shale piled together without mortar or whitewash'.[4]

In Caernarvonshire, J. Evans writes (1812)[5] 'in situations exposed to westerly winds the walls of dwelling houses are not unusually guarded with slates. These are applied to the walls squameously or clinker fashion, that is, each succeeding row upwards partially overlaying the one below... put on neatly with black or dark grey mortar (of quick or boiling lime and sharp sand, intermixed with coal ashes or forge cinders)'. The same feature is found in parts of Pembrokeshire (see p. 20) and latterly in some other districts.

Walls were sometimes colour-washed inside, the application of coat after coat of colouring giving the wall after many years a plastered appearance. Or they were lime-plastered. In a cottage at Brogynin, Penrhyn-coch, north Cardiganshire, which had dry-stone walling, such a plaster was discovered painted with a pleasing floral pattern and dado line in orange and dark red (plate 76) of early 17th-century type. A coin of Queen Elizabeth's period is reputed to have been found in the plaster. The site is of considerable Welsh interest since it is believed to have been the birthplace of Dafydd ap Gwilym, the famous 14th-century poet. The building concerned is, of course, of much later date, but Dafydd's own reference to the painted decoration of walls is pertinent :

---

[1] *Op. cit.*, p. 44.

[2] Evans, J.: *Letters . . . North Wales in the year 1708*, p. 66.

[3] Aikin, A.: *Journal of a Tour through North Wales* (1797), pp. 32-3.

[4] *Report*, p. 63.

[5] Evans, J.: *Beauties of England and Wales* (1812), XVII, pp. 322-3.

Ai gwaeth bod y mur gwyn
Dan y calch, doniog cylchyn,
No phe rhoddid, geubrid gŵr,
Punt er dyfod o'r paentiwr
I baentio'n hardd bwyntiau'n hoyw,
Lie arloes â lliw eurloyw,
A lliwiau glân ychwaneg,
A lluniau tariannau teg ?[1]

[Is it worse that the white wall, (the room's) uneven surround, is under the lime than if a pound were given to the painter, artificial (work)man, to come and paint fair spots and (to paint) an empty space with golden colour and other beautiful colours and (to paint) the shape of fair shields ?]

We have seen how in dry walling, the spaces between the stones were plugged with turf. Very often as in some of the circular 'pigsties', an outer covering of turf was found effective with such walls and when a mortar was used, it was generally clay—the *cymrwd clai* referred to by Peate above. This clay mortar was used in the Roman station at Caersws (Montgomeryshire) and continued in use for folk-building into the 19th century. A combination of stone and mud for walling was also met with: we have already referred (p. 28) to an example of this construction at Llandybie (Carmarthenshire) where the walls were made of river pebbles (*popyls*) and mud. In houses in this district too are found walls built of large stones on the inside and outside, with small pebbles in the core, all fixed with a lime and clay mortar. The Rev. Gomer M. Roberts informs me that though Llandybi'e produces a good supply of lime, Aber-thaw (Glamorganshire) lime was considered best for making this mortar and it was imported into the district from an early date.

Floors

'Native earth' was more commonly used throughout Wales for floors than it was even for walls. 'The floor', writes J. Evans in 1798 of a cottage near Barmouth (Merionethshire) 'was the native soil, rendered very hard and uneven from long and unequal pressure'.[2] Culley's description (*supra*) in 1867 of the 'ordinary form of cottage in south Wales' proceeds : 'The floor is usually of mud or puddled clay.' The present writer's own home had such a floor in its kitchen at the end of the 19th century and, describing the cottages of west Montgomeryshire in the 19th century, David Peate observes : 'Llawr

---

[1] Williams, Ifor and Roberts, Thomas : *Dafydd ap Gwilym a'i Gyfoeswyr* (1935), p. 25.

[2] Evans, J. : *Letters . . . North Wales in 1798*, p. 115.

daear a fyddai iddynt braidd yn ddieithriad, gosodid ychydig gerrig geirwon ar yr aelwyd'.[1] [Almost without exception, they had earthen floors, a few rough stones being placed on the hearth.] Mr. Sam Ellis describes certain farmhouses in the Garthbeibio district of Montgomeryshire in the late 19th century : 'Llawr pridd oedd yn Tyn-sietin gyda cherrig trwchus ar yr aelwyd. Ymddengys i mi fod cerddediad cenedlaethau ac ysgubell gwraig y tŷ wedi treulio llawr y gegin nes bod yr aelwyd ar dir ychydig yn uwch. Cofiaf fynd yno un noson pan yn hogyn ac eisteddwn ar stôl drithroed. Fe drodd y stôl oddi tanaf ac fe syrthiais wysg fy nghefn.'[2] [Tynsietin had an earthen floor with thick stones on the hearth. It seems to me that the feet of generations and the broom of the housewife had worn the kitchen-floor until the hearth was on a somewhat higher level. I remember going there as a boy one night and sitting on a three-legged stool. The stool turned over and I fell backwards.]

Of Llechog, in the same district, he writes : 'Cegin fawr, rhan ohoni'n llawr pridd. Parthied llawr y gegin, ni fedraf gofio'n iawn faint ohono a orchuddid gan gerrig. Cofiaf yn dda am Gatrin Morus yn porthi'r cŵn mewn twll yn y llawr.' [A large kitchen, part of the floor of earth. Concerning the kitchen floor, I cannot remember exactly how much of it was covered with stone. I well remember Catrin Morus feeding the dogs in a hole in the floor.] The reader may be reminded here of Heilyn Goch's 'hall' in *Breuddwyd Rhonabwy* !

In parts of Caernarvonshire, the hard earthen floors were washed with water containing soot, which in time gave them a smooth shiny surface.[3] On the hearth, white stones were used or decorations made with clay formed into small balls. This clay was dug in the Holyhead district and in Llŷn and sold in Caernarvonshire. These clay balls (or often dock leaves) were used for marking patterns, and such patterns were always to be found around the dresser and the long-case clock—on the *tyle* referred to above (p. 79)—in districts such as Bethel, Caernarvonshire. This custom of decorating floors of all kinds with geometrical patterns was found throughout Wales : the patterns were applied generally by the use of 'hearthstone'—a kind of whiting—and were renewed daily or at each washing of the floor. Examples noted at Solva, Pembrokeshire, in 1908 are illustrated (fig. 58). Another type of flooring met with in south-west Wales was a mixture of earth and lime, which properly mixed formed a good floor, 'with a smooth glazed surface. In some cases, bullocks' blood was added.

---

[1] *Op. cit.*

[2] In a letter dated 19th February, 1938.

[3] Information from Mr. Evan Rowlands, Llanllyfni.

The floor at Plas Watford, near Caerphilly, Glamorganshire, affords a good example of this type.

Fig. 58. Floor designs, Solva, Pembrokeshire, in 1908.

Giraldus Cambrensis has described[1] how the floors of the medieval houses were covered with rushes and green grass on which meals were partaken. This practice continued in at least one district of Caernarvonshire to within living memory. I am informed :[2] 'Mewn hen dai sydd yn adfeilion ar lechwedd y Bwlch Mawr, fe fyddai taenu brwyn a rhedyn ar y llawr a rhoi platiau pren ar y rhedyn sych ac yna gwledda ar y caws, y potas a'r cig a'r llaeth.' [In old houses now in ruins on the slopes of the Bwlch Mawr, rushes and fern would be strewn on the floor and on the dry fern were placed wooden platters, and then, feasting on the cheese, the broth and the meat and milk.] Mr. Ffransis Payne informs me that brick and stone floors were so strewn in parts of Radnorshire during his boyhood as tavern floors are still strewn with sawdust. The practice of using rushes also continued in the churches of Wales until a comparatively late date. John Evans (1798) describing the church at Mallwyd (Merionethshire) writes that 'the floor [was] covered with rushes, a practice almost universal through Wales'.[3] Cradock found that in 1776 the floor of Dolgelley (Merionethshire) church 'is only clay covered deep with rushes'.[4]

Mr. Evan Rowlands of Llanllyfni, Caernarvonshire, informs me that in his district he remembers—sixty years ago—the earthen floors being

---

[1] *Descriptio*, cap. X.

[2] By Mr. Evan Rowlands, Llanllyfni.

[3] Evans, J. : *Letters . . . North Wales in the year 1798*, p. 55.

[4] Cradock, Joseph : An *Account of some of the most romantic parts of North Wales* .(1777), p. 26.

sanded, and that this was known to him in the Rhondda Valley (Glamorganshire) as recently as twenty years ago. The practice was indeed widespread.

In the eastern half of Montgomeryshire where the half-timbered technique is normal, there are floors of attractive construction and design. These are the well-known 'pitched' floors formed of small stones or pebbles set on edge, cobble wise, forming geometrical patterns. These floors are now rapidly being destroyed. I found that housewives complained of the difficulty of keeping them clean, others—*sunt lachrymae rerum !*—wished to cover their floors with linoleum and the stones cut through it in a short time. Scores of these floors have therefore been torn up and relaid with tiles. As for the distribution of the pitching-technique, it is found in exterior work and in stables, etc., over a large area and is not confined to Wales. In housefloors, this technique is found in Montgomeryshire, Carmarthenshire (e.g. the Llandybie district) and Cardiganshire (e.g. Rhydlewis, Llangrannog, and the Llannonn district). Further inquiry may possibly reveal- a wider distribution. Wright[1] in his references to the word 'pitch', gives as a definition 'to pave with small uneven stones set up edgeways' and quotes its use from Lancashire, Cheshire, Derbyshire, Northamptonshire, Herefordshire, Hampshire, the Isle of Wight, Wiltshire, Somersetshire and Devonshire. It is obvious however that in several of these counties, the term is used for *external* paving but a quotation from west Somersetshire ('Will 'ee have the floor a-put in way brick or else will 'ee hab'm a-pitcht ?') may indicate that such floors are also known there.

M. F. H. Lloyd describing Abernodwydd, Llangadfan, Montgomeryshire,[2] writes : 'All rooms on the ground floor are paved with cobbles; this carefully executed floor is an interesting example remaining practically entirc.' I noticed when I visited the house that the initials of the? pitcher are worked in the floor in white pebbles.

Plasau Duon, Llanwnnog, Montgomeryshire, was described in 1904.[3] It was then stated that 'the floor of the kitchen is paved with small stones set edgewise in squares of alternate patterns, with a circle in the centre of the room enclosing a diamond square similarly treatcd'. 'As far as my experience goes' writes the then editor of *Mont. Coll.*, 'it is unique for such a position.' This floor was photographed in 1939 and is illustrated in plate 77. A floor of similar character but of a less pleasing design is found at Penrhiw, Trefeglwys (plate 78). The Trefeglwys district indeed formerly

---

[1] Wright, Joseph : *The English Dialect Dictionary* (1903), IV, p. 527.

[2] *Op. cit*, pp. 84-5.

[3] *Mont. Coll.*, 1904, p. 110.

had many examples. I am informed[1] as follows : 'Dyma rai o'r ffermdai y ceir hwynt: Penddôl, Pen-y-graig, Rhyd-y-carw, Talgarth, ac ymron bob un o'r tyddynnod lleiaf. Credaf fod yno un go dda ers talm ar gegin y Ffinnant. Ofnaf fod rhai wedi'u codi yn yr ugain mlynedd diwethaf a'u llorio efo *tiles* coch neu las.' [These are some of the farm-houses where they are found : Penddol, Pen-y-graig, Rhyd-y-carw, Tal-garth and nearly all the smaller *tyddynnod*. I believe that there used to be a good example in the kitchen at Ffinnant. I fear that some have been pulled up during the last twenty years and floored with red or blue tiles.] There are several examples too in Carno parish. Pryce in his 'History of the Parish of Llandysilio' (Montgo-meryshire)[2] writes : 'The farmhouses and cottages of that period [had] the floors paved with small pebbles, clay or cement, and occasionally with tiles or flagstones.'

Flag-stones were introduced in many areas where local supplies were available and such supplies 'overflowed' into neighbouring districts. The slate quarries of north Wales for instance provided flooring for a large area and in some parts of the north-Wales counties flagstone flooring was —and still is—a normal feature. In the same way, floors of Pennant stone are to be found in south Wales. The reconstructed farmhouse-kitchen in the National Museum of Wales is so floored from material acquired from a Brecknockshire farmhouse.

Roofs

Roof coverings in Wales as in neighbouring countries have consisted until recently of two classes of materials : thatch[3] and stone. These will be considered here in turn.

Thatch in the sense of vegetable matter, in Wales has consisted of many materials : turf, fern, heather, heath, rushes or reeds, and straw. Very often two or more of these materials were used together, but not always. Ap Vychan writes[4] of his home, Tan-y-castell, Llanuwchllyn, Merionethshire, as 'tŷ bychan a'i do o redyn y mynydd-dir' [a small house with its roof of mountain fern]. Bwlch Du, Mynydd Hiraethog, Denbighshire, on the road from Cerrig-y-drudion to Denbigh is described in 1916 as having a heather

---

[1] By the Reverend Stephen 0. Tudor, M.A., B.D. (letter dated 17th February, 1939), who was brought up at Rhyd-y-carw.

[2] *Op. cit.,* p. 258.

[3] The term 'thatch' is now only applied to roof coverings of vegetable matter and is so used here. But it should be remembered that the old English 'thack' originally applied to roof coverings of all kinds.

[4] *Cymru,* 1892, II, p. 14.

roof.[1] When I visited it in 1938, the roof had a heather under-thatch covered with rush thatching, the ridge being formed of sods.

An under-thatch indeed has always been a common feature. The Land Commissioners (1896) describe as normal—particularly of Carmarthenshire—a roof thus built: 'On the rafters are laid rough boughs and twigs as a lower layer, on which is again placed another layer, of rushes, heather or fem, which in turn is covered by a proper thatch of straw.'[2] It seems however that the lowest layer was often of wattle. This is illustrated in the Strata Florida (Cardiganshire) house, fig. 35. At Llanberis (Caernarvonshire), Williams writes (1892) of a 'tô o wiail plethedig'[3] —[a roof of woven rods]. At Tal-y-llyn (Merionethshire) the 1847 Education Commissioners state: 'The roofs are wattled.'[4] Of west Montgomeryshire, Peate writes (1887): 'Gwnelid y to trwy osod coed o'r cant i fyny i'r nenbren o bob tu ac yna plethid hwy wrth y nenbren a gwiail. Gosodid gwiail cryfion ar draws y rhai hyn ac yna toid yn gyffredin â brwyn yr hyn a wnaed yn drwchus ac a orffenid yn lled drefnus.'[5] [The roof was made by placing timbers from the wallplate up to the ridgepiece on both sides : they were then woven to the ridgepiece with withes. Strong withes were placed across them and the roof was then generally thatched with rushes, which was done thickly and finished off neatly.]

John Evans described (1798) the roofs of the cottages of parts of Caernarvonshire in some detail.[6] 'The walls are about six feet high over which are raised maiden poles not even stripped of their bark for rafters, and pegged at top and bottom; a few smaller ones interwoven serve the place of laths ; over these is placed heath or rushes, kept down by ropes of the latter, extending netwise over them.' Plate 79 illustrates the woodwork of a Caernarvonshire cottage (Tan-yr-ardd, Rhostryfan) which had a roof of rods tied together over the principal rafters, then covered with clods and a slate roofing on top.

Throughout the upland area where thatching was formerly widespread, the use of straw was limited. A writer in 1918 speaks of a cottage at Llanfihangel Glyn Myfyr (Denbighshire) the roof of which had a combination of rushes, straw and heather—'ei do o frwyn a gwellt a manrug

[1] *Cymru*, 1916, II, p. 79.

[2] *Report*, p. 693.

[3] Williams, W. : *Hynafiaethau . . . Plwyf Llanberis* (1892), p. 80.

[4] *Report*, p. 63.

[5] *Op. cit.*

[6] Evans, J. : *Letters . . . North Wales in 1798*, pp. 160-1.

y mynydd'.[1] Hughes and North[2] write of reed-thatching, by which presumably they mean rush-thatching, as formerly a common feature in the Snowdonian area. They point out that the thatch was tied with withes to wattling woven in and out of the rafters or in some examples pegged to them. Plate 37 shows a rush-thatched cottage in Cardiganshire. Rushes are now used in the Llandybie district of Carmarthenshire[3] but formerly straw was used and the rush thatch is found not to be so durable as straw. The old cottages had a straw thatch without exception as also did several of the farmhouses. Broom and heather together with fern were used to make a good foundation for the straw.

It was undoubtedly in the Vale of Glamorgan that the straw-thatching technique was most fully developed in Wales. Gwallter Mechain writes:[4] 'The origin of this neat thatching is in the prevailing practice of the county in hand-reaping their wheat-crops, without any confusion of ears and straw. A similar care is taken in thrashing on the floor. The stalks are crushed as little as possible. When taken up to be bound into whisps, called bellies, an iron hand-rake is sometimes used to comb out the loose or straggling straw. Sometimes the straw is drawn through an instrument, such as flax-dressers use, called a heckle. The butt-ends of the whisps are struck against the floor to make them even; which are then neatly bound with a twisted bandage of straw and laid aside for the thatcher's use. . . . The straw is very little crushed by the flail in thrashing; and even where thrashing machines are used, they are so constructed that the straw does not pass through them so as to be rendered thereby in their opinion of less value for thatch-work. . . . The best straw in the opinion of the thatchers is that growing on the strong soil of the blue and grey lias limestone from St. Donat's to Pennarth cliffs. . . Notwithstanding the neatness and thickness of the Glamorgan thatch-work, it is said it will not last without repairing for more than 15 to 18 years , whereas in the more slovenly manner in which thatching is done in other inland counties it frequently lasts from 20 to 25 years. There the straw is considerably crushed in thrashing and is thrown promiscuously to the side of a pond or river to be well watered. It is then drawn from the wet couch and bound into sizeable bundles and these again laid in regular wetted heaps of several feet or yards and every layer wetted in succession. When fermentation commences, which is known by the heating of the heap, then is the time to lay it on the building; the straw

---

[1] *Cymru*, 1918, I, p. 71.

[2] *Op. cit.*, pp. 45-6.

[3] Information from Reverend Gomer M. Roberts (letter dated 25th October, 1939).

[4] Davies, W. : *General View of the Agriculture and Domestic Economy of South Wales* (1815), I, pp. 140-3.

yielding a vegetable gluten which is supposed to render the thatch more firm and durable. . . Broom mixed with fermented straw makes a durable thatch.' Plate 49 illustrates a Vale of Glamorgan cottage straw-thatched in 1937.

There are two methods of thatching well illustrated in Welsh practice. The first is the scolp thatch whereby the under-thatch is first secured to the timbering of the roof by means of straw bands. 'Small whisps or pilions of straw, neatly bound, are laid across and bound to the spars of the roof writes Gwallter Mechain,[1] 'as a foundation for the upper covering which is laid at right angle to the former layer. The thatcher divides the prepared whisp into two or three handfuls, which he lays on in succession, holding them firmly at the top with his left hand, whilst he is smacking the butt-ends with his right hand, to force the straw into a level line parallel with the spars or roof; fastening each handful in succession with a bent and twisted stick called a scolp, and so proceeds until the roof be covered.' The term *scolp* or *scollop* is found both in Glamorganshire and in south Pembrokeshire 'and is found in Irish as *sgolb*, a thatching peg, and it seems to follow the so-called "Celtic-fringe" under variants as *scob, scope, scolp* and perhaps *scrobe* in Scotland, Ireland and Northumberland'.[2] In west Glamorganshire the form *sgilp* is also found. By this method therefore the top thatch is held down by 'ledgers' or rods which are secured by the hairpin-like scolps and by straw ropes held down in a similar manner (plates 82-4). Mr. T. J. David, probably the finest exponent of the thatching craft in Wales today, informs me that the underthatch is always sewn or bound to the roof. Today the sewing is done with tarred twine, but in the past in Glamorganshire long brambles were used for this purpose. Mr. David confirms Gwallter Mechain's description (above), particularly his statement concerning the 'best straw'.

The second method found in Wales of securing the thatch is the rope-thatch. By this method the thatch is held down by a net of ropes crossing at right angles, the ends of which were either weighted with stones which hung loose or were secured to stone or wooden pins set in the walls below the eaves (see plate 19). A good example of such a rope thatch is illustrated in *Cymru*, 1899, II, p. 101. The ropes—of straw or rushes, etc.—were made by means of the rope-winders still to be found in the countryside. Rope-thatching is found throughout the Keltic areas of the British Isles but now seems to be practised in Wales only on stacks, the wooden pegs being pushed into the sides.

---

[1] *Ibid.*, p. 140.

[2] Innocent, C. F.: *op. cit.*, p. 199.

The use of fissile stone for roofing has been known in Wales from at least Roman times and examples of stone roofing are well known from the various Roman sites. Stone tiles were of course much used in medieval times : note, for example, the reference to Corndon (Montgomeryshire) stone in the 15th century (above p. 129). Stone used for roofing in Wales can be divided into two main classes : (*a*) certain sedimentary and metamorphic rocks which have a fissile quality. But whereas slate may be cut in almost any thickness, rocks like shale and flagstone can only be split along the original plane of deposition into sheets the thickness of which is determined by that of the original beds. Such sheets were used for tiling on old buildings, e.g. a Roman villa at Llantwit Major (Glamorganshire) and many medieval buildings. The weight of such roofing generally necessitated a steep pitch in the roof. (*b*) Slate. There are several kinds to be found in Wales : in north Wales, the Cambrian and Ordovician strata of Caernarvonshire and Merionethshire and the Silurian strata of Denbighshire provide roofing slates. The Cambrian strata (the Bethesda-Llanberis-Nantlle area) provide purplish or green slates , the Ordovician strata (Blaenau Ffestiniog) provide slates darker in colour and finer in texture while the Silurian slates of Denbighshire are less smooth in texture and are less finely cleaved. In south Wales, the Ordovician rocks of Pembrokeshire and west Carmarthenshire provide pale grey, green or blue slates, some of the Pembrokeshire slates having a rough, spotted appearance.

Romano-British tiles were of various shapes, hexagonal, rhomboid etc. and some of these shapes persisted in parts of Wales until modern times. Several details illustrating this continuity of tradition could be mentioned. The builder of the Roman villa at Llantwit Major, wrote John Storrie,[1] 'had finished the ridge of the roof with channelled oolite stones, worked to make a water-tight ridge, and covering the junction of the upper rows of both sides; This seems to be also done at Cefn Mabli [Monmouthshire] where, the old style of roof being more in keeping with the character of the roof, the tilestone roof is still retained.' In the National Museum of Wales there are a number of (Pennant) ridge-stones from the Caerphilly (Glamorganshire) district. They are an inch in thickness and are in pairs cut to be interlocking (plate 80). By such an interlocking method, they were held only by their own weight while the tiles of the roof were secured by a dowel of wood driven into the timbering of the roof through holes in the tiles. The method seems to have been well-known in Wales and the border counties. Hughes and North refer too to ridges of clay and lime-and-hair mortar[2] and when ridge-tiles were used in the Caernarfon district

---

[1] 'A Genuine Welsh Antiquity', in the *South Wales News*, 27th August, 1901.

[2] *Op. cit.*, p. 61.

they were often coloured white and black or white and red alternately. Williams[1] refers to a house at Llanberis (Caernarvonshire) in 1806 which had a slated roof but with 'grass' (presumably clods) on the ridge and parts of the roof.

It was formerly the custom to bed stone tiles and slates on vegetable material such as hay, straw or moss. Innocent points out that in the 15th century, hay and straw were bought to be laid under the slating of St. Peter's Church, Oxford[2] and concludes that the custom was probably the survival of the roof covering of the earliest buildings. It also helped to keep out water and to make the house warm, since the earliest slates were hooked on to the wattling and there was no method of rendering them behind. An existing example (in ruins) of such a roof is mentioned above—Tan-yr-ardd, Rhostryfan (plate 79).

In north Wales, sphagnum moss was used for such bedding and from time to time the moss-man came round and with a long flat iron implement would tuck the fresh moss up under the slates from the outside.[3] Indeed these early slates, about ½ to ⅜in. thick, came to be known as *cerrig mwsog* (moss stone). Their precursors, the earliest type known in north Wales, were from ½ to ¾ in. thick and measured about 5 in. x 10 in. About the beginning of the 19th century, 'ton slates' (so called because they were sold by weight) made their appearance. They were similar in character to the cerrig mwsog 'but whereas the latter are generally not larger than 5 inches by 10 inches to 7 inches by 12 inches, the former are often enormous, 1 foot 6 inches by 2 feet not being at all uncommon'.[4] An example in the National Museum of Wales measures 4 ft. by 2 ft. 8 in. The next development was to fix the sizes of slates in the quarries. Though at first they retained their small and thick character, they were soon replaced by thin uniform slates which by their indiscriminate use have done much to ruin the beauty of the countryside. To quote William Morris :[5] 'Thin Welsh Blue Slates (one of the greatest curses of the age).'

The older small un-uniform Welsh slates are still to be seen on old buildings in many parts of the country : they were exported too and were used, for instance, on the roofs of some of the Cambridge colleges.[6]

---

[1] Williams, W. : *Hynafiaethau . . . Plwyf Llanberis*, p. 70.

[2] *Op. cit.*, p. 181.

[3] North, H. L. : *op. cit.*, p. 100.

[4] Hughes, H. H., and North, H. L. : *op. cit.*, pp. 46-7.

[5] *The Collected Works of William Morris*, Vol. XXII (1914), p. 409.

[6] Innocent, C. F. : *op. cit.*, p. 177.

Mr. Beynon Davies informs me that in central Cardiganshire, 'llechi Aberteifi' (Cardigan slates) have been used, a heavier, thicker and more brittle slate than those of north Wales. In roofing with these, the largest were fixed nearest the eaves, the size of the slates diminishing upwards towards the ridge. On outbuildings, an economy was effected by a reduced use of slates, a method known by the untranslatable term *tô brat*.

In several of the west Wales counties, from Pembrokeshire to Anglesey, where the winds are often of gale force, the roofs are weighted by slabs of quarried stone mortared on to the slates down each of the gables (plate 41)—a well-known feature too in Ireland.

In medieval times, thatch was required by law to be white-washed to reduce the danger of fire. The custom in Wales has survived to be transferred too to the slate roofs. Whitewashed thatch is still to be found occasionally in some of the west-coast villages while the slate roofs are cement- or white-washed. Mortar and cement indeed seem to have taken the place of moss for pointing slates, while the whitewash, which is of little practical use adds to the aesthetic value. This is well illustrated in many Pembrokeshire cottages where the white roofs, toned by the effect of the south-westerly winds, and in harmony with the walls, have a most pleasing effect.

The universal practice of whitewashing in the Welsh countryside down to recent times has already been noted. North has pointed out[1] how some Welsh churches continued the practice 'till quite recent times. Lewis's *Topographical Dictionary* mentions that many were whitewashed as late as 1833, some like Llanrug in Arfon, roof and all.'

Chimneys

In the past, the cottages and farmhouses of Wales have provided evidence of almost every stage in the development of the chimney. We may refer first to the simple hole in the roof. Early in the 19th century John Evans wrote of Caernarvonshire houses that 'many are destitute of chimneys, the smoke making its escape by an aperture at the extremity of the building'[2]— it is not clear whether this was in the roof or not, but it was probably the type he had described earlier (1798) in his letters : 'An aperture in the roof serves for a chimney. This is not made directly over the fire lest the rain should extinguish it but a little distance from the perpendicular line. The

---

[1] North, H. L. : *op. cit.*, p. 83.

[2] Evans, J. : *Beauties of England and Wales* (1812), XVII, p. 322.

smoke therefore as may be expected fills the place before it is able to obtain vent.[1] This is indeed the simplest type of 'chimney' possible.

A development from it was the introduction of the wattle-and-daub louvre. This was a three-sided canopy (the end wall forming the fourth side) of a conical shape fixed about 5 to 6 ft. above the fireplace with its. open apex in the hole in the roof (plate 81). It served to collect and guide the smoke from the fire up to the roof and out. These louvres were in almost all cases of wattle—often indeed almost fine basket-work, and daubed with clay or clay and cow-dung. Cow-dung is still considered by rural builders to be the finest lining possible for chimneys and the writer's father, who was architect for several houses in mid-Wales during the first thirty years of the present century, always insisted on its use. I find by enquiry that the practice is fairly general in the countryside, one of the reasons given being that dried cow-dung withstands the heat and 'hardens like iron' whereas mortar becomes brittle and friable.

Now we have already shown that as a general rule, the roofs of Welsh houses were wattled. We find then not only a wattled roof but a wattled louvre and it was natural that the wattling came to be projected above the ridge to form a chimney 'pot'. In thatched houses this was also thatched (plate 82). But in slated houses the wattled projection of the chimney could not be treated in the same manner as the roof. And so we find Evans describing the houses of the village of Llan-ym-Mawddwy (Merionethshire) in 1798 as having a 'roof. . . covered with broad coarse slates and the chimney formed by a hole surrounded for about two feet high with small sticks [the wattle] kept in place by a rush or hay rope'.[2] Aikin in 1797 had described the houses of Cwm Cynllwyd (Merionethshire) simil-arly : 'The roof is composed of broad irregular pieces of coarse slate, in which a large hole encircled by sticks that are fastened together by a straw rope serves the purpose of a chimney.'[3] In the 19th century however, when brick came into use in country building, the wattled chimney was sometimes encased in brick. Writing of the houses of Brecknockshire, Radnorshire and Cardiganshire, the 1847 Education Commissioners state: 'Brick chimneys are very unusual in these cottages: those which exist are usually in the shape of large cones, the top being of basketwork.'[4]

The inside of the louvre, it has been noticed, was daubed with clay or clay and cow-dung. To reduce the risk of fire, this daub was carried up

---

[1] Evans, J. : *Letters . . . North Wales in 1798*, p. 66.

[2] *Ibid.*

[3] Aikin, A. ; *op. cit.*, p. 33.

[4] *Report*, p. 56.

through the chimney and finished off neatly as a rim above the thatch on the outside (plate 83). So the exterior chimney gradually emerged, This clay rim and the wattle-work which formed its foundation were finally extended to form an exterior chimney of ordinary modern proportions (plate 84). It should be added that in some parts of west Wales, e.g. the New Quay district of Cardiganshire, the projecting wattle-work was encased with wooden boards (plate 85).

Doors, Windows, Partitions

This chapter would not be complete without some reference to miscellaneous details of construction which illustrate the persistence of old traditions in Welsh folk building. The references here are not intended to be exhaustive but only to indicate some features of interest.

We have already seen that the door hurdle was a feature of the houses of the early Laws and that it also figured in a Strata Florida (Cardiganshire) house which was in existence in 1888. Evans describing (in 1798) 'the cottages of Caernarvonshire', writes : 'door there is none : but this deficiency is supplied by a hurdle, formed of a few wattlings and rushes, which in bad weather is raised perpendicular to stop the gap'.[1] There are several references to such an arrangement.

But a feature often met with down to the second half of the 19th century was the harr-hung door. The harr and the hinge both reach in time to at least the Roman period. The hinged door is connected to its frame by a hinge and has been developed in so many ways that a detailed discussion of it is beyond the scope of this work. The harr-hung door however is fundamentally different. No hinge is required, and indeed no independent door-frame since the door is not fixed by means of such accessories.

The harr is formed 'by prolonging the hanging stile of the door so that its upper part, suitably shaped, runs into a hole in the lintel or into a projecting "ear", and its lower part or a pin attached thereto, is fixed in a hole in the threshold : actually the whole door then turns on itself and not on hinges'.[2] This form of door-hanging has a wide distribution in time and space from the ancient Egyptian and Etruscans to modern times. North (1906) mentions that such a door, 'not older than the 16th or 17th century', is to be found at Llanrhychwyn church, Caernarvonshire.[3] The method was undoubtedly a common one throughout the Middle Ages in Britain. Peate,

[1] Evans, J. : *Letters . . . in North Wales in 1798*, p. 161.

[2] Innocent, C. F. : *op. cit.,* p. 239.

[3] North, H. L.: *op. cit.,* p. 103.

writing in 1887, describing the doors of west Montgomeryshire cottages, states : 'Ni byddai uchter y tai hyn i'r cant ond tua dwy lath, ni fyddai'r drws yn fynych ond tua phum troedfedd, a byddai'n rhaid llamu tros wadn derw, neu drothwy, uchel i lawr y tŷ. Gosodid y drws i fyny drwy adael rhan o'i ochr yn hwy yn y ddeupen, y naill i fyned i le wedi ei baratoi iddo yn y trothwy, a'r llall i le cyffelyb yn y capan a dyna'r drws yn troi ar ei golyn.'[1] [The height of these houses to the eaves was only about two yards, the door was often only five feet, and one had to step over a high oak 'sole' or threshold to the floor of the house.   The door was set up by leaving part of its side longer at both ends, one end to go into a place prepared for it in the threshold and the other into a similar place in the lintel, and the door turns on its pivots.]

Windows have never been a prominent feature of folk architecture in Wales. There are many descriptions of houses whose only light was admitted through the doorway. In some instances there were 'lattices for the admission of light, formed by interwoven sticks'.[2] Such a construction described as a 'ventilation panel' is figured by Parkinson and Ould[3] in 'The Buttas' Falconry near Weobley. Hughes and North refer to the development of such a lattice form in wood : it was in use in the cottages in the 17th and 18th centuries.[4] One of these writers, H. L. North, suggests[5] that the wooden lattice with its shutter came in 'probably in the 14th or 15th century' and was followed by the glass lattice window with diamond lead-lights in the 16th and 17th centuries. He points out that good examples of early glazing were to be seen (1906) at Trefriw, Caernarvonshire. But it is interesting to note from Evans's description above that the primitive lattice, in its earliest wattled stage, was found in the same county at the end of the 18th century. Charles Ashton,[6] writing of rural houses in the 19th century, mentions 'tai ag un haner o'r ffenestri yn ddellt neu wiail plethedig'. [Houses with one half of each window of woven laths or withes.]

Hugh Evans, writing of the Merionethshire-Denbighshire border,[7] emphasizes how dark the houses were and how many of them had no window, one reason being the Window Tax.   Peate writes : 'Gadewid lle

---

[1] Peate, D.: *op. cit.*

[2] Evans, J. : *Letters. . . North Wales in 1798*, p. 160 , see also Downes, J. : *The Mountain Decameron* (1836), II, p. 146.

[3] Parkinson, J., and Ould, E. A. : *op. cit.*, plate lxvi.

[4] Hughes, H. H., and North, H. L. : *op. cit.*, p. 15.

[5] North, H. L.: *op. cit.*, p. 99.

[6] Ashton, C. : *'Bywyd Gwledig yng Nghymru' in Cofnodion Eisteddfod Genedlaethol Bangor* 1890, p. 40.

[7] Evans, H. : *op. cit.,* pp. 64-5.

bychan i ffenestr, bychan iawn yn ami fyddai hefyd, a'r gwydr yn aneglur.[1] [A small space was left for a window, very small it often was and the glass not transparent.] An examination of the plates in this volume will show that most of the windows in the older houses were indeed small and few of them were made to open, a fact which explains why windows were *broken* when an inhabitant died, so that his spirit might escape to heaven.

Finally, a type of partitioning which the present survey showed to have been general throughout Wales must be commented upon briefly. This is the 'in-and-out' boarding, illustrated here (plate 86) by an example from Penyberth, Llŷn, Caernarvonshire, a house with features dating back to the end of the 15th century and destroyed by the Air Ministry. In this kind of partition, the boards are not placed in line but alternately backward and forward or 'in-and-out'. This method gives the partition a false appearance of thickness. North[2] has remarked upon its presence as the main partition in the single-roomed cottages of pre-17th century date in Caernarvonshire and at the other extreme of the Welsh countryside I have seen it used with great effect in more than one farmhouse in Monmouthshire.

[1] Peate, D. : *op. cit.*
[2] North, H. L. : *op. cit.,* p. 99.

Epilogue

'Now let us end the talk about those qualities of invention and imagination with a word of memory and of thanks to the designers of time past. Surely it had been pity indeed, if so much of this had been lost as would have been if it had been crushed out by the pride of intellect that will not stoop to look at beauty unless its own kings and great men have had a hand in it. Belike the thoughts of the man who wrought this kind of art could not have been expressed in grander ways or more definitely, or, at least, would not have been; therefore I believe I am not thinking only of my own pleasure, but of the pleasure of many people, when I praise the usefulness of the lives of these men, whose names are long forgotten, but whose works we still wonder at...

'Let us admit that we are living in the time of barbarism betwixt two periods of order, the order of the past and the order of the future, and then, though there may be some of us who think (as I do) that the end of that barbarism is drawing near, and others that it is far distant, yet we can both of us, I the hopeful and you the unhopeful, work together to preserve what relics of the old order are yet left us for the instruction, the pleasure, the hope of the new. So may the times of present war be less disastrous, if but a little; the times of coming peace more fruitful.'[1]

---

[1] *The Collected Works of William Morris*, Vol. XXII, pp 111-12, 317.

Bibliography

THE following list is of works which were of direct value in the preparation of this book or bear direct reference to problems discussed in it. For a complete list of English works published before 1830 on travel in Wales, Welsh topography, history and antiquities—most of which were consulted —the reader should see W. J. Hughes's *Wales and the Welsh in English Literature,* where an exhaustive bibliography appears on pp. 168-78, 189-200. Works of a general historical character are not included here except where they bear specifically on the subject of this work but R. T. Jenkins and W. Rees's *A Bibliography of the History of Wales* (1931) should be consulted for works on, e.g., the political, social and economic background. Periodicals and journals appear in the list only when they contain extensive papers on the subjects discussed: passing references in them are mentioned in the footnotes but not in the list.

Abercrombie, P. and Kelly, S. A.: 'The .Wye Valley Regional Planning Scheme', in *The Welsh Housing and Development Year Book,* 1935, pp. 19-117.

Addy, S. 0. : *The Evolution of the English House.* 1910.

Agriculture, Board of:—
> *General View of the Agriculture of the count[ies] of Monmouth, Radnor, Cardigan, Carmarthen, Brecknock. [Each separately]* 1794.
> *General View of the Agriculture of North Wales.* 1794.
> *General View of the Agriculture of the county of Glamorgan.* 1796.
> *General View of the Agriculture in the county of Perth.* 1799.

Aikin, A. : *Journal of a Tour through North Wales.* 1797.

Allen, J. Romilly : 'Old Farm-Houses with Round Chimneys near St. David's,' in *Arch. Camb.,* 1902, pp. 1-24.

Ancient and Historical Monuments in Wales and Monmouthshire, Royal Commission on. County Inventories :—
> *Montgomery.* 1911.
> *Flint.* 1912.
> *Radnor.* 1913.
> *Denbigh.* 1914.
> *Carmarthen.* 1917.
> *Merioneth.* 1921.
> *Pembroke.* 1925.
> *Anglesey.* 1937.

Anon. : *A Trip to North-Wales.* 1742.

Ashton, C. : 'Bywyd Gwledig yng Nghymru', in *Cofnodion Eisteddfod Genedlaethol Bangor,* 1800, pp. 36-92.

Barber, J. T. : *A Tour throughout South Wales and Monmouthshire.* 1803.

Barnwell, E. L. : 'Domestic Architecture of South Pembrokeshire', in *Arch. Camb.,* 1867, pp. 193-204, 363-74; 1868, pp. 70-84.

Batsford, H. and Fry, C.: *The English Cottage.* 1938.

Bingley, W. : *A Tour round North Wales during the summer of 1798.* 1800.

Bosch-Gimpera, P.: *Etnologia de la Peninsula Iberica.* 1932.

Bowen, Ivor : *The Statutes of Wales.* 1908.

Brown, G. Baldwin : *The Arts in Early England.* 1925.

Brunhes, J. : *Geographic humaine de la France.* 1920-6.

Brunn, D.: *Fortidsminder og Nutidshjem paa Island.* 1928.

Bulleid, A. and Gray, H. St. George : *The Glastonbury Lake Village.* 1911.

Cambrian Directory, The. 1800.

Campbell, Ake : 'Irish Fields and Houses : a study of rural culture', in *Bedloideas,* V, 1935, pp. 57-74.

Campbell, Ake: 'Notes on the Irish House', in *Folkliv,* 1937, pp. 207-34, and *Folk-Liv,* 1938, pp. 173-96.

Cantrill, T. C.: 'The Hut-Circles on Gateholm, Pembrokeshire', in *Arch. Camb.,* 1910, pp. 271-82.

Cardozo, Maria : *Citania e Sabroso.* 1938.

Chaike, H. D.: *An Investigation into the causes of the continued high death-rate from Tuberculosis in certain parts of north Wales.* 1933.

Clark, Graham: *Archaeology and Society.* 1939.

Collingwood, R. G.: *The Archaeology of Roman Britain.* 1930.

Commons' Inclosure, Select Committee on : *Report and Minutes.* 1845.

Covernton, J. G.: 'Romano-British sites at Finchingfield', in *Transactions of the Essex Archaeological Society,* XXII, 1936-9, pp. 309-15.

Cox, A. H. (and others): 'The Geology of the St. David's District, Pembrokeshire',. in *the Proceedings of the Geological Association,* 1930, pp. 241ff.

Cradock, Joseph : *An Account of some of the most romantic parts of North Wales.* 1777.

Danaher, Kevin : 'Old House Types in Oighreacht Ui Chonchubhair', in *Journal of the Royal Society of Antiquaries of Ireland,* LXVIII, 1938, pp. 226-40.

Davies, Ellis : *The Prehistoric and Roman Remains of Denbighshire.* 1929.

Davies, Walter : *General View of the Agriculture and Domestic Economy of North Wales.* 1810.

Davies, Walter: *General View of the Agriculture and Domestic Economy of South Wales.* 2 vols. 1814.

Delamarre, M. J.-B.: 'Contribution a l'etude de l'habitat rudimentaire: les cabanes en pierre seche des environs de Gordes (Vaucluse)', in *Comptes Rendus du, Congres International de Geographic,* Paris, 1931, III, pp. 293-8.

Demangeon, A.: 'L'habitation en France, essai de classification des principaux types', in *Annales de geographie,* XXX, 1920, pp. 352ff.

[Dickinson, W.]: *Cumbriana.* 1875.

Downes, J. : *The Mountain Decameron,* 3 vols. 1836.

Education in Wales, Commissioners of Inquiry into the State of: *Report.* 1847.

Edwards, Griffith : 'History of the parish of Garthbeibio' (Hafotai, or Summer dwellings), in *Montgomeryshire Collections,* VI, 1873, pp. 27-8.

Ellis, T. P. : *Welsh Tribal Law and Custom in the Middle Ages.* 2 vols. 1926.

Employment of Children, Royal Commission on the : *Report.* 1842.

Employment of Children, Young Persons and Women in Agriculture, Commission on the : *Third Report.* 1867.

Erixon, Sigurd: 'Svenska gardstyper', in *Foreningens for svensk kulturkistoria tidskrift Rig,* 1919, pp. 1-39.

Erixon, Sigurd : *Kulturhistoriska avdelningen.* 1925.

Erixon, Sigurd: 'Some primitive constructions and types of lay-out, with their relation to European rural building practice', in *Folkliv,* 1937, pp. 124-55.

Evans, E. Estyn : 'Donegal Survivals', in *Antiquity,* 1939, pp. 207-22.

Evans, G. Nesta : *Social Life in Mid-Eighteenth Century Anglesey.* 1936.

Evans, Hugh : *Cwm Eithin.* 1931.

Evans, J. : *Letters written during a tour through North Wales in 1798.* 1804.

Evans, J. : *Letters written during a tour through South Wales.* 1804.

Evans, John: *The Beauties of England and Wales.* Vol. XVII. 1812.

Evans, T. C. : *History of Llangynwyd.* 1887.

Fenton, R. : *Historical Tour through Pembrokeshire.* Recent edition, 1903.

Fleure, Herbert J. . 'Problems of Welsh Archaeology', in *Arch. Camb.,* 1923, pp.225-42.

Forestry Commission : *Report on Census of Woodlands.* 1924.

Fox, Sir Cyril: 'Peasant Crofts in North Pembrokeshire', in *Antiquity,* 1937, pp. 427-40.

Fox, Sir Cyril: *The Personality of Britain.* 4th edit., 1943.

Fox, Cyril and Aileen: 'Forts and Farms on Margam Mountain, Glamorgan', in *Antiquity,* 1934, pp. 345-413.

Fox, Aileen: 'Dinas Noddfa, Gelligaer Common, Glamorgan. Excavations in 1936', in *Arch. Camb.,* 1937, pp. 247-68.

Fox, Aileen : 'Early Welsh Homesteads on Gelligaer Common, Glamorgan. Excavations in 1938', in *Arch. Camb.,* 1939, pp. 163-99.

Fynes-Clinton, 0. H. : *The Welsh Vocabulary of the Bangor District.* 1913.

Geological Survey : Memoirs :—
    Ammanford. 1907.
    Anglesey. 1919.
    Cardiff. 1912.
    Carmarthen. 1909.
    Flint, Hawarden and Caergwrle. 1924.
    Haver fordwest. 1914.
    Merthyr Tydfil. 2nd edit., 1932.
    Milford. 1916.
    Newport. 2nd edit., 1909.
    Pembroke and Tenby. 1921.
    Pontypridd and Maesteg. 2nd edit., 1917.
    Rhyl, Abergele and Colwyn Bay. 1885
    Wrexham. 1928.

Giffen, A. E. van : 'Der Warf in Ezinge, Provinz Groningen, Holland, und seine westgermanischen Hauser', in *Germania, Anzeiger der Romisch-Germanischen Kommission,* XX, 1936, pp. 40-7.

Gilpin, W. : *Observations on the River Wye and several parts of South Wales . . . in 1770.* 1782.

Godfrey, W. H.: *The English Staircase.* 1911.

Gotch, J. Alfred : *The Growth of the English House.* 1909.

Gotch, J. Alfred : *Old English Houses.* 1925.

Gould, S. Baring (and others) : 'Exploration of Moel Trigarn', in *Arch. Camb;* 1900, pp. 189-211.

Grieg, Sigurd : *Jernaldershus pa Lista.* 1934.

Griffith, Ll. Wyn : *The Wooden Spoon.* 1937.

Gruffydd, W. J.: *Owen Morgan Edwards, Cofiant,* I. 1937.

Harris, H.: *Rhondda MSS.* (in typescript in the National Museum of Wales). n.d.

Hatt, Gudmund : 'Prehistoric Fields in Jylland', in *Acta Archaeologica,* II, 1931, pp. 117-58.

Health, Ministry of: *Report of the Committee of Inquiry into the Anti-Tuberculosis Service in Wales and Monmouthshire.* 1939.

Historical Monuments, England, Royal Commission on :—
>*Herefordshire, I, South-west.* 1931.
>*Herefordshire, II, East.* 1932.
>*Herefordshire, III, North-west.* 1934.

Holme, C.: *Old English Country Cottages.* 1906.

Horsfall-Turner, E. R.: *Walks and Wanderings in County Cardigan,* n.d. [after 1902].

Howe, J. Allen : *The Geology of Building Stones.* 1910.

Hughes, H. Harold : 'Prehistoric Remains on Penmaenmawr (known as Braich y Dinas)', in *Arch. Camb.*, 1923, pp. 243-68.

Hughes, H. Harold and North, H. L.: *The Old Cottages of Snowdonia.* 1908.,

Hutton, W. : *Remarks upon North Wales.* 1803.

Hyde, H. A. : *Welsh Timber Trees.* 1935.

Innocent, C. F. : *The Development of English Building Construction.* 1916.

Jenkins, D. E. : *Bedd Gelert : its facts, fairies, and folk-lore.* 1899.

Jones, Edmund : *A Geological, Historical and Religious Account of the parish of Aberystruth.* 1779.

Jones, 0. Gethin : *Gweithiau Gethin.* 1884.

Jones, R. W. : *Hanes hen furddynod plwyf Llansannan.* 1910.

Jones, S. R.: *English Village Homes.* 1936.

Jones, Theophilus : *A History of the County of Brecknock.* 1805-9.

Jones, Thomas : *Gerallt Gymro : Hones y Daith Trwy Gymru : Disgrifiad o Gymru.* 1938.

Jones, T. Gwynn : 'Social Life as reflected in the Laws of Hywel Dda', in *Aberystwyth Studies,* X, 1928, pp. 103-28.

Jones, T. Gwynn : *Welsh Folklore and Folk Custom.* 1930.

Knoop, D. and Jones, G. P. : *The Medieval Mason.* 1933.

Labour, Royal Commission on: *The Agricultural Labourer. Vol. II. Wales.* Reports by Messrs. D. Lleufer Thomas and C. M. Chapman. 1893.

Labour, Royal Commission on : *The Agricultural Labourer : England, Monmouthshire.* 1893.

Land in Wales and Monmouthshire, The Royal Commission on : *Report, Minutes of Evidence etc.* 7 vols. 1896.

Lange, Konrad: *Haus und Halle : Studien zur Geschichte des antiken Wohn-hauses und der Basilika.* 1885.

Lauridsen, P. : *'Om dansk og tysk Bygningsskik i Senderjyiland',* in *Historisk Tidsskrift, 6, Række,* VI, pp. 43-113.

Laws, E. : *The History of Little England beyond Wales.* 1888.

Leland, J. : *Itinerary in Wales,* 1536-9. 1906 edit.

Lewis, E. A.: 'A Contribution to the commercial history of mediaeval Wales', in *Y Cymmrodor,* XXIV, 1913, pp. 86-118.

Lewis, E. A.: *The Welsh Port Books* (1550-1603). 1927.

Lewis, H. and (others): *Cywyddau Iolo Goch ac Eraill,* 1350-1450. 1925.

Ling, A. G. : 'Peasant Architecture in the Northern Provinces of Spain', in the *Journal of the Royal Institute of British Architects,* Set 3, Vol. 43, 1935-6, pp. 845-63.

Lloyd, Sir John Edward : *Hywel Dda.* 1928.

Lloyd, Sir John Edward : *History of Wales to the Edwardian Conquest.* 2 vols. New edition, 1939.

Lloyd, M. F. H. : 'Abernodwydd', in *Montgomeryshire Collections,* LXIV, 1935-6, pp. 84-5.

Lloyd, N. : *A History of English Brickwork.* 1934.

Loth, J.: 'L'Ystoria Trystan et la Question des Archetypes', in *Revue Celtique,* XXXIV, 1913, pp. 365-96.

Macalister, R. A. S. : *The Archaeology of Ireland.* 1928.

Malkin, B. H. : *The Scenery, Antiquities and Biography of South Wales . . . in 1803.* 1807.

Mathews, W. : *The Miscellaneous Companions.* 1786.

Matley, C. A.: 'The Pre-Cambrian Complex and Associated Rocks of South-western Lleyn', in *Quarterly Journal of the Geological Society,* LXXXIV, 1928, pp. 440-504.

Meidhre, Sean Mac Giolla : 'Some notes on Irish Farm-houses', in *Bealoideas,* VIII, 1938, pp. 196-200.

Meyer, Kuno : 'Eine Episode in "Tristan und Isolde" und das celtische Haus', in *Zeitschrift fur Romanische Philologie,* XXVI, 1902, pp. 716-7.

Monroe, L. : 'A Crutch Roof truss at Lloran Ganol, Montgomeryshire', in *Arch. Camb.,* 1933, pp. 122-5.

Monroe, L.: 'Plas Ucha, Llangar, Merioneth', in *Arch. Camb.,* 1933, pp. 80-7.

Morris, Meredith : *A Glossary of the Demotion Dialect.* 1910.

Morris, R. P. : *Cantref Meirionydd.* 1890.

Morris, William : 'The Influence of Building Materials upon Architecture' (1892), 'The External Coverings of Roofs' (c. 1890), in *The Collected Works of William Morris,* Vol. XXII, pp. 391-409. 1914.

Moss, Fletcher : *Pilgrimages to Old Homes mostly on the Welsh Border.* 1903.

Muhlhausen, L. : 'Contributions to the Study of the Material Culture of the Gaoltacht', in *Journal of the Cork Historical and Archaeological Society,* XXXVIII 1938 and XXXIX, 1939.

Nash-Williams, V. E.: 'An Early Iron Age Hill-Fort at Llanmelin near Caerwent', in *Arch. Camb.,* 1933, pp. 237-346.

Nash-Williams, V. E. : 'Sudbrook Excavations, 1936', in *Arch. Camb.,* 1936, pp. 314-16.

Newell, R. H. : *Letters on the Scenery of Wales.* 1821.

North, F. J. : *The Evolution of the Bristol Channel.* 1929.

North, F. J.: *Coal, and the Coalfields in Wales.* 1931.

North, H. L. : *The Old Churches of Arllechwedd.* 1906.

O'Curry, E. (edited W. K. Sullivan): *On the Manners and Customs of the Ancient Irish.* 3 vols. 1873.

Oliver, B. : *The Cottages of England of the 16th, 17th and 18th centuries.* 1929.

Olsen, Magnus : *Farms and Fanes of Ancient Norway.* 1928.

O'Neil, B. H. St. J.: 'Breiddin Hill Camp Excavations, 1934', in *Arch. Comb.*, 1935, pp. 161-2.

O'Neil, B. H. St. J.: 'Excavations at Breiddin Hill Camp, Montgomeryshire, 1933-35', in *Arch. Camb.*, 1937, pp. 86-128.

O'Neil, B. H. St. J.: 'Excavations at Caerau Ancient Village, Clynnog, Caernarvonshire, 1933 and 1934', in *The Antiquaries Journal*, XVI, 1936, pp. 295-320.

O Riordain, S. P. and O'Kelly, M. J. : 'Old House Types near Lough Gur, Co. Limerick', in *Feil-sgribhinn Eoin Mic Neill,* pp. 227-36. 1940.

Owen, A. : *The Ancient Laws and Institute of Wales.* 2 vols. 1841.

Owen, Elias: 'Arvona Antiqua', in *Arch. Camb.,* 1867, pp. 102-8; 1872, pp. 239-48.

Owen, Elias : 'On the Circular Huts sometimes called *Cyttiau'r Gwyddelod,* and their Inhabitants', in *Y Cymmrodor,* IX, 1888, pp. 120-40.

Owen, George : The Description of Penbrokshire. Edit. 1892.

Parkinson, J. and Ould, E. A. : *Old Cottages, Farm-Houses and other Half-Timber Buildings in Shropshire, Herefordshire and Cheshire.* 1904.

Peate, David : *Hen Ffyrdd a Hen Dai adfeiliedig Llanbrynmair.* (MSS. in private possession). 1887.

Peate, Iorwerth C. : *Guide to the Collection of Welsh Bygones* [in the National Museum of Wales]. 1929.

Peate, Iorwerth C. : *Y Crefftwr yng Nghymru.* 1933.

Peate, Iorwerth C. : *Guide to the Collection Illustrating Welsh Folk Crafts and Industries [in the National Museum of Wales].* 1935.

Peate, Iorwerth C. : 'Some Welsh Houses', in *Antiquity,* 1936, pp. 448-59.

Peate, Iorwerth C.: 'The Double-ended Fire-Dog' in *Antiquity,* 1942, pp. 64-70.

Peate, Iorwerth C.: 'The Pot-oven in Wales' in *Man,* 1943, pp. 9-11.

Pennant, T. : *The Journey to Snowdon.* 1781.

Pennant, T. : *Tours in Wales.* 3 vols. 1810.

Pessler, Wilhelm : *Handbuch der Deutschen Volkskunde.* Band 1-3, *passim.* 1936.

Petersen, Jan : *Gamle gdrdsanlegg i Rogaland.* 2 vols. 1933 and 1936.

Phillips, C. W. : 'The Excavation of a hut site at Pare Dinmor, Penmon, Anglesey', in *Arch. Camb.,* 1932, pp. 247-59.

Phillips, C. W. : 'The Excavation of a hut group at Pant-y-Saer in the parish of Mathafarn-Eithaf, Anglesey', in *Arch. Camb.,* 1934, pp. 1-36.

Pinnock's County Histories : *North Wales.* 1822.

Powell, A. H. : 'Country Building and Handicraft in Ancient Cottages and Farm-houses', in *The Studio Yearbook of Decorative Art,* 1920, pp. 27-48.

Pringle, J. and George, T. N.: British Regional Geology : South Wales. 1937.

Pryce, T E . 'Half-timbered houses of Montgomeryshire', in *Montgomeryshire Collections,* XVII, 1884, pp. 149-64, 359-88 ; XVIII, 1885, pp.155-68, XIX, 1886, pp.125-8, 351-4, XXI, 1887, pp.303-10 ; XXII, 1888, pp.257-60.

Rees, W. : *South Wales and the March,* 1284-1415- 1924.

Rees, T.: *The Beauties of England and Wales.* Vol. XVIII. 1815.

Rhys, J. and Brynmor Jones, D.: *The Welsh People.* 6th edit., 1913.

Richards, Robert: *Cymru'r Oesau Canol.* 1933.

Richards, T. : *Wales under the Indulgence,* 1672-1675. 1928.

R[ichards], W. : *Wallography or The Britton Describ'd.* 1682.

Richmond, I. A.: 'Irish Analogies for the Romano-British Barn Dwelling', in *The Journal of Roman Studies,* XXII, 1932, pp. 96-106.

Richthofen, Boiko Frhr. von: 'Zur Bearbeitung der vorgeschichtlichen und neueren kleinen Rundbauten der Pyrenaenhalbinsel', in *Homenagem a Martins Sarmento,* pp. 332-41. 1933.

Roberts, E. Stanton : *Peniarth MS. 67.* 1918.

Roberts, Gomer M.: *Hanes Plwyf Llandybie.* 1939.

Roberts, T. and Williams, I. : *The Poetical Works of Dafydd Nanmor.* 1923.

R[obinson], G. G.: 'Hut Dwellings in Montgomeryshire', in *Arch. Comb.,* 1880, pp. 25-30.

Robinson, G. W. : 'The Soils of Wales', in *Guide Book for the Excursion round Britain of the Third International Congress of Soil Science,* pp. 260-2. 1935.

Roussell, Aage : *Norse Building Customs in the Scottish Isles.* 1934.

Sayce, R. U. : ' "Hill Top Camps" with special reference to those of north Cardiganshire', in *Trans. Hon. Society of Cymmrodorion,* 1920-1, pp. 99-134.

Seebohm, F. : *The English Village Community.* 1915.

Shuffrey, L. A. : *The English Fireplace and its Accessories.* 1912.

Smith, B. and George, T. N. : *British Regional Geology : North Wales.* 1935.

Stanley, W. 0. : 'On the remains of the ancient circular habitations in Holyhead Island, called Cyttiau'r Gwyddelod, at Ty Mawr, on the S.W. slope of Holyhead Mountain', in *The Archaeological Journal,* XXIV, 1867, pp. 229-42.

Stapledon, [Sir] R. G. (edit.) : *A Survey of the Agricultural and Waste Lands of Wales.* 1936.

Stenberger, M.: 'Remnants of Iron Age Houses on Oland', in *Acta Archaeologica*, II, 1931, pp. 93-104.

Stenberger, M. : *Oland under aldre Jarnaldern.* 1933.

Strzygowski, J. : *Der Norden in der bildenden Kunst Westeuropas.* 1928.

Strzygowski, J. : *Early Church Art in Northern Europe.* 1928.

Tansley, A. G. : *The British Islands and their Vegetation.* 1939.

Thomas, F. W. L.: 'Notice of Beehive Houses in Harris and Lewis', in *Proc. of the Society of Antiquaries of Scotland*, III, 1857-60, pp. 127-44.

Thomas, F. W. L.: 'On the Primitive Dwellings and Hypogea of the Outer Hebrides', in *Proc. of the Society of Antiquaries of Scotland*, VII, 1866-8, pp. 153-95.

Thompson, A. Hamilton : *The English House.* 1936.

Trefois, Cl. V.: 'La Technique de la Construction rurale en bois', in *Folk*, 1937, pp. 55-73.

Vaughan, H. M. : 'A Synopsis of Two Tours made in Wales in 1775 and in 1811' in *Y Cymmrodor*, XXXVIII, 1927, pp. 45-78.

Vreim, H.: 'The Ancient Settlements in Finnmark, Norway : Cabins and Tents', in *Folkliv*, 1937, pp. 169-204.

Wade-Evans, A. W.: *Welsh Medieval Law.* 1909.

Ward, J.: *Romano-British Buildings and Earthworks.* 1911.

Warner, R.: *A Walk through Wales in 1797.* 1798.

Watson, J. : *British and Foreign Building Stones.* 1911.

Wheeler, R. E. M.: 'Roman and Native in Wales : an imperial frontier problem', in *Trans. Hon. Society of Cymmrodorion*, 1920-1, pp. 40-96.

Wheeler, R. E. M.: *Prehistoric and Roman Wales.* 1925.

[Wheeler, R. E. M.]: 'Hut-circles and cattle enclosures .. Blaenrhondda, Glamorgan', in *The Bulletin of the Board of Celtic Studies*, I, 1921-3, p. 70.

Wickham, A. K.: *The Villages of England.* 1932.

Wigstead, H. : *Remarks on a Tour to North and South Wales in the year 1797.* 1800.

Willans, J. B. : *The Byways of Montgomeryshire.* 1905.

Williams, G. J. : Hones Plwyf Ffestiniog. 1882.

Williams, H.: 'The Romano-British Site at Rhostryfan, Caernarvonshire', in *Arch. Camb.*, 1922, pp. 335-45 ; 1923, pp. 87-113.

[Williams], H. Cernyw : *Hynafiaethau Edeyrnion.* 1878.

Williams, Ifor : *Pedeir Keinc y Mabinogi.* 1930.

Williams, Ifor : 'Trystan ac Esyllt', in *Bulletin of the Board of Celtic Studies,* V, 1929-31, pp. 115-29.

Williams, Ifor and Roberts, Thomas: *Cywyddau Dafydd ap Gwilym a'i Gyfoeswyr.* 1935.

Williams, Ifor and Williams, J. Ll.: *Gwaith Guto'r Glyn.* 1939.

Williams, S. W.: 'An Ancient Welsh Farm-House', in *Arch. Camb.*, 1899, pp.320-5.

Williams, W.: *Hynafiaethau a Thraddodiadau Plwyf Llanberis a'r Amgylchoedd.* 1892.

Willis-Bund, J. W.: *The Black Book of St. David's.* 1902.

Young, Arthur: 'A Tour in Wales . . . during two visits in 1776 and 1778', in *Annals of Agriculture,* VIII, 1792, pp. 31-51. [A facsimile reprint was published in 1932 as No. 14 of a *Series of Reprints of Scarce Tracts in Economic and Political Science by* the London School of Economics].

Zangenberg, H.: *Danske Bendergaarde : Grundplaner og Konstruktioner.* 1925.

Index

(A) HOUSES AND SITES
(arranged under counties and localities)

(B) GENERAL

1 Braichmelyn, Dinas Mawddwy, Merionethshire. Note the use
of large boulders of igneous rock in the walling

2 Circular pigsty, Blaen Gwenffrwd, near Llanover, Monmouthshire.
The exterior has been rough-cast

Copyright : National Museum of Wales

3. Circular pigsty, Hendre, Pontypridd, Glamorganshire.

Copyright : National Museum of Wales

4. Circular pigsty, Penddeucae-fach, Bedlinog, Glamorganshire.

5. Circular pigsty. The Downs, Llantwit Major, Glamorganshire.

6. Interior of circular pigsty. The Downs, Llantwit Major, Glamorganshire,
showing the corbelling technique.

7. Circular pigsty, Blaen-ddôl, Usk Valley, Trecastle, Brecknockshire.

8. Charcoal-burners' hut, Rockley, Stainborough, Yorkshire.

Copyright : National Museum of Wales

9. Abernodwydd, Llangadfan, Montgomeryshire, 1937.

10. Farmhouse in the Hautes Alpes. The relationship between the dwelling house and cow-stalls here is essentially different from that in the Welsh long-house

11. Lan, Llandeilo, Carmarthenshire.

12. Ty'r celyn, Llandeilo, Carmarthenshire.

13. Blaenwaun, Llansadwrn, Carmarthenshire.

14. Cwmeilath, Llansadwrn, Carmarthenshire.

Photo: W.R.Hall

15. Llwyn-rhys, Llanbadarn Odwyn, Cardiganshire.

Photo: D. J. Davies.

16. Llwyn-rhys, Llanbadarn Odwyn, Cardiganshire.

17. Nant-y-ffin, Llandeilo, Carmarthenshire.

18. Ty'n-dolau, Llangeitho, Cardiganshire.

19. Ty'n-coed uchaf, Blaencaron, Cardiganshire : front.
Note the pegs for holding the thatch ropes

20. Ty'n-coed uchaf, Blaencaron, Cardiganshire : back.

Copyright : National Museum of Wales

21. Gwastad Gwrda, Abermeurig, Cardiganshire.

Copyright : National Museum of Wales

22. Gwndwn, Pencader, Carmarthenshire.

Copyright : National Museum of Wales

23. Coedlannau, Pencader, Carmarthenshire.

Copyright : National Museum of Wales

24. Doorway, Whithen, Pencader, Carmarthenshire, leading into feeding-walk.
The entrance into the kitchen can be seen on the right.

Copyright : Llew. E. Morgan.

25. Maes-y-bidiau, Abergorlech, Carmarthenshire.

Copyright : Llew. E. Morgan.

26. Erw Domi, Porth-y-rhyd, Carmarthenshire. An inhabited long-
house in ruinous condition

27. Hepste Fawr, Penderyn, Brecknockshire.

28. Hepste Fawr, Penderyn, Brecknockshire : view from
kitchen into cow-house.

29. Dinas Isaf, Pen-y-graig, Rhondda, Glamorganshire.

30. Dinas Isaf, Pen-y-graig, Rhondda, Glamorganshire: view from kitchen doorway into cow-house.

31

31. Ciloerwynt, Dyffryn Claerwen, Radnorshire.

Copyright : Llew. E. Morgan.

32. Cefh-hirfryn, Cynghordy, Carmarthenshire. Note the kiln-room.

Copyright : National Museum of Wales

33. Glan-'rafon, St. Harmon's, Radnorshire.

34. Llannerch-y-cawr, Cwm Elan, Radnorshire.

35. The deserted countryside: a view in the Brecknockshire Beacons upland: note the sites of two former houses and the indications of former ploughing.

Photo : W. R. Hall.

36. Cottage, Pont-rhyd-fendigaid, Cardiganshire, 1910.
(The old lady is wearing a Sunday School long-attendance medal)

37

37. Pensarn-mynach, Cribyn, Cardiganshire. The central 'hump' in the roof is the chimney opening. The addition on the right in (stone-work) is later.

Copyright : National Museum of Wales

38. Great Mains, Llaethdy, Radnorshire.

39. Ffynnon Goy Isaf, Llanychaer, Pembrokeshire: entrance into the *croglofft*

40. Paradise Cottage, Leighton, Welshpool, Montgomeryshire : *croglofft* entrance.

41. Llain-wen isaf, Llanychaer, Pembrokeshire : front.

42. Llain-wen isaf, Llanychaer, Pembrokeshire : back.

43. Carn-deifog fach, Llanychaer, Pembrokeshire :
the *tyddyn* in relation to the moor.

44. Carn-deifog isaf, Llanychaer, Pembrokeshire : interior, roof.

45. Ty'n-rhosgadfa, Rhosgadfan, Caernarvonshire.

46. Llainfadyn, Rhos-isaf, Caernarvonshire.

Copyright : *National Museum of Wales*

47. Cae Rhys, near Llanuwchllyn, Merionethshire, once the home of Sir Owen M. Edwards. The lower door replaces a window.

Copyright : *National Museum of Wales*

48. Bryn-mawr, Llanerfyl, Montgomeryshire : front.

Copyright : *National Museum of Wales*

49. Cottage, St Nicholas, Vale of Glamorgan

50. Gwrhyd Bach, St David's, Pembrokeshire : a recess

51. Llaethdy, St. David's, Pembrokeshire: interior view.

52. Llaethdy, St. David's, Pembrokeshire: interior view.

53. Hendre Einon, St. David's, Pembrokeshire

Photo : Herbert Felton, F.R.P.S.

54. Cottage at Selworthy, Somersetshire: note the form and position of the chimney.

55. Rhydonnen, Gellifor, Denbighshire.

56. Galch Hill, Denbigh.

Photo : James Watts

57. Plas Uchaf, Eglwysegl, Denbighshire.

Photo : James Watts

58. Lymore, near Montgomery; recently demolished

Photo : James Watts

59. Penrhos, east Montgomeryshire; demolished

Photo : James Watts

60. Trewern, near Buttington, Montgomeryshire.

Photo : James Watts

61. Maes-mawr, Caersws, Montgomeryshire.

Photo : James Watts

62. Penarth, near Newtown, Montgomeryshire.

Photo : James Watts

63. Talgarth, Trefeglwys, Montgomeryshire.

Photo : James Watts

64. Rhyd-y-carw, Trefeglwys, Montgomeryshire.

65. Cefncloddiau, Llawr-y-glyn—Staylittle district, Montgomeryshire.

66. Timbering of a barn in south Yorkshire, showing crucks.

Copyright : National Museum of Wales.

67. Glan-y-wern, Llandyrnog, Denbighshire, showing crucks.

Photo: W. J. Hemp

68. Cruck constructed building, Yale district, Denbighshire.

Copyright: Cambridge University Press

69. Cruck-constructed cottage, Hawarden, Flintshire.

Photo: W. J. Hemp

70. Crucks at Y Gilfach, Llanfihangel-y-Pennant, Merionethshire.

71. Cruck construction, Lloran Ganol, Llansilin,
Montgomeryshire - Denbighshire border.

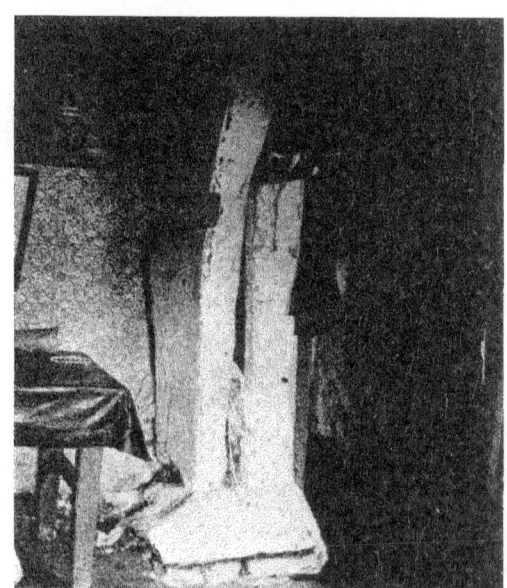

72. Llwyn-rhys, Llanbadarn Odwyn, Cardiganshire : interior view of cruck. 1901

82. Thatched chimney-'pot', Carmarthenshire.

81. Wattling of a chimney louvre, Carmarthenshire.

84. Developed wattle-and-daub chimney-pot, Carmarthenshire.

83. Rim of clay daub appearing above the thatch,
the beginning of a chimney-pot, Carmarthenshire.

Photo : Miss M. Wight

85. Chimney-pot of wooden boards. New Quay, Cardiganshire.

Copyright : National Museum of Wales

86. 'In-and-out' partitioning from Penyberth, Llyn, Caernarvonshire,
now in the National Museum of Wales.